Crime: *A Spatial Perspective*

CRIME:
A Spatial Perspective

Daniel E. Georges–Abeyie
AND
Keith D. Harries
EDITORS

New York COLUMBIA UNIVERSITY PRESS *1980*

Library of Congress Cataloging in Publication Data

Main entry under title:

Crime, a spatial perspective.

   Includes bibliographical references and index.
   1. Crime and criminals—Addresses, essays,
lectures.   2. Criminal anthropology—Addresses,
essays, lectures.   3. Environmental psychology—
Addresses, essays, lectures.   4. Crime and
criminals—United States—Addresses essays,
lectures.   I. Georges-Abeyie, Daniel E.,
1948–   II. Harries, Keith D.
HV6150.C74   364.2   80-14640
ISBN 0-231-04734-7

Columbia University Press
New York   Guildford, Surrey

CONTENTS

CONTRIBUTORS

EDITORS

Daniel E. Georges-Abeyie: Center for the Study of Crime, Delinquency and Corrections, Southern Illinois University.

Keith D. Harries: Department of Geography, Oklahoma State University.

AUTHORS

Patricia L. Brantingham: Department of Criminology, Simon Fraser University.

Paul J. Brantingham: Department of Criminology, Simon Fraser University.

Ronald L. Carter: Department of Geography, University of Houston at Clear Lake City.

Christopher S. Dunn: Center for the Study of Crime and Delinquency, National Institute of Mental Health.

Glenn M. Fishbine: Minnesota Crime Prevention Center.

David T. Herbert: Department of Geography, University College of Swansea, South Wales, United Kingdom.

Kim Quaile Hill: Department of Public Affairs, University of Houston at Clear Lake City.

Mitchell R. Joelson: Minnsota Crime Prevention Center.

Jack M. Kress: Attorney at Law, Albany, New York.

Carl Makres: Dallas Police Department, Planning and Research Division.

James F. Nelson: Department of Sociology, SUNY at Albany.

Woodrow W. Nichols, Jr.: Department of Geography, North Carolina University.

Gene E. Patterson: high school teacher in the south of France.

Phillip D. Phillips: WAPORA Inc., Chicago, Illinois.

Gerald F. Pyle: Department of Geography and Earth Science, University of North Carolina at Charlotte.

George Rengert: Department of Geography, Temple University.

Ralph A. Sanders: Research Scientist, Syracuse University.

Christopher J. Smith: Department of Geography, University of Oklahoma.

Larry K. Stephenson: Arizona Department of Health Services and Arizona State University.

Robert D. Swartz: Department of Geography, Wayne State University.

Hans Toch: School of Criminal Justice, SUNY at Albany.

Marshall A. Worden: Community and Rural Development Program of the Cooperative Extension Service, University of Arizona.

FOREWORD

WHAT AM I—an offbeat psychologist—doing, abusing a typewriter pretending to frame a book edited by geographers, a book that deals with "spatial aspects" of criminal offenses? Is this a gesture of ecumenical tokenism, a paternalistic pat-on-the-back? Is it trespass? A housewarming gift from an impudent stranger? Is it (to give me benefit of doubt) a mistake? Have I lost my way and am I forewording the wrong book?

The reason it is none of the above is because the distinguished contributors to this volume are at the forefront of an important development, one that changes interdisciplinary interfaces in remarkable ways, and produces new insights for us, including persons like me. The trend at issue is *ecology*, and it links us all because it enables us—as the editors of this volume point out—to combine "macro data" and the inferences drawn from them, with "micro data" and the understandings they yield.

The key lies in the link between man-and-circumstance, a link we have collectively ignored, or (to be more accurate) discovered early and neglected. One reason for the neglect is convenience, because we have—all of us—an affinity for methods that center on man and environment separately, and that we have trouble combining. The simple point we have forgotten—which this book rediscovers—is that we can better ask "Why" when we know "Where," "When," and "How."

Space is the stage on which man's behavior unfolds. Space provides the occasions for motives—the opportunities, temptations and pressures. Space conditions human relationships, brings people together and separates them. Space undergirds social climate, sets limits, inspires, beckons, frustrates, isolates, crowds, intrudes, liberates. It pretends vistas and forecloses them, yields privacy and violates it.

In relation to crime, space is what the aggressor must case and the victim fear. Space makes targets vulnerable or impregnable, presents proving grounds to wolves and obstacle courses to sheep. For the law, space makes pursuit and capture easy or difficult.

Such relationships not only operate in the short run individually, but in the long run, socially. Frustration, (space intrusive) can lead to aggression when an individual feels crowded, stressed, imposed upon, challenged, cornered and (in response) lashes out. The sequence, however, plays itself out indirectly, over time, with groups of persons subjected to common fates, as in riots, revolutions, wars and high-violence subcultures. Predatory behavior may cap migrations or demographic changes which place teenage gangs in competition, or leave unprotected wagon trains of the aged exposed to invading young settlers. Such confluences are no different for urban areas of transition, for grazers and homesteaders, frontiersmen and indians, colonizers and natives.

The concern of human ecology is defined as the relationship between people and their environments. The crux of the concern is "relationship," which implies a range from passive "adaptation" through "coping" to creative "mastery." Relationship connotes cycles of active and passive, in that our environment is the bed we make and subsequently lie in. More than most organisms, man creates the settings in which he acts; more importantly, he shapes the settings in which others must act, so that one person's effort-to-adapt creates adaptation problems for the next. Viewed in this way, the law places rough limits to antisocial adaptations. It tells me that I cannot create a congenial setting by eliminating or terrorizing people who disturb me, or by coveting and appropriating some of my neighbor's environment.

The contextual aspects of crime illuminate the motives of offenders, as well as the concerns of victims and bystanders. They help explain why burglars stay close to home, and why heat breeds violence; why robbery symbolizes concern and interracial crime distorts it; why rape victims are reticent and elderly victims self-insulating. Contexts pose questions about new crime and about old crime in new bottles—questions about crime in cars, supermarkets, suburban banks, and parks. Such questions relate to the target-connotations, the "temptation aspects" of crime, and to the habits and routines, aversions and fears, impulses and plans, goals and requirements of criminal offenders.

Mapping the contexts of human acts yields clues to human motives. The geographer and his brethren make the psychologist's and sociologist's task easier; they tell us what to look for so we can more sensibly speculate about patterns of human conduct, and about the stimuli that occasion them. They tell us where sequences of motives start, and where consequences of actions end. They place humanity in context, and protect us from parochial flights of fancy. For this reason, books like *Crime: A Spatial Perspective* are timely and important contributions to social science.

HANS TOCH
SUNY, Albany

Crime: *A Spatial Perspective*

INTRODUCTION

The study of crime from a spatial perspective is not new. Geographers and social ecologists have studied spatial relationships in urban environs for over fifty years, since University of Chicago sociologists Robert E. Park and Ernest W. Burgess published their textbook, *As Introduction to the Science of Sociology*, which they later expanded in conjunction with Roderick D. McKenzie.[1] Chicago School sociologists, under the leadership of Ernest W. Burgess, working among such giants as Clifford R. Shaw, Henry D. McKay, Clark Tibbitts, Roderick D. McKenzie, Nel Anderson, Louis Wirth, Harvey Zorbaugh, and others, collectively developed America's first large-scale theoretical approach to the study of the nature of crime and American urbanism, an approach which was spatial as well as sociological.

The social ecological approach first developed by the Chicago School of sociology has had its defenders as well as its detractors, yet its legacy has not only remained but grown and can be directly credited with the birth of numerous theoretical and research orientations firmly grounded in empirical research; one such theoretical and descriptive approach is that of the geography of crime of which the various contributors to this volume are the undisputed pioneers. This essentially descriptive spatial approach embraced by David Herbert, George Rengert, and others, takes cognizance of site and situational factors associated with what the Chicago School had labeled the criminal area, i.e., the area of crime occurrence and the area of criminal/delinquent residence, which may or may not coincide. More specifically, the geography of crime calls for either the macrolevel geographic analysis of criminal residence, criminal victimization, or crime occurrence (an attempt to aggregate the data to sociopolitical geographic units), or the microlevel analysis of crime and victimization data (i.e., site-specific crime data—the exact location of our "incident"). Thus, the geography of crime focuses on what lawyer/criminologist Richard Block calls the environmental factor in the "criminal event and its outcome."[2] This involves community ecology and structure—the time and day of week in which the "criminal event" occurred, the location of the crime, the type of victim and neighborhood disorganization, the residence of the perpetrator, as well as other socioeconomic and political factors which may be studied from a spatial perspective.

It is the belief of the editors of this volume that this work offers a comprehensive sampler of the social ecology and geography of crime, which can serve as a basic text in a course concerned with crime from a spatial perspective. It can also effectively supplement Harries' *Crime and the Environment*, Harries and Brunn's *The Geography of Laws and Justice: Spatial Perspectives on the Criminal Justice System*, or Georges' *The Geography of Crime and Violence: A Spatial and Ecological Perspective*,[3] just as it relates to other textbooks for undergraduate or graduate courses in urban problems, criminal justice, sociology, social ecology, urban geography, or the geography of crime. This volume also provides an excellent introduction to the orientation and work of some of our leading contemporary urban geographers and criminologists who have opted to analyze crime data from a spatial perspective. In addition it should help to draw attention to the relevance of spatially oriented crime analysis, as well as to the gap that exists between descriptive spatial analyses and holistic theories of crime causation, location, and criminal victimization. It is our hope that this book will further the growing interest in spatially oriented crime studies.

NOTES

1. Robert E. Park et al., *The City* (Chicago: University of Chicago Press, 1925).

2. Richard Block, *Violent Crime* (Lexington, Mass.: Lexington/Heath Books, 1977).

3. Keith D. Harries, *Crime and the Environment* (Springfield, Ill.: Charles Thomas, 1980); Keith D. Harries and Stanley D. Brunn, *The Geography of Laws and Justice* (New York: Praeger, 1978); Daniel E. Georges, *The Geography of Crime and Violence*. Resource Papers for College Geography, series 78:1 (Washington, D.C.: Association of American Geographers, 1978).

⇄ 1 ⇄

THE SPATIAL PERSPECTIVE

INTRODUCTION

The spatial approaches to the analysis of adult crime and juvenile delinquency manifest a rich academic tradition in both the United States and Great Britain. The inclusions in this section are exemplary of spatial analysis as conducted by geographers and criminologists, and offer outstanding summaries of works which typify the spatial approach found within the disciplines of sociology, geography, social ecology, law, and criminal justice.

The first article, by Christopher Dunn, offers an extensive review of the American social ecological and social geographical approach to the study of adult crime and juvenile delinquency, i.e., of research which utilizes the criminals' area concepts of crime (offense) occurrence and criminal (offender) residence. Dunn concludes that the value of crime area research will only be maximized by more complete and more accurate information about crime, especially information pertaining to the activities and actual behavior of participants leading up to and resulting in an offense or victimization.

David Herbert's "Urban Crime and Spatial Perspectives: The British Experience" is a comprehensive view of British criminological research with a spatial focus. Herbert notes that although British criminological research has a long record and a strong empirical tradition, the extent to which the spatial perspective on crime and delinquency has been developed is both limited and unsystematic. Herbert acknowledges that early observations on the apparent link between urbanization and levels of criminality have continued to be confirmed, though the general spatial arrangement of high crime rate areas in British cities has changed significantly since the later 1920s. He also posits the belief that as a single factor, the introduction of the public sector of housing, with its effect of altering the basic social geography of the city, has been the main explanation of this change. He states that as professional geographers become interested in the study of crime and delinquency for almost the first time, a number of useful roles await them. Analyses of the spatial ecology of crime, employing both traditional and innovative skills, continue to form a valuable research field and focus attention upon environmental qualities, both social and physical. Herbert concludes that attempts to understand the nature of the allocative processes, at societal and local levels, which may lead to the emergence of problem housing areas, are already adding considerably to the comprehension of spatial outcomes of British sociopolitical processes.

George Rengert advocates the position that geographic analysis must go beyond purely descriptive ecological studies and formulate some theoretical constructs which may lead to explanations of the criminal spatial structure. Rengert notes that the criminal area can be viewed as either the area of crime commission or the area of criminal residence, thus taking cognizance of the separate issues of *why* crimes occur and *where* crimes are committed. It is Rengert's position that most crimes which are not spontaneous responses to situational stimuli involve a decision process which probably includes considerable deliberation and weighing of alternative possibilities, both criminal and legal, with the "principle of least effort" playing a major role in the outcome of the decision-making process. Furthermore, the site of criminal residence and the site of the area of crime commission involve the concepts of accessibility and profitability; this site/situation complex may not be the same for both the juvenile delinquent and the adult criminal.

The concluding article in this section is by Jack Kress, a lawyer and criminologist who believes that on substantive, procedural, and perceptual levels, the legal environment of crime involves the spatial interrelationships of people (whether victims, offenders, or justice system personnel) and their surroundings. Kress notes that on a procedural level, the concepts of jurisdiction and venue provide boundaries beyond which criminal justice system personnel may not act, while other pragmatic geographic considerations affect the discretionary exercise of authority by police, court, and correctional officials. Kress observes that on a substantive level a close look at the basic penal code definitions reveals an underlying geographical framework, with certain crimes spatially circumscribed by their very nature and others by criminal justice practices.

⿻ 1 ⿻

Crime Area Research

CHRISTOPHER S. DUNN

IN LIGHT OF three recent excellent reviews of the literature adopting or advocating the ecological or spatial analysis of crime,[1] the need for yet another may not be readily apparent. In fact, even with such repeated attention, there has been little systematic discussion about findings and methods used by persons from *different* occupational roles who study the distribution of crime among areas. Police administrators may be interested in knowing only how much crime occurs in various precincts, whereas sociologists may be interested in the relationships between the distribution of crime and other social circumstances, or urban geographers in the relationships between crime and a variety of physical and related land use features. Knowing how much and what types of crime occur in particular areas may help police administrators make manpower allocation decisions, something for which sociologists interested in criminogenic processes rarely show concern. Similarly, sociologists and urban geographers who were able to identify patterns of relationships among crime occurrence, offender residence, physical and land use features, and social structure may be able to construct explanations for crime occurrence in terms of fundamental ecological processes, a capacity which the operational

The research assistance of Ann Hughitt, Center for Administration of Justice, American University, Washington, D.C., is gratefully acknowledged. The points of view or opinions presented herein are those of the author and do not reflect nor are intended to represent any official policies or positions of the U.S. Department of Health, Education, and Welfare.

This review was completed prior to January 1979.

and evaluative activities normally involved in policing do not readily possess, yet which is relevant for a broader range of crime control or social action programs. However, such broader issues may have only passing relevance for police administrators.

In contrast to such current insularity, it is useful to remember that one intent of early crime area researchers was to use the crime area study as a means of investigating complex social-ecological *processes* occurring in urban areas. Quite simply, crime as a behavioral phenomenon consists of a complex set of transactions of individuals with environments, environments which vary in setting, time, objects, participants, and activities. To understand this essential dynamic character of crime has required the evolution, application, and convergence of a variety of concepts, methods, and measurement tools from disciplines having inherently different foci. For example, "behavior setting" from psychology, "physical setting," "land use," and "density" from geography, "social disorganization" and "social control" from sociology, and "systems theory" from administrative science, all focus on central themes of *activity* and *process*. Thus, the fundamental importance of crime area research is its concern with the recognition, specification, and explanation of the multifaceted variation in social activities and processes rooted in an areal framework *as these relate to criminal behavior*.

I have argued elsewhere,[2] that the fundamental impediment to advancement of knowledge in this area of criminology is not conceptual but informational. Areas (behavior space) are not like the ancient concept of the "ether" of space, but more like Dr. Swain's environment of variable gravity.[3] Unfortunately, our typical crime area information, and more importantly, the capacity to make inferences therefrom, often fail to meet the criteria demanded by studies of social activities and processes. Therefore, this overview of findings also seeks to refocus attention on those capacities and limits of area studies.

Identification of High Crime Areas

Analyses of the distribution of offenders and/or offenses had their modern beginnings in nineteenth-century Europe. Guerry and

Quetelet in France and Rawson, Mayhew, and others in Great Britain all studied the differences in distribution of offenses or offenders within their respective countries. Each attempted to account for or explain different patterns of distribution in terms of a variety of social phenomena. However, most of these studies involved the analysis of crime among regions of countries, rather than within cities.

Shaw[4] has received much credit for initiating the empirical investigation of the distribution of delinquency within a city. The basic findings made by Shaw and his associates regarding spatial distribution of delinquency indicated that there was considerable variation in both rates of offenses and offenders among areas *within cities*. The general pattern identified in Shaw's early studies was that delinquent areas (concentrations of delinquents' residence) varied inversely in proportion to the distance from the center of the city. Where crime occurrence was plotted, it was also found to exhibit the same pattern. And these patterns were found to be relatively constant over time. Such areas tended to be characterized by physical deterioration, decreasing population, poverty, a high percentage of foreign-born and Negro population; furthermore, in those areas the community tended to function least efficiently as an agent of social control.

These findings about the distribution of delinquency led to the construction of a theory which suggested that community characteristics, including delinquency, were products of general processes common to most American cities. Briefly, the theory was a forerunner of current subcultural theory. Delinquency areas were viewed as products of social disorganization and lack of cohesion. Differential rates of delinquency reflected differences in social values, norms, and attitudes to which youngsters were exposed.

Since the social disorganization explanation was proposed, there has been a wide variety of research concerned with the association of delinquency and more specific social conditions. Although present crime area research is usually focused on specific characteristics of areas, the demonstration of areas of communities in which delinquency occurred and the description of these areas was nonetheless an important step in delinquency research. It specified those areas in which more intensive analyses of crime and its relation to social conditions were likely to be profitable.

Later research led to the finding that concentrations of delinquents occur in areas *adjacent* to the central business district and industrial areas. Shaw and McKay analyzed additional data from Chicago and concluded that "the rates of delinquents for many years have remained relatively constant in the areas adjacent to centers of commerce and heavy industry, despite successive changes in the nativity and nationality composition of the population."[5] Morris found that the distribution of *offenses* against property was closely related to concentration of commercial and industrial land use; however, concentrations of delinquents' residences were not.[6] He explained this difference by citing the fact that Croydon did not develop radially, and consequently, no well-defined zonal rate difference could be identified.

Schmid[7] demonstrated that crime in Seattle tended to decrease more or less in direct proportion to distance from the center of the city. However, he also found that certain offenses were more prominent in the center of the city while others were more highly concentrated in the "skid row" section. Check fraud and arrests of females for drunkenness both decreased in outward radial pattern. However, check fraud was most prevelant in the central business district, while arrests of females for drunkenness were concentrated in the "skid row" area.

Thus, the finding that the frequency of delinquency and crime decreases proportionate to distance from the center of the city is not the only characterization which can be made. Delinquency areas (areas high in resident juvenile offenders) are often adjacent to industrial and commercial land use areas. Such industrial and commercial areas often have concentrations of offenses. Moreover, different types of offenses are likely to be concentrated in different areas.

Association of Land Use with Offense Occurrence and Offender Residence Areas

The above findings raise the much broader issue of the relationship of land use to the distribution of delinquent or criminal residence and to the distribution of offense occurrence.

Shaw found that high rates of delinquency, truancy, and crime prevailed in areas which were "characterized by physical deterioration and declining populations."[8] These areas were also adjacent to the central business district and to large industrial centers. As such, they were in a process of transition from residential use to business and industrial use.

White studied the distribution of crime (offense occurrence) and criminals (offender residence) in relation to five independent variables, one of which was "percent land used for business purposes." He found that, in general, "the residences of felons and the location of their offenses are associated with business and industry."[9] In addition, offenses were apparently related to the distribution of factories. Most factories were concentrated in the central business district, but some factories were also located adjacent to a railroad which passed through a considerable portion of the city. White found that at certain points along it, where factories were located, the felony rate was "higher than in contiguous tracts at similar distances from the center business district."[10]

There is no question, however, that the examination of physical and land use characteristics in relation to the concept of differential social opportunity is extremely valuable. However, since the scope of possible crime occurrence settings is broad and diverse, and since different activities thrive under different conditions (e.g., intrafamily violence within households versus stranger-to-stranger violence in public places), it is instructive to turn to studies of specific offenses (viz., homicide, robbery, and burglary) to learn more about the association of crime occurrence with land use or particular areas.

Homicide

In a study of homicide in Cleveland,[11] offenses were found to be concentrated in a few areas. Three of twenty-eight social planning areas accounted for 62 percent of the homicide incidents in Cuyahoga County. These three areas had a combined seven-year homicide rate of 52.2 homicides per 10,000 residents aged 18 to 59, compared with the homicide rate for the entire city of Cleveland of 10.2 per 10,000 residents aged 18 to 59, and the overall Cuyahoga

County rate of 7.0 per 10,000 residents aged 18 to 59. These areas
were located near the center of the city and were adjacent to each
other; they were not, however, business or commercial areas, but
mainly residential. Generally, they were the areas with the "lowest
socioeconomic status, most undesirable neighborhood conditions,
greatest financial dependency, the most acute problems of space
and crowded housing conditions, the least stability of the population, the greatest social maladjustment and family and individual
adjustment problems, and the poorest health."[12] Pyle, using data
some fifteen to twenty years more recent than Bensing and
Schroeder's, also found that overall crime rates for Cleveland indicated the existence of a "crime concentration corridor."[13] Block
indicated that the present concentration of homicides in Chicago is
also similar: "Of the 2,389 homicides in Chicago between 1971
and 1973, 495 (21 percent) occurred in an area of 375 blocks. Two
percent of the blocks of Chicago accounted for 22 percent of the
homicides."[14]

Bullock also found that homicide was differentially distributed
throughout an urban area.[15] Using data on homicides in Houston,
Texas, between 1945 and 1949, he demonstrated that eighteen of
the city's census tracts, containing 32 percent of the population
age 21 and older, were the sites of 71 percent of the homicides.
Generally, these census tracts surrounded the central business district. Using census tracts high in homicide and census tracts low in
homicide, Bullock demonstrated that homicide rates were directly
associated with physical deterioration of dwelling units, racial
composition of the population, unemployment levels, and occupational class, and inversely associated with median education. Consequently, Bullock's findings parallel somewhat those of Bensing
and Schroeder.

Bullock, however, extended the analysis to a more complex level
than did Bensing and Schroeder by proposing an explanatory
scheme for the relationship of homicide to particular areas of
Houston. He stated that "strategic areas of the city became dy-
namically related to the occurrence of homicide through the basic
ecological process of segregation."[16] The consequence of segregation as an "ordering" or explanatory scheme vis-à-vis the distribution of homicide is that "in assorting people, (segregation) also

assorts institutions."[17] The assorting of institutions results in people of like kind gathering and engaging in interpersonal relations both of a congenial and of a conflicting nature. Bullock summarized his thesis by stating, "The basic ecological process of urban segregation centralized people of like kind, throws them together at common institutions, occasions their association on levels of intimacy, and thereby paves the way for conflicts out of which homicides occur."[18]

The thesis of ecological segregation as a contributory factor to differentials in urban homocide is not the only applicable explanation for ecological process/crime occurrence patterns. For one reason, available studies of homicide and other types of offenses suggest that segregation (viewed predominantly as residential segregation of races) is not a major differentiating factor. For example, it has recently been shown by Munford et al. that the relationship between high homicide occurrence and areas of low socioeconomic status holds for both predominantly white and predominantly nonwhite areas.[19] Even if this were so, however, it still does not follow that such a relationship to homicide or any other offense is direct and causative, as Bullock seems to impute by mentioning some supposed direct effects of ecological segregation (for example, residential race segregation leading to reduced social control leading to homicide). Wolfgang and Ferracuti, on the other hand, identified some of the cultural correlates of the segregation process as much more closely related to any cause/effect pattern than segregation itself.[20] Race differences in relation to the distribution of homicide notwithstanding, ecological segregation as the assorting of *institutions*, *resources*, and *culture* as well as people is more closely aligned with activity and process and is thus perhaps a more valid *ecological process concept* than segregation viewed solely as ethnic residential segregation.

Robbery

The offense of robbery exhibits a spatial distribution in urban areas which differs from that of homicide. Normandeau demonstrated that robbery in Philadelphia was concentrated in the central part of the city;[21] on its face, this seems to suggest that the spatial distributions of robbery and homicide are the same. A more detailed consideration of Normandeau's data showed, however, that "highway" robbery and "business" robbery were the predominant types of robbery setting, in contrast to the distribution of homicides, which occur mainly in private residences. Normandeau found that robbers committed their offenses at some distance from their places of residence, often in census tracts different from, but adjacent to, those in which they resided. Turner's thesis of attraction to opportunities available in the central part of the city was used to explain this relationship among offender residence, scene of offense, and social structural characteristics.[22] Turner noted the large proportion of robberies occurred on the street or against businesses (i.e., in places affording a greater opportunity for the commission of the offense), and since these situations or settings were most prevalent in the central areas of the city, offenders tended to gravitate there to commit robbery. Consequently, the sites of robberies usually tended to be associated with those structural characteristics which defined central city areas.

Schmid's study of crime distribution in Seattle provides ample evidence of the association of robbery with such social characteristics. Schmid showed that robbery occurred most often in areas characterized by a high percentage of unemployed males, a lesser number of school grades completed, lower median income and fewer people age 14 and over who are married. These structural variables, along with offenses such as larceny, auto theft, and, in particular, robbery, were highly loaded on a factor which Schmid termed "low family and economic status."[23] Thus, this factor, also referred to as the "urban crime dimension par excellence," represented in large measure the crime occurrence pattern in the central area of Seattle.

Robbery, then, as contrasted with homicide, occurs mainly in public and business settings, in places where targets are likely to be most lucrative in relation to the risk involved in separating that wealth from its keeper. Downtown or central areas of cities that have stores, commercial establishments, financial institutions, and are relatively attractive in relation to adjacent areas of low income and physical deterioration, fit well the requirements of such a setting.

Burglary

Burglary is an offense category which probably encompasses a wider variety of offender activities than homicide or robbery. Consequently, settings for burglary are likely to be more diverse. Scarr, in a recent study of burglary in metropolitan Washington, D.C., divided burglary into two kinds: residential and nonresidential. This difference, at least in the Washington area, was highly associated with another dichotomy, viz., daytime weekday burglaries were more likely to be residential burglaries and nighttime or weekend burglaries were more frequently nonresidential burglaries. This behavior-setting distinction turned out to be important in explaining differences in distributions of burglary in the two suburban counties studied from the pattern in the District of Columbia. Scarr noted that although concentrations of burglary, both residential and nonresidential, occurred in two suburban counties (Fairfax County, Virginia and Prince George's County, Maryland), residential and nonresidential burglaries in Washington were much more segregated simply as a function of the types of land use. He attributed the coexistence of suburban residential and nonresidential burglaries in the same areas to the existence of similar "levels of opportunity" for both types, and indicated that "The existence of shopping centers throughout F(airfax) C(ounty) and P(rince) G(eorge's) C(ounty) means that opportunities for both residential and non-residential burglaries will co-exist in the same geographic areas to a similar degree."[24] Therefore, the association of burglary with other social structural variables is to a large extent conditioned by the land use and target density functions. Where these functions are mixed, as in suburban areas, burglary is likely to be associated with different structural characteristics than in places where residential and nonresidential land use is more segregated, as in urban areas.

Land Use Summary

The discussion of the distribution of crime in relation to land use patterns has indicated four important points. First, crime occurrence (as distinct from residence of offenders) is more frequent in the central and interior areas of urban places. Second, these areas are generally ones in which levels of commercial activity are high and adjacent high-density residential development is in relatively poor condition, compared with other residential areas. Third, the quality of residential land use is related to crime occurrence. For example, the percent of dwelling units in an area which lacks major plumbing facilities, and the percent which need substantial repair, are often used as indicators of substandard housing, and hence are less improved, more physically deteriorated neighborhoods. Crime occurrence is often more frequent in such areas. Of course, it is difficult to determine when land use becomes a social phenomenon. Deteriorating housing has both physical and social correlates. Fourth, different land uses are often related to specific offenses; differences in available targets or potential victims are often noted as a function of the activities or structure of an area.

Association of Social Structural Components with Offense Occurrence and Offender Residence

Most studies of the relationships between crime and social structural phenomena concentrate on social variables falling into three categories: socioeconomic status, or class; family stability; and ethnicity.[25]

Socioeconomic Status (SES)

Early crime area studies indicated that areas of low socioeconomic status had high rates of delinquency. However, in 1954, Lander—reacting against a heavy concentration of area research which only partly supported that finding—identified a set of nontraditional SES variables which covaried with delinquency differently than traditional SES indicators such as median income and education. Lander indicated that the percentage of nonowner-occupied housing and of nonwhite population were also (as well as more strongly) associated with delinquency. He described this association as indicative of a general dimension of "anomie," which, it was argued, differed from socioeconomic status.[26]

Since Lander's study, a number of partial replications and critiques have been published, as have studies not concerned with the identification of explanatory mechanisms such as "anomie." In summary, the relationship of crime occurrence to socioeconomic status (as determined on an areal basis) is fairly clear. Education (measured by median grade completed) and home ownership (measured by percent of dwelling units owner-occupied) appear to be most highly, and inversely, correlated with crime occurrence or delinquency. In other words, areas of higher median education and more owner-occupied homes generally tend to be lower in crime and delinquency. In addition, median income is also negatively related to crime. Generally speaking, areal measures of both offender residence and offense occurrence are related to the SES indicators. As was the situation with the relationship of patterns of land use to crime occurrence, SES is related to different types of offenses in varying degree. Most of the evidence supporting this finding is taken from studies involving residence of delinquent. However, Schmid found that areas of nonresidential burglary occurrence were not related to median income or percent of owner-occupied homes, but were slightly related to median education.

Family Stability

The characteristic most commonly used in discussions of family status in relation to delinquency or crime at the areal level has been marital status. Generally, two different aspects of marital status have served as measures. First, there have been differentiations as to the percent of people in an area who are married, or conversely, the percent of people in an area not related to anyone in the household in which they reside. Schmid, for example, found moderate to strong negative associations between his marital status variable (percent 14 years and over who were married) and most of the specific offense variables.[27] Using another form of the marital status variable, Ferdinand found that there was a strong positive relationship between urbanization and the percent of delinquents from *voluntarily broken homes* (broken homes in rural areas were more likely to be involuntarily broken).[28]

Distinctly different areal measures of family stability were used by Quinney: percent age 50 and over, percent females in the labor force, and percent homes owner-occupied. He regarded these three variables respectively as: (1) "the tendency towards the preservation of the established order in an area (percent age 50 and over); (2) the extent to which traditional family patterns exist (percent females in labor force); and (3) the extent to which the dominant middle class value system exercises control over an area population (percent owner-occupied housing)."[29] It was found that these family status variables in urban areas were moderately related to some specific offense types but that the strength of the relationships varied with type of offense and type of family status variable. For example, percent females in the labor force exhibited much stronger associations with the specific UCR violent personal crimes of murder, forcible rape, and aggravated assault (Pearson's r = +.41, +.38, and +.38, respectively) than with robbery or with other property crimes.

As was the case with socioeconomic status in the period following Lander's study, the meaning of the association of family status indicators with rates of offenses known to police is not altogether clear, in part because some family status indicators are also strongly related to indices of socioeconomic status. Nevertheless, with certain cautions about the construct validity and multicollinearity of the areal indicators, it is recognized that family status, as measured by marital status or percent children not living with both parents, is related to delinquency. Although there are joint effects of both low SES and nonintact families in the highest delinquency rate areas, for other area types (for example, predominantly white and affluent), family disability is probably a more important independent factor in explaining delinquency rates than is socioeconomic status.

Ethnicity

The evidence from crime area studies indicates some degree of relationship among delinquency or crime occurrence, low socioeconomic status, and predominantly nonwhite or black areas. For the most part, however, the same studies also confirm that the race composition of areas has effects on crime distribution which are independent of socioeconomic status.

For example, Willie pointed out that socioeconomic status and family status had both joint and differential effects on the distribution of delinquency.[30] In so doing, he also showed that there were differences between nonwhite versus white areas regarding the importance which the two variables had in explaining delinquency rates. In both white and nonwhite areas, delinquency was highest where both socioeconomic status and family stability were low. However, family instability had a much greater effect on delinquency in white areas high in socioeconomic status than in nonwhite areas high in socioeconomic status. In contrast, delinquency was higher in nonwhite, low SES, stable-family areas than in white, low SES, stable-family areas.

The type of offense most prevalent in white versus nonwhite areas also has been found to vary. Chilton studied specific types of offenses comprising delinquency, in part to determine whether different types of offenses were related to differences in the race composition of areas.[31] He found that children from tracts with large Black populations were proportionately less frequently involved in car theft relative to other offenses, but appeared overrepresented when offenses such as robbery, assault, disorderly conduct and carrying concealed weapons were examined. In contrast, Black children were less likely than white children to be charged with running away, trespassing, truancy, vandalism, curfew violations, liquor violations, and traffic violations.

Another difference in delinquency areas with which race is associated was demonstrated by Turner. He calculated both rates of offenses (i.e., where offenses occurred) and rates of offender residence (i.e., where offenders resided). He then showed that race was more important in predicting high-offender residence areas than in predicting high offense areas.[32] As Turner noted, the weaker association of blacks with high-*offense* areas is clearly accounted for by the existence of areas in the central part of Philadelphia which were high in offenses but low in resident offenders.

Three factor analytic studies of crime in relation to structural variables also demonstrate the independent relationships of race composition with offenses and arrests. Schmid, Boggs, and Schmid and Schmid all found that the variable indicating race composition of an area either (1) defined a factor different from one on which socioeconomic status indicators were heavily loaded, or (2) was related to a crime factor to which socioeconomic status indicators were not strongly related.

The proposition that the relationship of race composition and the distribution of crime or delinquency indicates more than only deleterious effects of low socioeconomic status appears to be substantiated by crime area studies. A number of differences seem to occur. First, some structural variables related to delinquency or crime occurrence affect non-white areas differently than white areas. In particular, where socioeconomic status is not a problem family instability is related to higher rates of delinquency in white areas than in non-white areas. Second, types of offenses vary according to the race composition of an area. For example, Chilton found that nonwhite areas exhibited higher rates of offenses against persons, whereas offenses in white areas were mostly property offenses. Turner's findings in this regard are also similar. Third, race (percent nonwhite) was related more strongly to offender residence areas than areas of offense occurrence. Fourth, race composition (percent nonwhite) defines or is related to different crime occurrence dimensions than are socioeconomic status variables.

Summary of Crime Occurrence Patterns

The extant research (to date based mainly on official data) shows clearly that different levels and types of crime are associated with different land use patterns and social structural characteristics, depending upon the particular area of occurrence or offender residence.

Generally, higher rates of reported personal attack crimes prevail in lower-class residential areas of cities. Often, these areas are predominantly black, which therefore results in an association between percent black and personal attack crimes. This association is probably due to some extent to the effects of low socioeconomic status in these areas. However, ample evidence suggests that socioeconomic status and race are not identical in respect to effects on crime distribution. Consequently, explanations of crime production and distribution have evolved, based on some of the cultural differences often observed among areas which differ in socioeconomic status and race composition.

Higher rates of property crimes are usually reported to characterize the central business areas of cities. One explanation often given is that the attributes of central business areas present the most favorable circumstances—availability of targets, accessibility, relative anonymity—for commission of such offenses. Higher rates of property crimes are reported in these areas, and therefore, an association is noted with the land use and structural attributes which characterize such areas. Thus, property crimes are associated with percent land used for business purposes, with areas of having greater proportions of single or unrelated individuals, with areas of relatively higher rates of unemployment, with areas of lower income, and less strongly, with areas of high percent black population.

However, it has been shown that the distribution of property crimes among areas also differs as a function of some *characteristics of the offense.* For example, *suburban* residential and nonresidential burglaries occurred in generally the same areas, thereby largely reflecting the greater mix of residential and commercial land use in suburban areas. Urban burglary types (residential versus nonresidential) were more separated, quite possibly as a function of the segregation of residential and commercial land uses.

Some of the differences exhibited by types of crime and characteristics of the offense, in relation to land use and social structural phenomena, are taken into account by a few crime area studies utilizing multivariate analytic techniques. Generally, these studies have been undertaken to describe various dimensions of urban crime areas. For example, Boggs extracted four offense-occurrence/offender-residence factors using twelve specific offenses and six offender characteristics as variables. Turner described two general kinds of delinquency areas; Schmid specified urban crime area dimensions (factors) using a large number of crime occurrence, offender residence, and offender attribute variables.[33]

Explanations for Crime Occurence Patterns:
The Inference to Process

It is understandable that discussion centering on the implications and applications of crime area research has been inhibited. The large amount of research, the lack of integration and summary of findings, and the technical nature of some of the research have all contributed to the absence of discussion about implications and policy. Perhaps more importantly, there are some difficult problems in logic and inference in deriving explanations that purport to be of processes but are typically of patterns.

Schmid's classic study serves as a beginning point for discussion of that point. Subsequent to a detailed analysis of the distribution of rates of various offenses and arrests in Seattle, Schmid presented a short discussion of six alternative hypotheses that could possibly be used to account for the patterns of crime. These hypotheses included the following:

1. the "ecological segregation/contingent control" hypotheses— that the higher frequency of crime in one milieu than in another may be a reflection of greater opportunities, profitableness, relative availability of targets or victims, and other conditions, increasing the probability of occurrence of offenses of a particular kind or that have special characteristics;
2. the "drift" hypothesis—that certain areas tend to attract offenders;
3. the "differential association/cultural transmission" hypothesis—that particular areas are characterized by distinct subcultural patterns of delinquency and crime;
4. the "social alienation" hypothesis—that particular areas are characterized by social isolationism, anonymity, impersonal interpersonal relations, and interstitial conditions, all of which breed deviant behavior;
5. the "anomie" hypothesis—that delinquency is a function of anomie in an area or, in other words, the disturbance or disruption of the collective order, the external regulating force

which defines norms and goals and governs behavior; deviant behavior occurs when a social structure restricts or closes access to approved goals for some part of the population;
6. the "illegitimate means/differential opportunities" hypothesis—that differentials in access to illegitimate means (Cloward and Ohlin),[34] have a basic spatial dimension, especially in reference to opportunities for illegal activity, such as (1) specific setting of offense (stores, banks, warehouses, etc.) or (2) specific occupational position of the offender (handler of money or other commodities).

If one inventoried the crime area patterns described previously with these hypothetical mechanisms or explanations of occurrence and distribution, one would find that it is frequently difficult to specify precise conclusions about processes that flow from crime area research findings. One reason is that, as "explanations," the empirical findings often are forced toward a relatively higher degree of generality, in essence, a movement from pattern to process. Another reason concerns the focus of tasks performed by most providers of the raw data used in crime area research. That is to say, while such explanations of social processes or mechanisms are of interest per se to sociologists and social psychologists, the tasks of police officials and criminal justice planners require attention to somewhat different considerations. Many policing functions (e.g., preventing or deterring crime, responding to service calls, apprehending suspected offenders) are rooted in "site-specific" frameworks. Many forms of crime or criminal activity involve a distinct and specific location of occurrence. The policing function in general recognizes this aspect of crime in that it is organized, for the most part, on a decentralized local basis. In effect, the police are required to be where the action is. In order to meet this requirement, the police must also, therefore, know where the action is, and consequently, they have traditionally developed their own sources of information and manipulated that information in ways not designed to address generalized, theoretically grounded explanations of ecological processes, but to address specific questions and tasks.

It is interesting to note that in spite of this occupational dissonance, most crime area researchers have relied on official police crime statistics or information. Yet such measurement programs rarely include information about behaviors of offenders and victims or about situational contexts of offenses, in effect, about activities. Consequently, it has been difficult for crime area researchers to examine the geographic and sociological variability of phenomena that are more accurately representative of ecological processes that produce or promote various behaviors or adaptive responses including, but not limited to, crime.

Information about characteristics of crime incidents and behaviors of participants is sometimes collected by police. However, it is rarely systematically refined and summarized. Nor are many attempts made to analyze the patterns of behaviors and situations characterizing crime incidents in terms of their distribution among homogeneous areas or in terms of their association with attributes of various areas. Consequently, crime area research has been somewhat limited in its application to specific policing tasks, and is presently stagnant in its role for advancing criminological theory.

However, such analyses are quite valuable and clearly relevant as the central theme of crime area research. For example, Cartwright and Howard, in a little-noted but seminal study began to specify relationships between *ecological* or *area attributes* of gang neighborhoods and *dimensions of gang behavior*. They found, for example, that a "suburb" factor, having heavy loadings on such area attributes as persons per household, percent females 14 and over in labor force (negative loading), percent dwelling units built between 1950 and 1960, and percent single dwelling units, was strongly positively related to a "stable corner-boy activity" factor indicating such gang activities as sports, social activities, gambling, loitering on street corners, truancy, and joy riding.[35] Another moderate positive association was indicated between a "socioeconomic status" factor and an "authority/ protest" gang behavior factor, defined by auto theft, driving without a license, and public nuisance behaviors.

According to Cartwright and Howard, these sets of information allowed for "an unusual opportunity to take area research beyond the stages of geographical delineation and association between ecological variables and delinquency rates." They also stated that, with the derivation of ecological factors and gang behavior factors, it became possible to engage in "precisely the kind of further enquiry intended by Shaw and McKay."[36] According to Shaw and McKay, the study of such a problem as juvenile delinquency only began with a study of its geographical location. Shaw wrote that its purpose was to reveal "the areas in which delinquency occurs most frequently, and therefore marks off the communities which should be studied intensively for factors relating to delinquent behavior."[37]

Thus, Shaw and his colleague, some years ago, and Cartwright and Howard relatively recently, all espouse the necessity of *understanding relationships between environment and individual actions in order to understand a behavioral phenomenon such as crime occurrence.*

Thus, the future of ecological research about crime is intimately connected with the extent to which power of behavioral information about crime is maximized. To a certain degree, this can be accomplished by modest analytics; innovations such as those relating incident characteristics to specific area attributes (Dunn) or more seminal studies about crime/environment interactions (e.g., Cartwright and Howard; Peterson).[38] Yet to an even larger extent, the value of crime area research will only be maximized by more complete and more accurate information about crime, especially information pertaining to the activities and actual behavior of participants leading up to and resulting in an offense or victimization.

NOTES

1. J. A. Wilks, "Ecological Correlates of Crime and Delinquency," appendix A in Task Force Report: *Crime and Its Impact: An Assessment.* Task Force on Assessment, the President's Commission on Law Enforcement and Administration of Justice (Washington, D.C.: U.S. Government Printing Office, 1967), pp. 138–56; K. D. Harries, "Intraurban Crime Patterns," in *The Geography of Crime and Justice* (New York: McGraw-Hill, 1974), pp. 61–88; J. Baldwin, "British Areal Studies of Crime," *The British Journal of Criminology* (July 1975), 15(3):211–27.

2. C. S. Dunn, *The Patterns and Distribution of Assault Incident Characteristics Among Social Areas* and *Patterns of Robbery Characteristics and Their Occurrence Among Social Areas.* U.S. Department of Justice, Law Enforcement Assistance Administration, National Criminal Justice Information and Statistics

Service, Utilization of Criminal Justice Statistics Analytic Reports 14 and 15, respectively (1976).

3. Kurt Vonnegut, *Slapstick* (New York: Del, 1976).

4. C. R. Shaw, *Delinquency Areas* (Chicago: University of Chicago Press, 1929); and Shaw and H. D. McKay, *Report on the Causes of Crime*, vol. 2, National Commission on Law Observance and Enforcement (Washington, D.C.: U.S. Government Printing Office, 1931).

5. C. R. Shaw and H. D. McKay, *Juvenile Delinquency and Urban Areas* (Chicago: University of Chicago Press, 1942), p. 315.

6. T. M. Morris, *The Criminal Area* (London: Routledge and Kegan Paul, 1957).

7. C. F. Schmid, "Urban Crime Areas: part II," *American Sociological Review* (1960), 25:655–78.

8. Shaw, *Delinquency Areas*, p. 203.

9. R. C. White, "The Relation of Felonies to Environmental Factors in Indianapolis," *Social Forces* (May 1932), p. 499.

10. *Ibid.*, p. 500.

11. R. C. Bensing and O. Schroeder, Jr., *Homicide in an Urban Community* (Springfield, Ill.: Charles Thomas, 1960).

12. *Ibid.*, p. 184.

13. G. F. Pyle, "Spatial and Temporal Aspects of Crime in Cleveland, Ohio," *American Behavioral Scientist* (November/December 1976), 20(2):188.

14. R. Block, "Homicide in Chicago: A Nine-Year Study (1965–1973)," *The Journal of Criminal Law and Criminology* (1976), 66(4):510.

15. H. A. Bullock, "Urban Homicide in Theory and Fact," *Journal of Criminal Law, Criminology, and Police Science* (January-February 1955), 45:565–75.

16. *Ibid.*, p. 569.

17. *Ibid.*, p. 567.

18. *Ibid.*, p. 567.

19. R. S. Munford, R. S. Kazer, R. A. Feldman, and R. R. Stevens, "Homicide Trends in Atlanta," *Criminology* (August 1976), 14(2):213–31.

20. M. E. Wolfgang and F. Ferracuti, *The Subculture of Violence* (London: Tavistock, 1967).

21. A. Normandeau, "Trends and Patterns in Crimes of Robbery." Ph.D. dissertation, University of Pennsylvania, 1968.

22. S. Turner, "Ecology of Delinquency," in T. Sellin and M. Wolfgang, eds., *Delinquency: Selected Studies* (New York: Wiley, 1969), pp. 27–60.

23. Schmid, "Urban Crime Areas: Part I," pp. 533–36.

24. H. A. Scarr, *Patterns of Burglary*, 2d ed. U.S. Department of Justice, Law Enforcement Assistance Administration, National Institute of Law Enforcement and Criminal Justice (June 1973).

25. C. S. Dunn, "The Analysis of Environmental Attribute/Crime Incident Characteristic Interrelationships." Ph.D. dissertation, State University of New York, Albany (1974).

26. B. Lander, *Toward an Understanding of Juvenile Delinquency* (New York: Columbia University Press, 1954).

27. Schmid, "Urban Crime Areas: Part i," p. 530.

28. Thomas N. Ferdinand, "Offense Patterns and Family Structures of Urban, Village, and Rural Delinquents," *Journal of Criminal Law, Criminology, and Police Science* (March 1964), 55(1), 86–93.

29. R. Quinney, "Structural Characteristics, Population Areas, and Crime Rates in the United States," *Journal of Criminal Law, Criminology, and Police Science* (1966), 57:51.

30. Charles V. Willie, "The Relative Contribution of Family Status and Economic Status to Juvenile Delinquency," *Social Problems* (1967), 14:326–35.

31. R. J. Chilton, "Middle-Class Delinquency and Specific Offense Analysis," in E. W. Vaz, ed., *Middle-Class Juvenile Delinquency*, pp. 91–101 (New York: Harper & Row, 1967).

32. S. Turner, "Ecology of Delinquency."

33. C. F. Schmid and S. E. Schmid, *Crime in the State of Washington*, Law and Justice Planning Office (Olympia, Wash.: Office of the Governor, 1972); Schmid, "Urban Crime Areas. Part ii," pp. 676–78.

34. Richard A. Cloward and Lloyd E. Ohlin, *Delinquency and Opportunity* (Glencoe, Ill.: Free Press, 1961).

35. D. S. Cartwright and K. I. Howard, "Multivariate Analysis of Gang Delinquency: I-Ecologic Influences," *Multivariate Behavioral Research* (July 1966), 1:359–67.

36. *Ibid.*, p. 365.

37. Shaw, *Delinquency Areas*, p. 8.

38. E. Petersen, *A Reassessment of the Concept of Criminality: An Analysis of Criminal Behavior in Terms of Individual and Current Environment Interaction* (New York: Halstead Press, 1977).

Ꙩ 2 Ꙩ

Urban Crime and Spatial Perspectives:
The British Experience

DAVID T. HERBERT

WHAT MIGHT BE termed the spatial ecology of crime has a long, though often incidental record of research and study in British cities. The spatial characteristics of crime had not escaped the attention of a number of criminologists, and although none of these could be labeled as geographers they did employ some of the basic graphical tools of description and analysis. Phillips[1] has identified the cartographic tradition of analyzing crime statistics, with its origins in France, and this mode of analysis is discernible in early British studies. Mayhew noted the regional variation in crime rates,[2] and with Booth demonstrated the fact of "crime areas" in London and sought to characterize them.[3] Another contemporary writer in the nineteenth century observed: "There is a thieves' quarter in all large towns, well known to the police and better known to the thieves."[4] Tobias has reexamined the Vauxhall district of Liverpool,[5] about which Hume had written: "The area, which poverty claims for its own, contains within it small localities which are specially devoted to crime, vice and immorality."[6] Tobias obtained access to contemporary statistical material and was able to show that those parts of Vauxhall which Hume had labeled as criminal also possessed distinctive social profiles though no precise measure of their criminality was recorded.

This general interest in the spatial ecology of crime has continued in British criminological research through to the modern period, despite the disclaimers of writers such as Mannheim, who suggested that "ecological theory . . . has gradually retreated into the background in the decades after 1945."[7] A useful summary of British areal studies of crime and delinquency has been provided by Baldwin,[8] who was able to identify at least twenty studies, about half of which had been published in the previous decade. Baldwin provided a classification for this group of studies which may be used as a framework from which to develop the present discussion. He was concerned with identifying the main weaknesses of the ecological approach. These were, first, that all such studies are based upon official measures of criminality; second, that reliance upon small-area statistics raises the central question of ecological fallacy; and third, that "areal" was a better description of these studies than "ecological" because of the symbolic connotation of the latter phrase. These first two weaknesses are broadly recognized in these studies and are normally used to qualify results. There are data problems, noted by Smith and by Hindess,[10] which are known, but official statistics form the only comprehensive sources. Some recent British studies[11] using a variety of techniques to identify "hidden delinquency," have provided some assurance that official statistics are accurate indicators of the relative incidence of offenders. While small-area statistics contain the ecological fallacy problem, practitioners have learned to use their findings with circumspection.

Baldwin suggested that British areal studies fell into three broad types.[12] There was first a group in which an areal component emerged but was largely incidental to the main purposes of the research. Ferguson,[13] for example, suggested that some housing schemes had very high offender rates but did not include any detailed portrayal of the distribution of delinquency in Glasgow; while Downes,[14] although analyzing patterns of crime commission and delinquency residence, was centrally interested in subcultural rather than ecological theory. In the remaining two studies in this first group, Mays[15] focused on the delinquent activities of eighty slum boys but his prime concern was not spatial, while McClintock[16] presented a number of maps relating to violent offenders in London but these were merely used to complement other forms of data.

As a second group of studies, Baldwin identified those in which areal analysis was an end in itself.[17] Some of these were strongly influenced by Shaw and McKay's work[18] on crime and delinquency "areas" and their zone and gradient generalizations. Castle and Gittus[19] completed a study of social defects in Liverpool from which they felt able to confirm the main features of the Chicago model. Wallis and Maliphant[20] worked with a small sample base and gross areal units for London but presented a series of patterns of delinquency residence and were, interestingly, able to confirm a general persistence of high-rate areas over time by comparing their results with those of Burt.[21] Edwards[22] studied the distribution of delinquency in Newcastle and added an interesting dimension by calculating prevalence rates. These rates, calculated for a cohort born in 1949, reached 23.5 percent for the city as a whole and 51.4 percent in the highest-rate ward. Baldwin[23] reviewed two studies in this group which had used multivariate statistical techniques to analyze crime data, those by Giggs[24] and by Brown, McCulloch and Hiscox,[25] but was critical of the ways in which both of these had employed their methodologies and interpreted their results.

In his final group of studies, Baldwin[26] listed those which had used areal analysis as means to an end. It is this group which contains most potential and its development can be discussed at greater length below. Earlier studies in this category included the widely acknowledged work by Morris[27] which, besides providing an overview of ecological studies, contained detailed areal analyses and a discussion of the segregation processes which led to the emergence of problem areas. Sainsbury's analysis of suicide in London[28] was an explicit attempt to integrate the two levels of aggregate analysis and case studies of individuals; whilst Jephcott and Carter[29] first reduced the scale of their areal analysis to a point at which they could identify "black" and "white" streets within a high-rate delinquent area in Nottingham, and then sought to investigate the "climate of opinion" within these streets by extensive qualitative analysis. Lastly in this group, Lambert[30] focused a Birmingham study upon criminality in the context of race relations. High crime areas, marked also by physical deterioration and decay, were those in which colored immigrants became trapped by social processes, but Lambert was able to show that immigrant crime rates per se were actually low within the high-rate areas.

Research Directions

There are several directions in which most recent research into crime, which has some level of spatial content, is proceeding. Interestingly, geographers are now becoming directly involved in this research for almost the first time. Firstly, there are continuing studies in the spatial ecology tradition which seek both to depict further the spatial patterning of both offenses and offenders and to examine the environmental correlates which exist. While examples can be drawn from the environments of crime commission and of crime residence, it is in the former that new research endeavor may well be concentrated. Secondly, there are attempts to use the methodology of residential differentiation as a basis for the systematic analysis of delinquent behavior and, more specifically, of the social environments of delinquency areas. This is a research direction classified by Baldwin[31] as using "area as means to an end."[31] Thirdly, there are attempts to locate and identify some of those sociopolitical processes which are the antecedents of "problem areas." Within the British context, the recent emergence of "problem estates" as one product of public sector housing has provided a unique opportunity to study the genesis of a delinquency area.

These provide convenient compartments within which the progress of a spatial perspective on British urban crime can be discussed. One or two more general points may serve as a useful context for this discussion. It must be acknowledged that British criminal statistics[32] are probably less amenable to geographical analysis than their American counterparts. Statistics are published annually in some detail but the administrative police units for which regional and local data are available are very large and do not match those used for other regional statistical returns. McClintock and Avison,[33] in the most comprehensive national-scale analysis which is available, showed that while recorded crime had moved from an average annual growth rate of 5 percent in the 1920s and 1930s, through a period of fluctuation, to a rate of around 10 percent since 1955, variations by regions did not appear to be great. As a general point, therefore, there are a number of major problems concerning data sources which involve questions of availability, suitability, and representativeness.

Another general point concerns the ways in which British geographers are likely to enter the study of crime. There is clearly some scope for specialist spatial analysis and for the involvement of professional geographers as "spatial consultants" on interdisciplinary projects.[34] It is also possible and perhaps desirable, however, that geographers in studying crime will do so within the framework of a more general methodology appropriate for the analysis of urban social problems. A schema for such a methodology, which is discussed in more detail elsewhere,[35] might identify a series of "levels" of analysis within which geographers might work. Such levels could proceed from that of the political economy to that of resource allocation and "managerialism" as antecedents of urban problems, and to a further level of analysis based upon local environment.[36] In the context of crime, the antecedents of particular interest are the sociolegal systems which both define the legality or otherwise of behavior and operate the policing, recording, and penal system. The tenor of this argument, therefore, is that while crime and delinquency do of course have special features, they can be analyzed in the context of a more general problem-oriented geographical methodology.

British Areal Studies

The term "areal" here is reserved for those studies, or sections of studies, which use available statistics to identify spatial distributions. Relatively few British studies have made any explicit attempt to replicate the Shaw and McKay[37] spatial generalizations and, of these, the Castle and Gittus study[38] has already been cited. Reason for this is mainly that there is a general awareness of those structural changes in British cities, principally related to the impact of public sector housing, which have made what Robson called "the game of hunt the Chicago model,"[39] redundant. As large numbers of people were redistributed from inner city to peripheral council estates, patterns of known offenders were also redistributed. Numerous studies demonstrate that simple gradients of crime and delinquency rates no longer obtain and that clusters of high rates appear in both central and peripheral areas. Morris[40] showed that this pattern existed in Croydon; Timms analyzed 976 adult criminals and 989 juvenile delinquents in Luton and concluded: "The rooming house districts, the slums, and the older Council estate. These are the main 'problem areas.'"[41]

Areal studies have generally shown an awareness of the need to distinguish between distributions of offenders and offenses. The distinction is important, as figures 2.1 and 2.2 illustrate, with the offender pattern (figure 2.1) displaying the two sets of clusters in

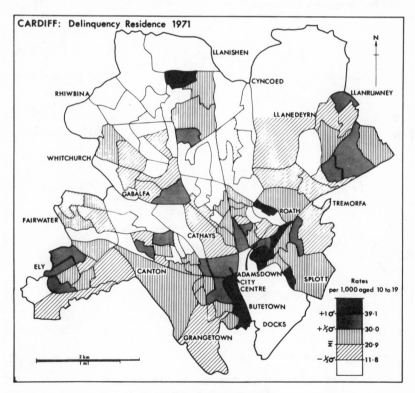

Figure 2.1. Offender Pattern

inner city and peripheral estates, and the offense pattern (figure 2.2) revealing ι strong concentration upon the high "opportunity environment" of the inner city. Davidson, Weir, and Irving[42] suggested that while council rehousing schemes had redistributed offenders, their offenses were still committed in the inner city. Several studies of offender patterns have been able to distinguish among types of offenders,[43] and Davidson[44] has examined the spatial ecology of shop-lifting in Hull (see also Baldwin and Bottoms).[45] Other studies have brought areal analysis down to a microscale. Both Morris[46] and Jephcott and Carter[47] mapped individual data to show clusters within estates and street-by-street variations. Figure 2.3 shows a distribution of individual known juvenile offenders for one Cardiff estate in 1971. While clusters are

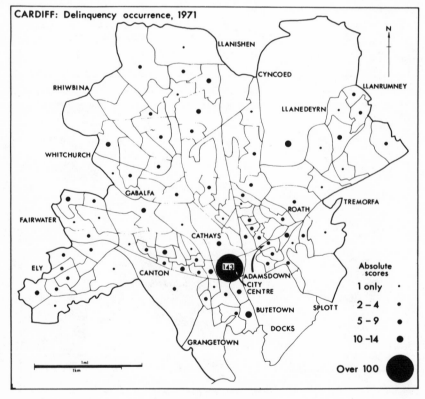

Figure 2.2. Offense Pattern

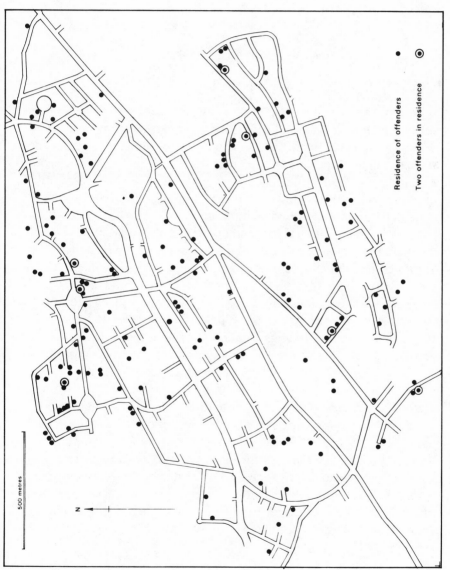

Figure 2.3. Distribution of Known Juvenile Offenders

clearly discernible, there were insufficient longitudinal data to examine their persistence over time, though some of the social networks could be estimated.[48]

Ecological Analyses

Offender Rates and Environment Variables

A considerable literature has been generated by the possibilities of measuring the levels of association between offender rates and other measurable qualities of urban environments. Again, the lineage of this type of analysis goes back well into the nineteenth century with Mayhew[49] providing an early example of a correlative exercise. Small-area statistics from national censuses have only been generally available in Britain since 1961 but have since been used as bases for multivariate analyses.[50] Giggs[51] adopted a principal components procedure to analyze his data set of fifty-six variables but did not separate dependent and independent variables. Gittus and Stephens[52] advocated a canonical analysis of separate data sets and this procedure was followed by Herbert.[53] Many of these types of multivariate analysis are most likely now to confirm existing findings rather than provide new insights, and procedures which test limited hypotheses are potentially more rewarding. Baldwin and Bottoms[54] used a series of regressional analyses to identify relationships in their Sheffield study. Among their findings were the suggestion of a "social disorganization" group of diagnostic variables and the notion of a "housing class" hypothesis was that when offender rates were categorized by "housing classes," that is, owner-occupiers, council-rented, private-rented, mixed, there were consistent differences between some offender rates even when social class was controlled. A replication of this hypothesis for Cardiff data[55] was able to confirm its partial validity, with owner-occupied areas consistently having the lowest offender rates.

Where Offenses Occur: The "Prone Environment"

Oscar Newman's essay on defensible space[56] has provided something of a catalyst in research concerned with the environments in which offenses occur. British work in this mode is ongoing, but to date only Mawby[57] has reported his findings in detail. Mawby's work is a development from the Sheffield study,[58] some aspects of which provide a foundation for his analysis. Using data for four estates labeled council housing (CH) and council flats (CF) with high (H) or low (L) *offender* rates, Mawby found that when rates per 1,000 for residential *offenses* were calculated, a contrasted pattern (CHH 85.1; CFH 29.9; CLF 20.2) appeared. This and similar findings led Mawby to question the general validity of Newman's thesis. Highest rates in this example were not in the high-rise apartments, as might have been expected and, more generally, Mawby thought that many of the concepts from Newman's *Defensible Space* were ambiguous. In another reported investigation, Mawby obtained data on twenty-seven telephone kiosks in Sheffield which had been vandalized an exceptional number of times. His evidence suggested that when levels of usage were controlled, a relationship did exist between visibility and level of vandalism. This appeared to support one of Newman's ideas but again it was ambiguous. The rate was low relative to use in publicly visible kiosks but was very high in absolute terms simply because of greater usage. While there are few studies to report in this category, both the level of interest and scope for research is high.

The Sheffield study[59] has also provided the most detailed analysis of the travel characteristics of offenders and distance relationships between place of residence and place of offense. Spatial distribution of offenses showed a very high level of concentration in and around the city center, with 23.7 percent of offenses being committed within a half mile of the center and 50.9 percent between one and three miles. Using an index relating to the location of industrial and commercial properties to measure opportunities, Baldwin and Bottoms found a strong correlation between this index and offense rates but not a total explanation of the pattern. The city center contained more offenses than could be accounted for simply by the level of opportunities. There was also no support for the hypothesis that offense and offender areas were synonymous. On analyzing distances travelled by offenders to place of offense, the Sheffield study was able to confirm the earlier finding[60] that crime in general and juvenile delinquency in particular is a very local phenomenon. While there are differences among types of offenders—older offenders travel further—and offenses, three-quarters of young offenders commit most types of offense within one mile of their homes.

Delinquency Areas—Problem Estates

While the idea of delinquency areas has a long tradition, it presents a number of difficulties both conceptually and empirically. Gill[61] suggested that as a concept it draws upon three sociological theories—the ecological approach (why people live where they do), the subcultural approach (how localized and distinctive life styles exist), and the social reaction approach (how labels are given to individuals and areas). Gill's study of Luke Street in Liverpool exemplifies how these theories can be combined. Practical problems arise because as an area, and thus an aggregate, approach the question of ecological fallacy arises. Even proponents of the delinquency area idea have to accept that it contains many nondelinquents. This may in part be a reflection of the inadequacy of official statistics and methods of interpretation. A recent study of prevalence rates for Newcastle[62] suggested that in the "worst" ward a majority of a cohort born in 1949 were known offenders. Gill, examining one area in Liverpool, found that of sixty-nine families, forty-one had at least one offender and between them there were 429 recorded offenses. Armstrong and Wilson have argued that all youths who live in particularly bad areas become stigmatized: "The youth who live in a delinquent area has a good chance of being labelled delinquent. His moral character may become a question of open debate, and be challenged more frequently."[63] While these observations are correct, it remains true that many nondelinquent youths live in delinquency areas. The concept is one of relative differences between various districts of a city; it also has to acknowledge that other factors—such as home, school, or special interest group—may counterbalance the "area effect." Again, the idea of delinquency area, in common with other area approaches, is vulnerable to criticism on the grounds that it tends artificially to isolate the influence of space, location, and territory and neglects the structural and social processes which are also involved. However one defines delinquency areas, there will be many offenders outside them, as there are nonoffenders within. These are real problems which qualify a delinquency area approach but do not invalidate it. Aggregate and individual approaches (and policies) are not alternatives but may complement each other. Delinquency areas identify local circumstances which may promote high offender rates and localities to which ameliorative resources may be allocated.

While some British criminologists would doubt, in an increasingly mobile society, whether "crime areas" still exist,[64] virtually all would agree that there are still delinquent neighborhoods. Many faced the practical problem of drawing a boundary around this type of area:

> What we are saying is that within a broad zone which can be drawn upon a map a very substantial number of people commit offences . . . the majority of residents in that zone may not be offenders . . . but there are sufficient who are criminal . . . for us to be able to say that the area as a whole is "delinquency producing."[65]

Most recent studies have suggested that "areas" can be sharply demarcated where strong physical or social barriers exist.[66] Damer, in his study of "Wine Alley,"[67] suggested that part at least of the explanation for its persistence was due to the fact that it was a clearly defined ecological unit.

British experience of major public sector rehousing projects in the last half of the century has allowed a detailed scrutiny of the ways in which some kinds of delinquency areas—the "problem estates"—have emerged. In some British cities, the majority of known offenders now reside in these peripheral estates rather than in inner-city areas. One effect of this change has been to dismiss finally the cruder expressions of architectural determinism which would see substandard housing and other deficiencies of the built environment as prime causes of criminality, and has shifted attention to social processes and the mechanisms of the housing market. Gill, writing on a particularly "bad" area of Liverpool, stated: "It was local planning and housing department policies that produced Luke Street. The action of the police and the stereotyping of Luke Street as a 'bad' area were crucial but secondary processes."[68] There is a majority view[69] that the larger estates of the 1920s and 1930s are the most problematic, but some studies[70] found recent estates to possess similar levels of difficulty.

Several researchers have attempted to form or classify possible explanations for the emergence of these problem estates. Baldwin[71] identified three lines of explanation and assessed the merits of each of these in the light of the Sheffield study.[72] First, there were those theories which focus upon the allegedly high rates of population turnover on delinquent estates and relate these to "social disorganization." Giggs[73] had some suggestion of this in his Barry study, though he allied it with additional stresses associated with residential upheaval. As a theory, however, the "turnover" idea does not square with the evidence that high delinquency rates are often a feature of stable areas. The second line of explanation, concerned with the paucity of social and recreational facilities, particularly for youngsters, on problem estates, was also identified by Gill.[74] Although this is clearly a problem over a wide range of housing projects, there was no direct evidence in the Sheffield study to link delinquency and level of provision in a direct way. In addition to the deficiency of facilities, Gill also noted the absence of opportunities in the key fields of employment and education in areas which have the "worst of everything." The third explanation for problem estates favored by both Baldwin[75] and Gill centered around the role of the housing departments.

This line of explanation can be examined rather more closely because it both ties in with recent work by urban geographers (though not necessarily directly linked with crime) and it also is an active research front with a spatial perspective. Urban geographers concerned with the housing market have shown an increased interest in what might be termed the "managerialist" perspective. While all would regard the analysis of local decision makers, managers, or "gatekeepers" as important, there are differences of opinion on the significance of their roles. Pahl[76] view them as critical figures regardless of the encompassing macrostructure of society, Lee[77] regards them as subservient to the form of the political economy within which they operate. The key "gatekeepers" in the context of problem estates are the local authority housing managers who allocate tenancies among the various council properties.[78] A direct assumption of some studies is that local authorities operate a "dumping" policy whereby tenants are preselected on a grading system based on present circumstances and assessed "social status." Gill listed some housing officials' descriptions of Luke Street families which included phrases like: "not suitable for new property," "suitable dock area only," "suitable West End only," and "not suitable for corporation to rehouse."[79] Timms stated of his study in Luton: "The older and less well-equipped an estate, the more likely it is to serve as a repository of problem families."[80] Whereas individual studies have come to conclusions of this kind, it has proved difficult to demonstrate that such policies have been practiced on a large scale. Evidence is not always available, policies will change over time and the multitude of considerations which may relate to a particular decision are often difficult to disentangle. Baldwin, on investigating this simple segregation policy hypothesis for Sheffield, found it to be too crude for several reasons. First, there was some choice among council estates, and slum clearance tenants, perhaps the potential "worse," seemed to be given more choice than others. Allocation policy was therefore a filter which might reinforce segregation but not initiate it. Second, the ability of the housing manager to direct was subject to the levels and locations of vacancies at any one point in time and voluntary exchanges played a significant part in the system. Third, an analysis of the distribution of tenants with criminal records showed some differences among estates but not enough to explain why some were "problem" and some were not.[81] For Baldwin, the local authority allocation policy was an involved variable but was not sufficient in itself to explain "problem estates"; Gill[82] was less convinced that this role was secondary.

Several writers have attempted to elicit the role of the allocation policy in comparison with other factors in the "creation" of problem estates. Wilson[83] argued that the additional factors to be considered were the existence of self-selection processes among tenants, based upon the level of rents and their image of how a particular estate would suit them. The Sheffield study[84] found that a majority of residents on a problem estate had no real concern about the level of crime, had no intention of moving and had a prime complaint that they were neglected by local improvement agencies. The problem estate in Sheffield had a low waiting list, "aspiring" tenants were trying to get off, those who stayed and those who accepted vacancies were indifferent to its reputation. Gill was much less willing to accept the self-selection idea and the notion that "like seeks like":

> Luke Street originated from a process of residential selection which can relegate some areas to the bottom of a hierarchy of desirability: the families who are least able to compete in the struggle for better accommodation in the private or public sector, end up living there.[85]

The question remains of how these estates acquire reputations in the first place. In this the characteristics of the very first tenants seem critical. The Sheffield study[86] showed that one such problem estate was initially used to relocate several notorious gang leaders and gang members in the 1930s; in Cardiff[87] there is some evidence that whole groups of Irish and therefore "different" people were moved from the worst inner-city areas to a particular estate in the 1930s. Another clue was provided in Sheffield[88] from the ways in which two estates—one problem, one not—were populated. The relatively good estate had taken its tenants off a long waiting list and largely from the nearby area; the problem estate had been tenanted at a time of low demand and had taken very recent applicants on the waiting list who were drawn from widely disparate sources. These facts have not been forgotten by the local community and are used to stigmatize the estate.

This idea of "stigmatization" is important and is linked to the theory that reputations, once established, are perpetuated—perhaps undeservedly—because the area is labeled as problematic. Damer's study of a Glasgow estate is the most detailed case study of this kind so far published.[89] His "Wine Alley," an estate built in 1934 and having just over 500 houses and 2,000 population, had an atrocious reputation with local people and officialdom alike. He found it, however, to be a fairly ordinary Glasgow manual workers' community. Its emergence as a problem estate was strongly tied to its recruitment of occupants from distant parts of the city and the resentment of this fact by the local Govan people. Wine Alley was regarded by municipal officials as typified by rent arrears, vandalism, crime, delinquency and sociopsychological problems. Its persistence was aided by ecological factors but it was more a product of labeling than of the realities of its occupants' behavior. Gill found much to support this contention and the need for a dynamic historical approach.[90]

Analyses of the emergence of problem estates have therefore highlighted a series of interrelated social processes, both internal and external, which contribute to their existence (see figure 2.4). These include local authority housing policy, self-selection among tenants, and labeling—factors which identify Gill's three strands of sociological theory noted above. Most writers have looked for ways in which the image can be improved and unfavorable reputations changed. Byrne[91] advocated more active attempts to disperse problem families and achieve more social mix; other ideas might include determined efforts to upgrade environments and improve social provision. These are local environmental solutions which policies of "positive discrimination" might achieve; other levels for action would seek to reform those sociopolitical processes, resource allocation procedures and housing management systems, which play significant roles in the emergence of problem estates.

Finally, in the context of problem estates and delinquency areas in general, British geographers have become increasingly interested in the possible existence of "area effects." Such effects have been considered in several contexts[92] as a "contagion" or "contaminating" process within particular neighborhoods; elsewhere the notion of measuring local climate of opinion[93] and personal social environment[94] within delinquency areas has similar objectives. A study completed on these lines[95] used an area sampling framework to select pairs of areas which were similar in terms of delinquency rates. The substantive finding was that in delinquency areas there were social modes and codes of behavior, held to some considerable level of consensus by the areas' residents, which constituted a negative externality for the local population as a whole and particularly for its youth. It was from these qualities of the personal social environment that some understanding of the prevalence of delinquent behavior might be obtained.

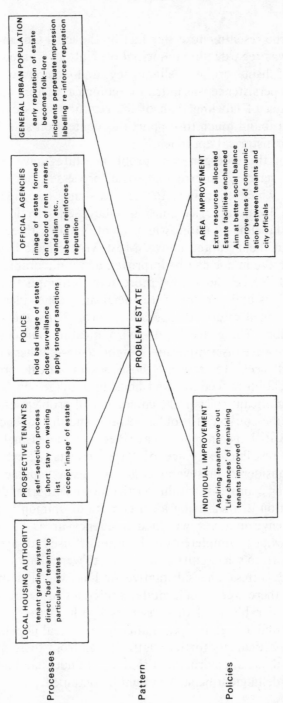

Figure 2.4. Social Processes and Problem Estates

Processes

LOCAL HOUSING AUTHORITY
tenant grading system
direct 'bad' tenants to
particular estates

PROSPECTIVE TENANTS
self-selection process
short stay on waiting
list
accept 'image' of estate

POLICE
hold bad image of estate
closer surveillance
apply stronger sanctions

OFFICIAL AGENCIES
image of estate formed
on record of rent arrears,
vandalism etc..
labelling reinforces
reputation

GENERAL URBAN POPULATION
early reputation of estate
becomes folk-lore
incidents perpetuate impression
labelling re-inforces reputation

Pattern

PROBLEM ESTATE

Policies

INDIVIDUAL IMPROVEMENT
Aspiring tenants move out
'Life chances' of remaining
tenants improved

AREA IMPROVEMENT
Extra resources allocated
Estate facilities enchanced
Aim at better social balance
Improve lines of communic-
ation between tenants and
city officials

Conclusions

This chapter has identified some of the main research directions which may contribute to a better comprehension of the geography of urban crime in Britain and which, in turn, will add an extra dimension of understanding to an already well-developed field of criminological studies. The scope for developing the analysis of spatial perspectives is considerable, both in the more traditional study of patterns and the spatial ecology of crime and delinquency, and in the emergence of newer perspectives which incorporate investigation of those complex sociopolitical processes which may be regarded as the antecedents of delinquent patterns, areas, and behavior. The lesson for British geographers turning to the analysis of crime is that they have the opportunities to apply and develop their traditional skills of spatial analysis but need not be deterred from drawing insights from new perspectives and methodologies.

NOTES

1. P. D. Phillips, "A Prologue to the Geography of Crime," *Proceedings of the Association of American Geographers*, (1972), 4:59–64.

2. Henry Mayhew, *London Labour and the London Poor* (London: Griffin Bohn, 1862).

3. Charles Booth, *Life and Labour of the People* (London: Williams and Margate, 1891).

4. W. H. Holland, "Professional Thieves," *Cornhill Magazine* (1862), 6:645.

5. J. J. Tobias, "A Statistical Study of Nineteenth Century Criminal Area," *British Journal of Criminology* (1976), 14:221–35.

6. Abraham Hume, *Conditions of Liverpool*, cited in Tobias, "Statistical Study," p. 221.

7. Hermann Mannheim, *Comparative Criminology* (London: Routledge and Kegan Paul, 1965), p. 532.

8. J. Baldwin, "British Areas Studies of Crime: An Assessment," *British Journal of Criminology* (1975), 15:211–27.

9. David M. Smith, "Crime Rates as Territorial Social Indicators," Queen Mary College, London, Department of Geography Occasional Paper No. 1 (1974).

10. Barry Hindess, *The Use of Official Statistics in Sociology* (London: Macmillan, 1973).

11. A. E. Bottoms, "Offender Patterns and Housing Allocation Policies," Unpublished conference paper, University of Sheffield, England (1977).

12. Baldwin, "British Areas Studies of Crime."

13. T. Ferguson, *The Young Delinquent in His Social Setting* (London: Oxford University Press, 1952).

14. David M. Downes, *The Delinquent Solution* (London: Routledge and Kegan Paul, 1966).

15. John B. Mays, *Growing Up in the City* (Liverpool: University of Liverpool Press, 1954).

16. Frederick H. McClintock, *Crimes of Violence* (London: Macmillan, 1963).

17. Baldwin, "British Areas Studies of Crime."

18. Clifford R. Shaw and Henry D. McKay, *Juvenile Delinquency and Urban Areas* (Chicago: University of Chicago Press, 1942).

19. I. Castle and E. Gittus, "The Distribution of Social Defects in Liverpool," *Sociological Review* (1957), 5:43–64.

20. C. P. Wallis and R. Maliphant, "Delinquent Areas in the County of London: Ecological Factors," *British Journal of Criminology* (1967), 7:250–84.

21. Cyril Burt, *The Young Delinquent* (London: London University Press, 1925).

22. A. Edwards, "Sex and Area Variations in Delinquency Rates in an English City," *British Journal of Criminology* (1973), 13:121–37.

23. Baldwin, "British Areas Studies of Crime."

24. J. A. Giggs, "The Socially Disorganized Areas of Barry: A Multi-Variate Analysis," in Harold Carter and Wayne K. D. Davies, eds., *Urban Essays* (London: Longman, 1970), pp. 101–43.

25. M. J. Brown, J. W. McCulloch, and J. Hiscox, "Criminal Offences in an Urban Area and Their Associated Social Variables," *British Journal of Criminology* (1972), 12:250–68.

26. Baldwin, "British Areas Studies of Crime."

27. Terrence P. Morris, *The Criminal Area* (London: Routledge and Kegan Paul, 1957).

28. Peter Sainsbury, *Suicide in London* (London: Chapman and Hall, 1955).

29. Pearl A. Jephcott and Michael P. Carter, *The Social Background of Delinquency*. Unpublished report, University of Nottingham, England (1954).

30. John Lambert, *Crime, Police and Race Relations* (London: Oxford University Press, 1970).

31. Baldwin, "British Areas Studies of Crime."

32. British criminal statistics are published annually by the Home Office, with a supplementary volume of regional statistics.

33. Frederick H. McClintock and N. Howard Avison, *Crime in England and Wales* (London: Heinemann, 1968).

34. Dr. R. Norman Davidson has this role in an ongoing survey of crime and delinquency at the University of Hull.

35. David T. Herbert and David M. Smith, eds., *Social Problems in the City: A Geographical Approach* (London: Oxford University Press, 1979).

36. Smith, *Crime Rates*; and D. T. Herbert, "Crime, Delinquency and the Urban Environment," *Progress in Human Geography* (1977), 1:208–39.

37. Shaw and McKay, *Juvenile Delinquency*.

38. Castle and Gittus, "Distribution of Social Defects."

39. Brian T. Robson, *Urban Analysis* (Cambridge: University of Cambridge Press, 1969), p. 132.

40. Morris, *Criminal Area*.

41. D. W. G. Timms, "The Spatial Distribution of Social Deviants in Luton, England," *Australia and New Zealand Journal of Sociology* (1965), 1:38–52.

42. R. Norman Davidson, David T. W. Weir, and Henry W. Irving, "Analysis of Urban Areas, Report to Social Science Research Council, University of Hull, England, Department of Geography (1974).

43. D. T. Herbert, "An Areal and Ecological Analysis of Delinquency Residence: Cardiff 1966 and 1971," *Tijdschrift voor Economische en Sociale Geografie* (1977), 68:83–99.

44. R. Norman Davidson, "The Ecology of Shoplifting," Discussion paper, University of Hull, England, Department of Geography (1976).

45. John Baldwin and Anthony E. Bottoms, *The Urban Criminal* (London: Tavistock, 1976).

46. Morris, *Criminal Area*.

47. Jephcott and Carter, *Social Background of Delinquency*.

48. Herbert, "Areal and Ecological Analysis."

49. Mayhew, *London Labour and the London Poor*.

50. Small-area statistics are generally available for British censuses 1961, though some figures on these bases for a few cities were released for 1951.

51. Giggs, "Socially Disorganized Areas of Barry."

52. Elizabeth Gittus and Chris J. Stephens, "Some Problems in The Use of Canonical Analysis," Discussion paper, University of Newcastle-upon-tyne, England (1973).

53. Herbert, "Areal and Ecological Analysis."

54. Baldwin and Bottoms, *Urban Criminal*.

55. D. T. Herbert, "Urban Crime: A Geographical Perspective" in Herbert and Smith, eds., *Social Problems in the City*.

56. Oscar Newman, *Defensible Space* (New York: Macmillan, 1972).

57. R. I. Mawby, "Defensible Space: A Theoretical and Empirical Approach," *Urban Studies* (1977), 14:169–79; and "Kiosk Vandalism: A Sheffield Study," *British Journal of Criminology* (1977), 17:30–46.

58. Baldwin and Bottoms, *Urban Criminal*.

59. Ibid.

60. McClintock and Avison, *Crime in England*.

61. Owen Gill, *Luke Street* (London: Macmillan, 1977).

62. Edwards, "Sex and Area Variations in Delinquency Rates."

63. G. Armstrong and W. Wilson, "City Politics and Deviancy Amplification," in Ian Taylor and Laurie Taylor, eds., *Politics and Deviance* (Harmondsworth, England: Penguin, 1973), pp. 61–89.

64. J. Mack, "Full-Time Miscreants, Delinquent Neighborhoods, and Criminal Networks," *British Journal of Sociology* (1964), 15:38–53.

65. J. B. Mays, "Delinquency Areas: A Re-assessment," *British Journal of Criminology* (1963), 3:216–30.

66. Gill, *Luke Street*.

67. S. Damer, "Wine Alley: The Sociology of a Dreadful Enclosure," *Sociological Review* (1974), 22:221–48.

68. Gill, *Luke Street*, p. 187.

69. Timms, "Spatial Distribution of Social Deviants."

70. Giggs, "Socially Disorganized Areas of Barry."

71. J. Baldwin, "Urban Criminality and the Problem Estate," *Local Government Studies* (1975), 1:12–20.

72. Baldwin and Bottoms, *Urban Criminal*.

73. Giggs, "Socially Disorganized Areas of Barry."

74. Gill, *Luke Street*.

75. Baldwin, "Urban Criminality and the Problem Estate."

76. R. E. Pahl, "Socio-political Factors in Resource Allocation," in Herbert and Smith, eds., *Social Problems in the City*.

77. R. Lee, "Economic Bases of Social Problems" in Herbert and Smith, eds., *Social Problems in the City*.

78. F. Gray, "Selection and Allocation in Council Housing," *Transactions*, 1, Institute of British Geographers (1976), pp. 34–46.

79. Gill, *Luke Street*, pp. 26–28.

80. Timms, "*Spatial Distribution of Social Deviants*," p. 47.

81. Baldwin, "Urban Criminality and the Problem Estate."

82. Gill, *Luke Street*.

83. Roger Wilson, *Difficult Housing Estates* (London: Tavistock).

84. Baldwin and Bottoms, *Urban Criminal*; and Baldwin, "Urban Criminality and the Problem Estate."

85. Gill, *Luke Street*, p. 182.

86. Baldwin, "Urban Criminality and the Problem Estate."

87. Herbert, "Urban Crime."

88. Bottoms, "Offender Patterns and Housing Allocation Policies."

89. Damer, "Wine Alley."

90. Gill, *Luke Street*.

91. David S. Byrne, "Problem Families: A Housing Lumpen-Proletariat," Working paper in sociology no. 5, University of Durham, England (1974).

92. R. J. Johnston, "Contagion in Neighborhoods: A Note on Problems of Modelling and Analysis," *Environment and Planning* (1976), 8A:581–85.

93. W. J. H. Sprott, "Nottingham," in John B. Mays, ed., *Juvenile Delinquency, the Family, and the Social Group* (London: Longman, 1972), pp. 30–32.

94. D. T. Herbert, "Urban Deprivation: Definition, Measurement and Spatial Qualities," *Geographical Journal* (1975), 141:362–72.

95. D. T. Herbert, "The Study of Delinquency Areas: A Geographical Approach," *Transactions 1*, Institute of British Geographers (1976), pp. 472–92.

ꙮ 3 ꙮ

Spatial Aspects
of Criminal Behavior

GEORGE RENGERT

RECENT GEOGRAPHICAL STUDIES which concern criminal activity have been somewhat confusing, since generally it is not clear whether the investigators are attempting to explain *why* crimes take place or whether they are explaining *where* crimes occur. Furthermore, studies which purport to examine the cause of crime usually do not explicitly determine whether the important variables should deal with the residence of the criminal, the location of the criminal act, or with some other supposed influence on crime which has distribution in space. In short, there is a general lack of theoretical development.

What is needed is increased focus on specific aspects of the criminal environment. We need to go beyond purely descriptive ecological studies and formulate some theoretical constructs which may lead to explanations of the criminal spatial structure.

As a beginning, we must define what is meant by a "criminal area." Specifically, can we ever get at the full spatial meaning of crime if we cannot separate why crimes occur from where crimes are committed? In other words, we must separate the *cause* from the *effect* (i.e., the exact site or physical location of the incident).

In this paper, an analytical framework is developed which should shed light on the distinction between *why* crimes are committed and *where* they are committed. Specifically, it is argued that since most criminal behavior is rational, it can be organized into a model of criminal decision making.[1] This model is used to illustrate the conceptual difference between factors which are believed to be related to the *causes* of crime and those which are more related to the distribution of crime occurrences.

The Criminal Decision Process

There is considerable literature on the causes of crime, most of which focuses on economic, sociological, and/or pathological factors. Recently, however, criminologists have been attempting to tie together certain of these diverse postulates into a more general theory of criminal behavior. Cloward and Ohlin suggest an approach which seems especially relevant to geographers.[2] Specifically, they suggest that individuals have been instilled with certain goals and/or aspirations by society which they strive to accomplish. Where legitimate means of accomplishing these aspirations are continually blocked, the individuals are likely to turn to "deviant behavior" rather than to accept their lot and its accompanying frustrations.[3] Therefore, throughout life, each individual is faced with choices concerning means of attaining life's goals—some are socially acceptable while others are termed deviant or criminal behavior.

The thrust of much contemporary research in criminology is toward identification of these aspirations and the barriers which are placed in the path of their legitimate attainment. However, it may in fact be that the barriers are less important than would be a conscious weighing of the relative advantages of alternative means (both legitimate and deviant) of attaining goals governed by the classic "principle of least effort." There seems to be no reason to believe that an individual will consistently choose legal behavior if it also consistently involves more effort and less reward than criminal behavior (considering the probability of apprehension and social stigma in this decision process).

However, whatever the cause of their choice, at some point in their life cycle individual criminals must have decided to commit what has been defined as a criminal act. For most crimes which are not spontaneous responses to situational stimuli, this decision process probably included considerable deliberation to weigh alternative possibilities—both criminal and legal. This is true even

of most juvenile crimes which the layman tends to consider unplanned malicious behavior. Criminologists have found that even
this youthful behavior is usually quite purposeful.[4] Therefore, once
the individual has decided to consider a criminal act, then there
must be final planning as to how and ultimately where to commit
the crime.

In line with this reasoning, we can model most criminal behavior as a two-stage decision process.

Decision   to Consider a Criminal Act in association with

Decision   on How and Where to Commit the Crime leads to

A criminal Act

Initially, the individual weighs alternatives in deciding whether or
not to commit a criminal act. Then, once the individual has decided to consider a criminal act, final planning of how and where
to commit the crime precedes any actual crime. On the other
hand, "situational crimes" occur when an individual is confronted
with an opportunity (how and where to commit the crime) which
then must be evaluated in terms of whether or not to commit the
crime. The total cause of crime thus is composed of a set of factors of which the "decision to consider a criminal act" and the
"how and where to commit the crime" are subsets. We can gain
considerable insight into criminal spatial structures if we can
identify the factors related to each of these subsets in turn. In fact,
most past research has dealt only with the first.

Geographers, however, may offer special expertise to investigations of where crimes are committed, since this involves a singularly geographic concept. Thus, by concentrating attention on
either one or the other of the two integrated criminal decisions, we
can alleviate much of the confusion which surrounds all-inclusive
explanations of criminal behavior.

Operational Variables

In the search for operational variables, to explain where a crime
takes place, it is once again important to emphasize that the
residence of the criminal is not an all-pervasive variable. The
search for a location for a criminal act may be associated with
many of the same types of factors geographers traditionally

analyzed in intraurban and interurban migration studies (especially search behavior).[5] The criminals, in searching for locations for criminal acts, are rationally attempting to approximate a set of criteria which they have established in the planning process.

The ideal location for a specific criminal act, therefore, seems to depend largely on the varying spatial structure of the criminal's environment as well as on the type of crime they intend to commit. In the empirical example presented in this paper, we are going to restrict our analysis to urban crimes—crimes which take place within the political boundaries of an urban area. Given the varying spatial structure of our major cities, the objective of the criminal may be served better in any of several locations, depending on the type of crime the individual intends to commit.

The central idea here is that there are different underlying objectives associated with different types of crimes, and these underlying objectives occasion different types of spatial behavior on the part of the criminal. For instance, an arsonist/vandal obviously entertains a different set of objectives than does a robber/ burglar. In the first instance, it seems that the primary objective of the criminal is both monetary reward (in the case of a shop owner making a fradulent insurance claim or of extortion by organized crime) and psychic pleasure (in the case of pyromaniacs), while in the second, monetary reward is more likely to be the primary objective.

In the light of such distinctions, grouping all criminal acts into one aggregate group for investigating factors which underlies the choice of a crime location would appear to ignore many potentially important differences between crimes which may contribute to an explanation of their relative spatial incidence. A helpful approach might be to group criminal acts into categories (prior to investigations of crime locations) based on primary objective of the criminal in committing the crime.

Monetary Gain	Psychic or Social Pleasure	Physiological Needs
Arson	Arson	Narcotics
Robbery	Vandalism	Alcoholism
Burglary		
Kidnapping		

Three types of objectives (or rewards) are identified as underlying certain types of criminal behavior: the major objective of robbers, burglars, and kidnappers is monetary gain; arsonists and vandals, on the other hand, are said to strive for psychic pleasures from their activities; finally alcoholics and narcotic addicts are more likely to be driven by physiological needs and desires.

The optimal location for satisfying any of these three objectives would vary throughout the urban spatial structure. For criminals with these objectives in mind, there are areas of the city which would bring larger monetary rewards or offer a greater number of opportunities for committing property crimes than other areas. On the other hand, areas with abandoned and/or public buildings provide opportunities for vandals and arsonists. These features are distributed unevenly throughout a city and provide varying degrees of opportunities for the prospective criminal.

The possibility of being apprehended is another consideration in criminal spatial planning. Since the probability of being caught also varies over urban space, there is no reason to assume spatial indifference concerning this matter in the criminal decision process. For example, in addition to the spatial variation in police protection, neighborhood attitudes toward crime and law enforcement officers are also a crucial determinant of potential criminal apprehension. In areas where residents have become accustomed to criminal behavior, crime can be committed with a relatively small chance of being apprehended. Law enforcement officers receive little or no aid in their investigations while neighbors and friends may harbor the suspect, protecting him from apprehension.

At the other extreme, other neighborhoods contain residents who consider the police valuable partners in their attempt to control crime. In these areas, full cooperation is given in an investigation and few people would be willing to conceal the criminal's identity. Here, police work is more efficient and fewer officers can do a more thorough job than in less cooperative areas. Of course, these are only a few of the many considerations which determine relative police efficiency. The rational criminals can subjectively evaluate a region of the city and rate their chances of being apprehended for a crime committed there. Although these rankings may vary for individuals, some semblance of aggregate agreement is expected.

The two goals of personal gain and avoidance of apprehension can be combined into an operational model of criminal spatial behavior. It is suggested that the individual criminal attempts to maximize the personal rewards gained by a criminal act while at the same time attempting to minimize the probability of being apprehended by choosing among alternative locations for the crime. There may in fact be trade-offs between personal safety and returns from the crime. Although there would be individual differences in such trade-offs for any given crime, it should be possible to identify generally optimal areas for the criminal act. Then, if we assume perfectly rational criminals with complete knowledge of the relevant spatial structure of the city, they would tend to choose this area for their criminal acts.

Operational Definitions of the Proposed Model
Using the Crimes of Arson and Vandalism

To operationalize the model of criminal spatial behavior as outlined above, one must keep in mind the specific reward the criminal is striving for. In the case of pyromaniac-induced arson and vandalism, locations for committing these crimes which offer the greatest likelihood of success are in places which are not cared for regularly. Abandoned properties are especially enticing since they can be set afire or wrecked with little likelihood that the act will be interrupted by a resident or caretaker. In this paper, therefore, opportunities for arsons and vandals are defined spatially as the number of vacant or abandoned homes per square mile. It is assumed that as the number of abandoned homes increases in a neighborhood, service establishments will lose their economic base and be abandoned also. Therefore, the relative number of abandoned homes per area is considered to be a measure of the total opportunities for vandalism and arson in an area.

Police efficiency, on the other hand, is somewhat less easy to operationalize in an a priori fashion. However, the results of police activity can be measured on an area basis by computing the ratio of case clearances to case occurrences for major crimes committed in an area. This provides a measure of police efficiency by area of the city, efficiency which is assumed to be perceived by the individual criminal.

Measures thus exist for each objective of an arsonist or vandal in the proposed model of criminal activity outlined above. Data concerning police efficiency were supplied for each police district by the Philadelphia Police Department.[6] The number of vacant homes per square mile was compiled from the 1970 census tract returns from Philadelphia.[7] The present analysis focuses on twenty-two police districts; the census figures were aggregated to this level (figure 3.1).

An Empirical Test of the Model

To combine measures of police efficiency and the number of vacant homes within each police district into a single measure of desirability without giving undue weight to either, each was converted into standard scores and graphed (figure 3.2). Assuming that the marginal utility of criminal opportunity is equal to that of apprehension, we can draw a line at 45-degree angle through the population defining a unity function ($X = Y$). Along this line, the chance of apprehension varies directly with opportunity for committing the criminal act. Therefore, deviations from the unity function should measure the relative desirability of a police district as the location for arson or vandalism. The rank of desirability in each police district is illustrated in table 3.1.

According to the proposed model, Police District 9 is the most attractive for arson and vandals in Philadelphia, followed by District 16. Conversely, District 7 is the least attractive, followed by District 14. The question now turns to how well the proposed model conforms to the actual distribution of arsons and vandalisms per square mile in Philadelphia (table 1). The zero order linear correlation between the two distributions yields an r^2 of .58. Therefore, if we assume equal awareness of individual arsonists and vandals of the desirability of specific regions of the city for crime locations, our model explains 58 percent of the variance in the observed pattern.

However, if we relax the constraint on equal awareness and

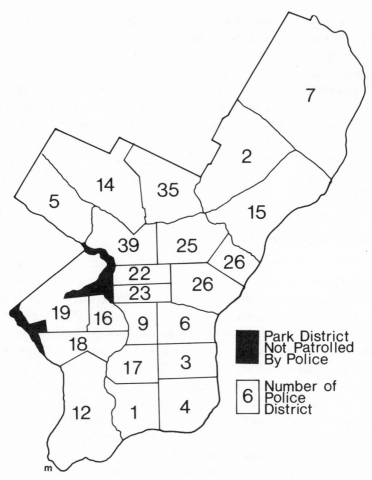

Figure 3.1. Philadelphia Police Districts

instead assume that *aggregate* familiarity with and accessibility to the city decreases from the central business district (CBD), we should obtain an even higher explanation. For instance, if all residents were to rank all areas of the city in order of their familiarity, the sum of ranks should be highest for the CBD and decrease with distance from it. Therefore, we can modify our model by including this variable (distance from the CBD) as a measure of the relative awareness of the opportunities that exist in each police district. When distance from City Hall to the center of each police district is added to the model, the percent of the variation explained in a linear model (multiple regression) increases to .73. Thus, it seems that not only the existence of opportunities but also awareness of and accessibility to the same is an important component of criminal behavior.

We must keep in mind, however, that generally socioeconomic status of residents also increases with distance from the CBD and with a decreasing proportion of vacant homes. Therefore, although the measures used in this study fit well into the identified theoretical postulates, there is a possibility that the negative correlation of distance from the CBD with arson and vandalism is

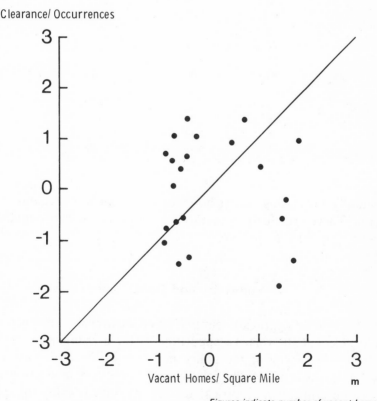

Figures indicate number of vacant homes.
Figure 3.2. Unity Function on Standard Scores

Table 3.1.
Arson and Vandalism by Police District

Police District	Arson and Vandalism	Rank Order of Desirability
1	82	20
2	133	9
3	116	8
4	176	19
5	157	13
6	189	12
7	307	22
9	168	1
12	443	15
14	207	17
15	278	10
16	175	2
17	169	4
18	143	18
19	147	21
22	283	6
23	106	3
24	156	11
25	188	16
26	273	14
35	244	7
39	149	5

actually measuring accessibility to socioeconomic regions of the city. Therefore, further research is required to substantiate the generalizations made here.

Summary and Conclusions

A model of aggregate criminal behavior is proposed which takes into account the relative opportunities for a criminal act and the relative efficiency of the police per area of the city. This model yields a measure of the relative desirability of a location for a specific crime. An empirical test of the model, using the city of Philadelphia and the crimes of arson and vandalism, resulted in 58 percent of the variance in the actual pattern explained by the model. When the model is modified to account for aggregate relative familiarity with and accessibility to the regions, explanation increased to 73 percent of the variance in the actual distribution. However, the aggregate model is derived from concepts relating to individual decision making. In other words, the aggregate model describes the pattern that would result if the decision-making assumptions of the individual hold. Still, we cannot say that these individual decisions caused the aggregate pattern. The resulting spatial pattern is necessary support but not sufficient proof of the individual decision-making process outlined above.

Needed at this point is further evidence of the search behavior of criminals in their choice of a location for a specific crime. Not only must the present model be tested using other crimes representing varying criminal objectives, but also data at the individual level is required to shed light on the actual travel behavior of a criminal in the journey from home to crime location. Do specific areas of the city actually attract criminals from long distances? This latter information should be especially enlightening in the effort to comprehend criminal activity patterns. In all these objectives, geographers have much to offer and as yet have only begun to contribute.

NOTES

1. In this paper, only planned crimes are considered. Violent and nonviolent unplanned reaction to a specific triggering situation are believed to be a different type of crime which should be analyzed separately from planned criminal behavior.

2. Richard A. Cloward and Lloyd E. Ohlin, *Delinquency and Opportunity: A Theory of Delinquent Gangs* (New York: Free Press, 1960).

3. *Ibid.*, p. 163.

4. This point is illustrated nicely by H. H. Bloch and Arthur Niederhoffer, *The Gang: A Study in Adolescent Behavior* (New York: Philosophical Library, 1958), pp. 198–99.

5. See, for example, Lawrence A. Brown and Eric H. Moore, "The Intra-Urban Mitigation Process: A Perspective," *Geografiska Annaler* (1970), 5(52B):1–13.

6. Philadelphia Police Department. Summary of Part II Crimes (1970). Mimeo.

7. U.S. Bureau of Census. Census Tract Returns for Philadelphia (1970).

⌖ 4 ⌖

The Spatial Ecology
of the Criminal Law

JACK M. KRESS

Criminal Procedure

ALL CRIMINAL LAW is usually spoken of as having both a substantive and a procedural component. Criminal procedure is concerned with the various legal steps of the criminal justice system, from police investigation through parole revocation. The relevance of criminal procedure to the geographer is apparent. Underlying all aspects of criminal law enforcement, for example, is the unifying legal concept of "jurisdiction," which refers to the very power or authority of any criminal justice agency to make any decision, exercise any discretion, or take any action whatsoever with regard to a particular criminal case. Lawyers speak of sovereign nations or states exercising jurisdictional powers, usually limited by their geographic boundaries. No nation exercises any jurisdictional control over any foreign national outside the bounds of that nation. In the United States, governmental powers are further limited by the federal system, which created a national government and fifty often sovereign states.[1]

The principal bases of a government's jurisdictional authority are territory and nationality, with the former being of primary significance. In America, the criminal jurisdictional powers of the national government are narrowly circumscribed with regard to matters lying within the purview of any individual state.[2] At the common law, every crime was considered to have but one situs or locus and, apart from the District of Columbia or certain federal reservations, the situs of a crime will normally lie within the boundaries of one of the states, and that situs typically establishes territorial jurisdiction even today.

Indeed, the criminal law may be seen perhaps as a last bastion of "states' rights," with the state wherein the crime was committed usually exercising exclusive jurisdiction over all subsequent action with regard to prosecution of the offense. (Sometimes there is concurrent federal/state jurisdiction over a given criminal case, but this is rare, applying most commonly only to interstate auto theft or bank robbery cases.) Criminal law is probably the most geographically bounded of all our laws, with ever decreasing zones of authority. Not only do penal codes vary by state (and important ordinances vary by local community), but enforcement is almost never larger than county-wide. Prosecutors, judges, sheriffs, are most often elected county officials in America. The jurisdiction of these agencies, therefore, is usually sharply limited to the narrow confines of a single local county.

While the subject of jurisdiction is undoubtedly the most pervasive geographic concern in the criminal justice system, other procedural laws concern the geographer. The laws of search and seizure circumscribe police behavior and establish zones of privacy beyond which law enforcement agents may not proceed.[3] A defense attorney may seek a change of venue if his or her client has been subjected to "pervasive and prejudicial" publicity in a given county.[4] Jurors are supposed to be chosen in a manner likely to represent a fair cross-section of the community.[5] Probation and diversion services are normally functions of the local counties. While prisons are often located far from the urban centers where inmates come from, the outcomes of prison riots are often decided by courts situated in the same county as the prison. (Prisoners' rights advocates, for this and other reasons, urge the construction of prisons and jails nearer to the central cities.)

Finally, on the subject of procedural law, we might mention the role of the geographer in the courtroom. Over the years, state rules of evidence have placed strict (and to the lay person, strange) restrictions on the admissibility of such tools of the trade as maps, charts, photographs, diagrams, or illustrations. Indeed, a sizeable caselaw has developed over the rather minor matter of whether or not jurors or witnesses may take a "view" of the scene of the crime.[6]

The Geographic Framework of the Substantive Criminal Law

Having briefly demonstrated the palpable significance of an understanding of criminal procedural law to the geographer, it will be instructive to detail the value of what might on the surface appear to be of lesser concern—substantive criminal law. Ever since the landmark efforts of the American Law Institute in formulating the Model Penal Code,[7] modern penal statutes have been divided into specific substantive offenses and general procedural provisions. New York's penal code, often held up as a model and major codification reform effort, was adapted from the Model Penal Code and formally adopted in 1967. It will thus provide a convenient reference to understanding these issues, especially with regard to particular substantive offenses, although reference will also be made to practices in other jurisdictions.

Substantive criminal law defines what conduct is to be considered criminal and prescribes the punishment for such conduct. It includes the definitions of specific crimes and defenses as well as general principles of liability, such as the usual necessity for a crime to involve a *mens rea* (a guilty mind or criminal intent) and an *actus reus* (a culpable action). Specific offenses in New York are grouped into ten overall categories, then subdivided into more generally recognized offenses within each of these categories. These offenses are then aggravated in turn by degree, with greater penalties accruing to those criminal acts wherein the basic foundation offense was committed in some particularly exacerbating manner. Although the overall category or the specific crime may imply a spatial relationship, it is most often with regard to the mitigating or aggravating factors considered in charging and sentencing offenders that geographical considerations arise. Using the structure of the New York State Penal Code as a guide, we will consider these in order. The following is a list of New York's ten overall offense categories:

Title G –Anticipatory Offenses
Title H –Offenses against the Person Involving Physical Injury, Sexual Conduct, Restraint, and Intimidation
Title I –Offenses Involving Damage to and Intrusion upon Property
Title J –Offenses Involving Theft
Title K –Offenses Involving Fraud
Title L –Offenses against Public Administration
Title M–Offenses against Public Health and Morals
Title N –Offenses against Public Order, Public Sensibilities and the Right to Privacy
Title O –Offenses against Marriage, the Family, and the Welfare of Children and Incompetents
Title P –Offenses against Public Safety

Title G refers to anticipatory offenses, which include attempts to commit other crimes and might thus more logically be discussed within the other categories.[8] Similarly, what the reader probably thinks of as "aiding or abetting" is today usually spoken of as facilitation and solicitation.

Title H, however, provides us with a series of clear illustrations of the geographical precepts which underlie penal code distinctions, on both substantive and procedural levels. The first Title H offense is assault, i.e., the causing of physical injury to another person. On a substantive level, the aggravating factors are the degree of injury caused and the weapon employed. In the systemic *implementation* of the sections, however, the location of the offense is operationally significant. If the assault occurs in the home, even if the injury verges on death and the weapon is a gun, the offense is for all practical purposes treated as a "minor" family matter. Usually the criminal court will not even have jurisdiction and the case will be transferred to Family Court; many states openly acknowledge this through the creation of a distinct assaultive category referred to as "wife beating."[9] If the assault occurs in a bar, then, practically again, even if the participants are sober, the police will treat the offense as a lower-order "barroom brawl."[10]

Perhaps the most insidious version of this is in the treatment of ghetto assaults. While the reader is probably aware that minority group members feel harassed and "overarrested" by the police, *within the ghetto* the opposite is often the case. A stabbing that would be viewed as a serious matter for full prosecution in a middle-class suburb is often viewed by criminal justice system officials as a trivial matter when the same offense occurs in the ghetto.[11]

Homicide is, of course, only an especially aggravated form of assault. The modern degree structure has sought to eliminate what were once specifically spatial considerations, but these have only become more hidden, arising instead in the exercise of prosecutorial or judicial discretion. The 1909 Penal Law (replaced by New York's 1967 revision), for example, explicitly addressed death resulting from the reckless operation of vehicles, vessels, and steamboats. Such vehicular homicide cases (which still form the bulk of the homicide caseload in most jurisdictions) are dealt with as relatively insignificant. This reflects to some extent a societal statement as to the value of geographical mobility. Motor-vehicle-related offenses (such as speeding and driving while intoxicated) are even taken out of most penal codes and placed in separate traffic codes with less severe penalties.[12] Yet the victim of a vehicular homicide is just as dead as one shot by a gun. As another example, even if bank robberies became epidemic, we would not want to be even mildly frisked upon entering a bank; yet we allow the most intrusive bodily searches at airports.[13] These infringements of life and civil liberties all take place in the name of freedom to travel.

Sex offenses are the third Title H offense division. While the public image of the rapist is a stranger who strikes from the bushes, the more commonly encountered situation involves a man and a woman who already know one another.[14] Yet the modern (?) New York penal law defines "female" as "any female person who is not married to the actor,"[15] so as specifically to immunize husband-wife rape from criminal prosecution. In practice, moreover, the "stranger" image makes the arrest and successful prosecution of most rapists an unusual thing.

Kidnapping is the final Title H category and this is by definition a clearly spatial crime. The gravamen of the offense is the abduction and the removal of the victim and principal aggravating actors are the duration of the abduction and distance of the removal. While skyjacking and political kidnapping are the most dramatic examples of this offense, the most commonly encountered version is the "self-help" abduction by a parent of his or her own child during a custody battle.[16]

Title I provides the best illustrations of direct statutory language confirming a spatial analysis. Burglary is, indeed, the paradigm spatial crime. Historically, for example, burglary was not thought of as a property crime—as we often think of it today; rather it was an offense against the security of the habitation itself.[17] It was a law designed to safeguard against nighttime intrusion upon one's dwelling. This trespassory offense is still the most serious form of burglary, with the type of premises involved creating the primary distinctions between degrees of the offense. Nondwelling buildings, fences, and real property such as a vacant lot provide, respectively, the lesser degrees of this trespassory offense.

Arson is a crime also typically defined in terms of the type of structure set afire, whether dwelling, commercial building, or other type of property. So too is the less serious property offense usually referred to as malicious mischief. Historically, the earliest of the latter statutes punished vandalism caused to specifically named structures: piers, booms, dams, bridges, milestones, etc. While modern statutes tend to lump these all in together, enforcement and sentencing policy do not and greater penalties are clearly meted out to criminal mischief occasioned to such spatially related structures as bridges and road signs. Indeed, the most heavily penalized variant of criminal mischief today relates to tampering with the property of a common carrier or public utility.[18]

Title J, involving theft offenses, offers a rich history for the geographer. Larceny was traditionally defined as involving a caption (a taking) and an asportation (a carrying away) of the property of another. While a caption requirement remains, the drafters of the model penal code urged the abolition of the asportation requirement; it nevertheless continues to exist in all but a handful of states.[19] Although the removal distance need not be great, no conviction may thus be obtained without the asportation requirement being met. Moreover, while the value of the property involved is the most frequent aggravating factor statutorily encountered, a number of states similarly enhance penalties when the property is taken from the person or from the dwelling house of the victim.

Criminologists have coined a spatial phrase distinguishing systemic reaction to "crime in the suites" as opposed to "crime in the streets." The former phrase is meant to encompass all forms of white-collar crime while the latter relates to the concern of the average citizen that it is unsafe to walk about because one may be "mugged." "Mugging" is legally referred to as robbery[20] and is the crime of greatest concern to the average citizen. It is the crime by which the quality of municipal life is often measured, and one which effectively determines the spatial relationships people walking about a community will have with one another. Although it is a personal crime of violence, we know it by its location: we speak of a bank robbery, not of the robbery of bank tellers; we speak of a train robbery, not of the robbery of individual passengers; or a street mugging, not the robbery of a particular pedestrian.

Several lesser theft offenses, such as joy riding or fare jumping (theft of services), are obviously spatially circumscribed by their very nature. Others, such as jostling, pickpocketing, fraudulent accosting, or fortune telling call forth the mental image of a carnival crowd where these offenses may usually take place.

As detailed in *Title K*, fraud offenses, usually relate to the crime-in-the-suites characterization referred to above. Forgery, falsification of business records, and commercial bribery are seen as crimes by and against the business community and are treated accordingly by criminal justice system personnel. These are crimes that for the most part may only be committed within a business enterprise. The police and prosecutorial resources allocated to these offenses are miniscule when one considers the amount of property loss involved. Issuing a bad check is the most frequently occurring of these offenses; it is of course the one committed by the most impecunious defrauder and is thus not truly in the white-collar crime category.

Title L relates a series of crimes that are committed only in connection with the workings of the criminal justice system itself. While escape from a prison may be the most obviously spatially bound crime, perjury can only take place before an official proceeding, resisting arrest necessitates the presence of a police officer, and bail jumping involves the failure to timely appear in court. Tampering with a witness, bribing a juror, and manufacturing false evidence all relate to court proceedings, as does criminal contempt of court.[21]

Title M refers to what are often called "victimless" crimes—drugs, gambling, prostitution, and obscenity. Much has already been written as to how these are spatially related offenses which represent not so much "public health and morals" as indeed the morals of one segment of society which may be in conflict with others.[22] Numbers in Harlem, or betting on cock fighting in the barrio, are often considered appropriate by local community standards, but not by those of the state as a whole. In one sharply contrary example, however, the United States Supreme Court has dictated that local community standards may indeed govern obscenity cases, even though those standards may be at variance with the state as a whole.[23] Certainly, different drug classifications have tended to be *class* classifications as well, with much of the movement to decriminalize marijuana occurring only after marijuana abuse was found to have occurred in the white, middle-class suburbs. While prostitution can and does occur anywhere, virtually every American city has some red-light district where almost anything goes, be it Boston's "combat zone" or New York's Eighth Avenue and 42nd Street. Such an area is often seen as a societal safety valve, or, less benignly, as a device to ensure comparatively less destruction and property value loss in favored areas selected for stricter enforcement. The spatially appropriate "house of prostitution" is of course worthy of mention here.

Again, these issues weigh differentially in different communities. Moreover, in cataloguing substantive distinctions, we should not ignore the macro spatial distinctions discovered through interstate as well as intrastate comparisons. In our federal system, criminal laws are separately created in each of the fifty states and what carries a potentially severe penalty in one state may be legal in another. The reader will be familiar with the decriminalization movement involving substances as diverse as marijuana and laetrile, or activities as varied as consensual homosexuality and abortion. Even within states, one can find "wet" and "dry" counties situated one next to the other, or, in Nevada, counties where prostitution is legal and others where it is a crime. We also have the recent development of legalized casino gambling expanding away from Nevada and now being available in New Jersey as well.

With the various possessory offenses, such as drugs and weapons, the law often makes an interesting spatial inference. There is an evidentiary principle referred to as the "in plain view" doctrine which states that the usual Fourth Amendment requirement for a search warrant is unnecessary if the contraband is observed out in the open—in plain view. A further inference is made in many states, with a statutory presumption that, if a drug, or a weapon—or even a gambling slip—is discovered by police in plain view of all the occupants of a car or a room, then *each* of the occupants is presumed to be equally in possession of the contraband in question.[24] While this occasionally defies reason, it is intended to obviate prosecutorial difficulties in assigning specific ownership to one among many.

Title N describes twenty-six offenses, most of which force the justice system into elaborating upon geographical distinctions. The title indeed begins by drawing the legal distinctions between public and private places. Section 240.00 (1) defines the concept of a public place in very broad terms:

"Public Place" means a place in which the public or a substantial group of persons has access, and includes, but is not limited to, highways, transportation facilities, schools, places of amusement, parks, playgrounds, hallways, lobbies and other portions of apartment houses and hotels not constituting rooms or apartments designed for actual residence.
"Transportation Facility" means any conveyance, premises or place used for or in connection with public passenger transportation, whether by air, railroad, motor vehicle or any other method. It includes aircraft, watercraft, railroad cars, buses, and air, boat, railroad and bus terminals and stations and all appurtenances thereto.[25]

These definitions relate to the crime of riot, inciting to riot, unlawful assembly and the ubiquitous offenses of disorderly conduct, loitering, and public intoxication. These latter three offenses tend to be the catchalls of the criminal justice system. Through one or the other of these offenses, all across America, strangers to the locale are typically arrested for looking and/or being "out of place." These are the offenses which derive from the common law's "breach of the peace" and refer to the securing by the governmental authority of geographical safety, security and—albeit perhaps unintended—immobility. These are the offenses that relate to tying up traffic, wandering about public places, begging, annoying people on the street by one's intoxication, and generally making a public nuisance of oneself.

New York's loitering provision[26] perhaps best exemplifies how the law at both its tedious and its most frequent seeks to impose sanctions upon moving about in an undesired manner to places from which the authorities would rather the person stayed away. Subparagraph 6 provides the most universal expression of this position:

A person is guilty of loitering when he:
  6. Loiters, remains or wanders in or about a place without apparent reason and under circumstances which justify suspicion that he may be engaged in or about to engage in crime, and, upon inquiry by a peace officer, refuses to identify himself or fails to give a reasonably credible account of his conduct and purposes. . . .

If we would have quoted this passage and said that it referred to South Africa's requirement that each citizen carry an identity card, then we would not have been surprised.

Similarly, various institutions are privileged to be able to prohibit persons from coming to them, even though they are theoretically public. See, for example, the above definition of transportation facility, or see the loitering subparagraph which prohibits a person who

  5. Loiters or remains in or about a school, college or university building or grounds, not having any reason or relationship involving custody of or responsibility for a pupil or student, or any other specific, legitimate reason for being there, and not having written permission from anyone authorized to grant the same. . . .

It may be maintained that these offenses are *only* "violations" and thus only subject the offender to a maximum imprisonment of fifteen days in jail. Nevertheless, it is hard to deny that that is a penal sanction. Moreover, it is hard to deny the police practice of using these disorderly conduct and loitering provisions for dragnet purposes, i.e., the roundup of undesirable persons. When the politicians order a "clean-up" of Times Square or any seedy area, it is typically under these catchall provisions that the grand sweep of persons is "authorized."

Other Title N provisions, such as the prohibitions against public lewdness and offensive exhibition, are the laws that keep nudist colonies private and which seem almost to amount to a penal code variation of a zoning ordinance, i.e., that type of law which most clearly and directly restricts activities to specific locations even when they are not considered "criminal."

Eight of the Title N offenses are classified as "offenses against the right to privacy." Such a classification is a modern one and an extremely interesting one in that the right to privacy has no direct constitutional genesis, but has increasingly been seen to be manifested in the "penumbra" of the Bill of Rights provisions to the Constitution.[27] That is, today we more and more recognize that people are entitled to be protected from the prying eyes of others, are endowed with a right not to be harassed by others, are protected from eavesdropping, and, in short, are endowed with a right to protect and have a space or place of their own.

Title O deals with offenses against the family such as bigamy and adultery and points out that the state is so concerned with securing the institution of the "home" that it places in the Penal Code prohibitions against activities which many would regard as completely civil and private. Nevertheless, it is here that the criminal law demonstrates the solemnity and sanctity with which it treats the institutions of marriage, the family and the home. Indeed, the spatial concept of abandonment is designated a felonious offense within this modern penal code:

> A person is guilty of abandonment of a child when, being a parent, guardian, or other person legally charged with the care or custody of a child less than

fourteen years old, he deserts such child in any place with intent to wholly abandon it.[28]

Title P relates to the uses of firearms and other dangerous weapons and here, too, the concept of transportation is not merely a justifying, jurisdictional one—as it might be with respect to a federal prosecution—used to secure the jurisdictional right to prosecute a given case. The very transport of a weapon, in and of itself, without license, becomes a felonious offense. The places in which weapons may be legally used are similarly sharply delineated.

Summary

Procedural criminal law encompasses such obviously spatial concepts as jurisdiction, venue, and search. It is therefore a rich source to study for the geographer seeking integrative relationships with the law. Nevertheless, even substantive criminal law issues may be seen to revolve about geographic concerns. The purpose of this essay has not been to explore in depth all the multifarious spatial concepts existing in the criminal law, but to present an overview which will hopefully whet the appetite of the student of geography to explore a vast area largely ignored in geographic literature.[29]

NOTES

1. U.S. Constitution, Amendment X; *McCulloch v. Maryland*, 17 U.S. (4 Wheat.) 316 (1819): John R. Green, "The Bill of Rights, the Fourteenth Amendment, and the Supreme Court," *Michigan Law Review* 46:869 (1948).
2. See Alexander Hamilton, *The Federalist Papers*, nos. 80–82.
3. See *Katz v. United States*, 389 U.S. 347 (1967); and *Chimel v. California*, 395 U.S. 752 (1969).
4. *Sheppard v. Maxwell*, 384 U.S. 333 (1966).
5. *Witherspoon v. Illinois*, 391 U.S. 510 (1968); and *Taylor v. Louisiana*, 95 S.Ct. 692 (1975).

6. See, for example, *People v. Crimmins*, 307 N.Y.S. 2d 81 (1969).

7. American Law Institute, *Model Penal Code.* Proposed Official Draft (New York: ALI, 1962).

8. Even here, however, the reader should know that the difference between a criminal attempt and nonculpable "mere preparation" often rests on the physical proximity or "nearness" to crime completion. See, for example, *People v. Rizzo*, 246 N.Y. 334 (1927); *Commonwealth v. Peaslee*, 177 Mass. 267 (1901); and *State v. Kleier*, 69 Idaho 491 (1949).

9. New York Family Court Act, Section 115. For a recent and fascinating discussion of police treatment of "battered wives," see *Bruno v. Codd*, 407 N.Y.S. 2d 165 (1st Dept., 1978).

10. For an extended analysis of such exercises of police discretionary power, see Kenneth Culp Davis, *Police Discretion* (St. Paul, Minn.: West Publishing, 1975).

11. See, for example, Henry P. Lundsgaarde, *Murder in Space City: A Cultural Analysis of Houston Homicide Patterns* (New York: Oxford University Press, 1977).

12. New York Vehicle and Traffic Law, Section 1180.

13. See also the analogous situation with regard to "border" searches. *Almeida-Sanchez v. United States*, 413 U.S. 266 (1973).

14. See generally, Vivian Berger, "Man's Trial, Women's Tribulation: Rape Cases in the Courtroom," *Columbia Law Review* 1 (1977), 77.1.

15. P. L. Section 130.00 (4).

16. See cases collected at Annotation, "Kidnapping or Other Criminal Offenses by Taking or Removal of Child by, or under Authority of, Parent or One in Loco Parentis." *American Law Reports*, (1951), 77:317.

17. P. L. Article 140.

18. P. L. Section 145.20.

19. Wayne R. LaFave and Austin W. Scott, Jr., *Criminal Law* (St. Paul, Minn.: West Publishing, 1972), pp. 631–33.

20. P. L. Article 160.

21. Ronald Goldfarb, *The Contempt Power* (New York: Columbia University Press, 1963).

22. See, for example, Sanford Kadish, "The Crisis of Overcriminalization," *The Annals* (1967), 374:157; and Jerome Skolnick, "Coercion to Virtue: The Enforcement of Morals," *Southern California Law Review* (1968), 41:588.

23. *Miller v. California*, 413 U.S. 15 (1973).

24. See, for example, P. L. Section 220.25.

25. The term "transportation facility" is defined in P. L. Section 240.00 (2).

26. P. L. Section 240.35.

27. See *Griswold v. Connecticut*, 381 U.S. 479 (1965); *Roe v. Wade*, 410 U.S. 113 (1973).

28. P. L. Section 260.00.

29. Editor's note: concurrent with the preparation of this essay, a spatial treatment of laws and justice embodying some of the issues raised by Professor Kress was published. See Keith D. Harries and Stanley D. Brunn, *The Geography of Laws and Justice: Spatial Perspectives on the Criminal Justice System* (New York: Praeger, 1978).

⇄ 2 ⇄

EMPIRICAL SPATIAL
ANALYSIS

INTERURBAN

The comparison of cities has intrinsic appeal to lay persons and scholars alike. Superlatives are not only generated by chambers of commerce; almost everyone sees something good or something bad about the particular city they live in. The growth of quality-of-life studies in the last decade and the generally increased level of interest in social indicators has spurred the comparative analysis of cities. Such comparisions have appeared in magazines found in the supermarket racks as well as in the sophisticated social science journals, and no aspect of the quality of life in cities has been more controversial than the crime rate. Small-town residents have learned to pity big-city dwellers who apparently cannot step out of their homes after sunset without the very high probability of being victimized. The large-city residents (it seems from the small-town perspective) turn their homes into fortresses. Relative levels of crime have been debated fiercely. New York has been perceived by many as the crime capital of the United States, with other big cities such as Chicago or Detroit following closely. In addition, the extraordinarily high homicide rates of southern cities periodically surface's in the media only to be dismissed as an inevitable part of southern culture. In this section of the book, containing three papers, distinctly different approaches are taken to intercity comparisons by a sociologist, a criminologist-planner team, and a geographer.

The Uniform Crime Reports of the F.B.I. have been the subject of criticism—even ridicule—for many years. In the last decade we have seen the development of an important alternative to the Uniform Crime Reports (UCR), in the form of the National Crime Survey (NCS). In the first paper, James Nelson presents a comparison of the UCR and the NCS in twenty-six American cities. The reader may recall that the UCR are based on reports by the public to the police. The NCS data are based, as the name implies, on a survey approach gathering, from a large sample of people, information about their crime victimization experiences. For various methodological and procedural reasons it is unlikely that the UCR and NCS data would reveal identical values even where definitions of crime are identical in both measurement systems. One of Nelson's key findings is that NCS and UCR rates correlated strongly for some crime categories, weakly for one, and were evidently independent or negatively related for other categories. In broad terms, crime involving theft tended to be associated with fairly strong correlation between NCS and UCR rates; on the other hand, personal victimization unrelated to theft did not exhibit such an interrelationship.

Another part of Nelson's study involved regressing NCS and UCR rate differences on some ecological variables. A key finding in this part of the paper was that nontheft-related crime pattern differences were intercorrelated with ecological variables more strongly than theft-related crimes. Nelson concludes that city characteristics were not important in the recording of rates of what he calls "well-defined and serious crimes," but such characteristics did appear to have some relationship to the less sharply defined personal crimes. Nelson's findings provide significant new insights into the differences between the two key data bases in the study of crime. A knowledge of such differences can be vital whether the researcher is relying on the UCR or the NCS or both. Such information is particularly critical if we are to know with any certainty whether interurban crime rate comparisons have validity.

The second paper, by Paul and Patricia Brantingham, builds on a number of earlier interurban studies, including those of Ogburn, Schuessler and Slatin, Harries, and Flango and Sherbenou. The originality of the Brantinghams' approach lies in their focus on a very specific aspect of the socioeconomic structure of cities, namely the mixture of employment and occupation as it relates to crime rates. The analysis is related not only to prior studies in intermetropolitan ecology, but also to the literature of criminal opportunity and criminal motivation. The employment and occupational structure is seen as a key dependent variable in the explanation of crime rates because occupation is such a significant surrogate for an individual's social and economic status; for all intents and purposes, occupation is social class. Occupational mixtures, then, may represent differential class structures, which in turn may represent differential distribution of motivations for crime.

The analysis is based on crime rate, economic specialization, and occupational and other ecological data for SMSA's with at least 250,000 people in 1970. In broad terms, data on economic specialization represented crime opportunities while data on socioeconomic status represented possible motivation. It was found that murder and assault were related to motivational variables. Burglary, larceny, motor vehicle theft, and robbery related to measures of opportunity. Measures of both opportunity and motive related to rape. The Brantinghams conclude that the understanding of differences in crime rates between cities is enhanced by consideration of measures of what they call "aggregate opportunity structures."

The third paper, by Marshall Worden, provides a temporal perspective on the correlates of metropolitan crime in two specific years, 1960 and 1970. Using data for 120 SMSA's, Worden takes into account total metropolitan characteristics as well as the attributes of central cities and the areas outside central cities—what may be regarded as census-defined suburbs. Worden finds that the absolute differences between central cities and the' areas outside them were generally insignificant. This leads him to focus his explanation on the concept of relative, rather than absolute deprivation. Of particular interest in the Worden paper is the structural contrast between models developed for 1960 and 1970. Conspicuously important is the role of the youthful minorities in the central city in the explanation of 1970 crime rates.

Increasing concern with the quality of life concept and the seemingly growing influence of interurban analysis on migration decisions, particularly among the more literate segment of the population, provides new challenges for social scientists interested in this type of analysis. In spite of the limitations of the NCS, it does provide a rich new data source, which, with refinements, may provide a new level of accuracy and general credibility for interurban comparisons. The costs associated with the administration of the NCS in all cities over a given threshold size in the U.S. may well be prohibitive. On the other hand, some extension of coverage could be useful in terms of improved understanding of the relationship between crime patterns and regional variations in culture, as well as relationships of the types considered by the Brantinghams and by Worden. In the following section the level of resolution shifts to the intraurban scale.

卐 5 卐

Alternative Measures of Crime

A Comparison of the Uniform Crime Reports and the National Crime Survey in Twenty-Six American Cities

James F. Nelson

BOTH THE National Crime Survey (NCS) and the Uniform Crime Reports (UCR) estimate the number of criminal acts committed in different places and times. These estimates are based on methodologies designed for different purposes. The UCR is designed to measure the extent of reported crimes. The NCS is a multipurpose project that, among other things, is designed to produce time series data on crime, to show how personal, household, business and environmental characteristics are related to the chances of being victimized, to estimate the consequences of crime, and to describe characteristics related to official crime reporting. The question raised is: do the NCS and the UCR measure similar amounts of criminal activity? This question needs to be answered because NCS data are frequently used to estimate how demo-

This paper was prepared for presentation at the annual meeting of the American Society of Criminology in Dallas, Texas, November 1978. The work was partly supported by Grant Number 75-SS-99-6029, awarded to the Criminal Justice Research Center by the Statistics Division, National Criminal Justice Information and Statistics Service, Law Enforcement Assistance Administration, U.S. Department of Justice. Points of view or opinions stated in this document are those of the author and do not necessarily represent the official policy or policies of the U.S. Department of Justice or the Criminal Justice Research Center. The author is indebted to James Garofalo, Michael Gottfredson, and Michael Hindelang for helpful comments on earlier drafts, and to David Van Alstyne for assistance in collecting the data.

graphic characteristics—like sex, race, marital status, household type, etc.—affect the chances of being victimized. If the UCR and the NCS measured the same underlying crimes, then patterns found in the NCS data should also underlie the UCR crimes rates. For example, the NCS victimization rate patterns could be used to locate persons, households, and businesses with unusually high UCR rates. However, if the UCR and the NCS rates did not measure the same basic criminal activity, then it would be inappropriate to use the NCS data to make inferences about UCR rates. In this case, the reliability of either or both the UCR and NCS rates would be uncertain.

The analysis of how the UCR is related to the NCS begins by describing the NCS methodology. Differences between reporting procedures and sources of bias are discussed. NCS rates are then correlated with UCR rates for seven crimes. These correlations show that the NCS rates are closely related to UCR rates for theft, but not personal crimes. The analysis is concluded by regressing UCR and NCS rates on ecological variables. These regressions show that the relationship of ecological variables to crime rates frequently depends upon whether UCR or NCS rates are used to measure crime.

The NCS Program

The National Crime Survey was designed to assess the character and extent of criminal victimization through representative probability sampling of households and commercial establishments. It consisted of a continuous national survey and surveys taken in selected cities. In the national sample, the same households and businesses were interviewed every six months for a period of three and one-half years. Households and businesses were continually rotated into and out of the survey. In the city surveys, respondents were interviewed one time. The NCS was designed and executed for the Law Enforcement Assistance Administration by the U.S. Bureau of Census.

The NCS city survey data collected during 1974 and 1975 were used to construct crime rates in this paper. In these city surveys, household and business respondents were asked questions on attempted and completed victimizations during a twelve-month period preceding the interview. Victimizations that were reported to have occurred during 1973 were recorded in Boston, Buffalo, Cincinnati, Houston, Miami, Milwaukee, Minneapolis, New Orleans, Oakland, Pittsburgh, San Diego, San Francisco, and Washington D.C.; during 1974 in Chicago, Detroit, Los Angeles, New York, and Philadelphia; and during 1974 and part of 1975 in Atlanta, Baltimore, Cleveland, Dallas, Denver, Newark, Portland, and St. Louis. Sampling procedures and descriptions of all NCS project are given by Garafalo and Hindelang.[1]

Differences between and Biases in NCS and UCR Data

Although the NCS and the UCR used the same definitions of crimes, they are not expected to produce the same crime rates because of differences in populations and because of methodological shortcomings. The UCR and the NCS were based upon slightly different populations. The NCS city surveys recorded crimes against persons 12 years of age or older living within each city, regardless of whee the crime occurred. The UCR recorded crimes that occurred within each city, regardless of the victim's age or residence.

Differences in age of victim and location of the crime are not expected to account for differences between UCR and NCS rates. Presumably few children were involved in the crimes to be analyzed here. Even if they were involved, relatively few children report such crimes to the police. Differences in where the crime occurred—namely, that all UCR crimes occurred within each city whereas NCS crimes could have occurred anywhere—are not expected to produce large differences in UCR and NCS rates because nearly all of the victimizations recorded in the NCS occurred within the victim's home city. Garofalo[2] showed that 93 to 94 percent of all personal victimizations reported in the NCS city data occurred in the resident's city.

Differences in the residences of the population in UCR and

NCS data are expected to affect crime rates because the number of persons within a city is ordinarily larger than the number of residents. Only the residential population was at risk of being victimized in the NCS reports, whereas the entire population within a city—including residents, workers, tourists, etc.—was at risk in the UCR. The crime rates calculated later in this paper partially adjust for these differences by varying the size of the denominator for UCR and NCS rates.

Perhaps the most important methodological difference between the NCS and the UCR is that the NCS was based upon representative samples of city populations but the UCR was based upon the population of victims who chose to report their victimizations to local police authorities. The NCS was expected to find more crime than the UCR because many nonserious crimes that normally go unreported to the police are likely to be brought out in an interview explicity designed to study crime.

The effectiveness of the NCS at uncovering crimes not reported to the police can be partially evaluated by examining the percentage of crimes reported to the NCS interviewer that were also said to have been reported to the police. The NCS city data show that about one-third of the simple assaults, about one-half of the personal robberies, rapes, aggravated assaults, and household burglaries, and about three-fourths of the motor vehicle thefts reported to the NCS were said to have been reported to the police. The reporting of business victimizations was higher than the reporting of personal and household crimes. In general, the NCS uncovered considerably more victimizations than were reported to the police.

If respondents reported all crimes to the NCS interviewers, then the percentages of crimes said to be reported to the police could be used to estimate the number of crimes that occurred but were not officially reported. Unfortunately, several studies suggest that not all crimes were reported to the NCS interviewers. The San Jose Methods Test of Known Crimes[3] showed that not all crimes reported to the police were also reported to NCS interviewers. This study was based upon a sample of 394 persons who reported a crime to the police. They were interviewed with the NCS form to learn how accurately the police report would correspond to the survey responses. The study showed that 48 percent of the assault victims, 67 percent of the rape victims, 76 percent of the robbery victims and 90 percent of the burglary victims reported the recorded police victimization to the NCS interviewer. This means that over half of the assault and about one-third of the rape victims did not report to the NCS interviewer the victimization that had been reported to the police. These figures demonstrate that persons were hesitant or forgot to discuss some crimes with NCS interviewers.

A somewhat different study of the relationship of police records and NCS reports was made by Anne Schneider in Portland, Oregon.[4] She searched police files for crimes that were reported in the NCS to have occurred within Portland and were said to have been reported to the police. Based on small samples sizes, Schneider found that only 19 percent of the robberies, 34 percent of the assaults, 60 percent of the auto thefts and 74 percent of the burglaries that were reported in the NCS and said to have been reported to the police could be found in police records. She suggested that the crimes may not have appeared in police files because persons did not actually report them to the police, or because the police either did not record them or lost the recording.

One reason NCS reports may not have appeared in police records is that police departments were supposed to attempt to validate reported crimes, but NCS interviewers were supposed to accept reported crimes at face value once the crimes had been clearly specified. Validation procedures may have resulted in actual crimes not being recorded in police records, whereas lack of validation procedures may have resulted in some noncriminal acts being recorded as crimes in the NCS. Research is needed to learn how validation procedures affected UCR rates and how they could affect NCS rates.

Several problems with recall of past crimes affected the reliability of NCS data presumably more than the reliability of UCR data. One such problem is that persons may have recalled victimizations that occurred more than twelve months before the interview as if they occurred within twelve months of the interview. Murphy and Cowan[5] addressed this issue with the National Crime Survey of households taken during 1974 and 1975. They compared the crime rates for persons who initially entered the study with those who were already in the study. Interviews of persons already in the study were bounded by past interviews, so that victimizations discovered in prior interviews would not be recorded as if they occurred in the most recent six-month survey period. Interviews of persons initially entering the study could not be bounded. Their data suggest that rates for unbounded interviews were about 44 percent higher than rates for bounded interviews for assaults, and 39 percent higher for burglaries. In other words, NCS city rates would have been lower if bounded instead of unbounded interviews were used. This does not necessarily mean that city crime rates were overestimated, because other effects, like forgetting or hesitating to report some victimizations, deflate the rates.

Another problem that occurred in the NCS is that respondents frequently could not distinguish the details of related victimizations. If a respondent experienced at least three victimizations of a similar type and was unable to recall the details of each separate victimization, then these victimizations were recorded as a series victimization and information on only the most recent victimization was recorded. The number of incidents involved in the series was coded into four categories: three to four victimizations, five to ten victimizations, eleven and more, and don't know. Most reports using the NCS data have excluded these incidents from rate calculations because information on each incident and the exact number of incidents is not available. Series victimizations were also excluded from most rate calculations in this paper.

Using the national NCS data, Shenk and McInerny[6] showed that omitting series victimizations substantially underestimates the number of personal victimizations.[6] Their data suggest that excluding series victimizations may underestimate the number of assaults and rapes by 30 to 40 percent, the number of robberies and burglaries by 15 to 20 percent, and the number of motor vehicle thefts by 3 to 4 percent.

In summary, the UCR and the NCS crime rates are not expected to be the same because they were based upon slightly different populations and had methodological shortcomings. The NCS measured victimizations of city residents age 12 and over wherever they occurred, whereas the UCR measured victimizations within city limits regardless of residence or age of the victim. The UCR rates are expected to underestimate the amount of crime because not all persons reported crimes to the police, and because not all crimes reported to the police were recorded. NCS rates are expected to be inflated because respondents frequently recalled victimizations that occurred more than twelve months before the interview as if they occurred within twelve months of the interview, and because the NCS did not attempt to validate the occurrence of reported victimizations. On the other hand, NCS city rates are expected to be deflated because not all crimes were reported to NCS interviewers, and because series victimizations were not included in NCS rate calculations. Rate deflation is especially likely to occur for personal crimes of assault and rape.

These methodological problems show that it is unreasonable to expect UCR and NCS rates to be identical. The question is: are the NCS rates related to the UCR rates? If they are strongly related, then patterns found between victimization rates and other variables in the NCS data set should also be found for UCR rates. This question will be addressed by calculating the NCS and the UCR rates to be as compatible as possible and then measuring the correlation between these rates in the twenty-six cities sampled by the NCS.

Calculation of NCS and UCR Rates

Seven types of crime measured in the NCS were found to be definitionally compatible with crimes reported in the UCR of 1973 and 1974. The number of aggravated assaults, simple assaults, motor vehicle thefts, and rapes were estimated in both reports. The number of robbery incidents both with and without a weapon were available in the UCR. They were estimated in the NCS by totaling the number of personal and commercial robbery incidents separately from armed and unarmed robberies. The total number of household and commercial burglaries which were available in the UCR were estimated in the NCS by adding the number of household burglaries to the number of commercial burglaries.

Crime rates were estimated by dividing the number of each type of crime by the size of the population exposed to the crime. Adjustments were made for differences in the sizes of the populations at risk of being victimized by basing the NCS rates on the city's residential population and by basing the UCR rates on the estimate of the number of persons who used each city on a daily basis. The procedure used to estimate the exposed population for UCR rates is available from the author on request.

Relationships between NCS and UCR Rates

Regression analysis was used to measure the relationship between the UCR and the NCS rates. The amount of variance explained in the NCS rates by the UCR rates showed that the NCS and the UCR rates were strongly related for motor vehicle theft and robbery with a weapon, moderately related for burglary, weakly related for robbery without a weapon, and were independently or even negatively related for aggravated assault, simple assault and rape.

An examination of the scatterplots showed that rates for burglary, motor vehicle theft and robbery were consistently higher for NCS than for UCR rates. One possible reason for this pattern is that not all persons or businesses reported victimizations to the police. To correct for reporting difference, NCS rates were recalculated for persons and businesses who said they reported each crime to the police. These rates were then correlated with the UCR rates. The relationship between UCR and NCS rates considerably increased for robbery without a weapon and only slightly increased for other crimes. As before, the NCS rates for aggravated assault, simple assault, and rape were independent of each other.

Several refinements in the measurement of NCS assault and rape rates were used to increase the correlation between UCR and NCS rates. First, the aggravated assault rate was recalculated to include only persons who suffered an injury. This removed from the NCS rate persons who experienced minor aggravated assaults that may not have been officially recorded as aggravated assaults by the police. The correlation of aggravated assault with this refined measure equalled −.28, showing that differences between UCR and NCS aggravated assault rates could not be explained by differences in the injuries suffered by persons reporting these crimes.

Second, the number of series victimizations for aggravated assault, simple assault, and rape were added to the number of nonseries victimizations for each of these crimes to learn if the lack of relationship between UCR and NCS rates could be due to omitting series victimizations. The correlations of these rates with UCR rates equalled −.02 for rape, −.09 for simple assualt, and −.48 for aggravated assault. Thus, the lack of a positive relation between UCR and NCS rates for assault and rape was not due to omitting series victimization. In fact, adding series victimizations to aggravated assault rates is disturbing because it strongly suggests that NCS and UCR aggravated assault rates were inversely related to each other. Neither of these refined measures were used in subsequent analyses.

In general, NCS and UCR rates were moderately to strongly related to each other for victimizations characterized by theft, but were unrelated or even negatively related to each other for personal victimizations not characterized by theft. The lack of a relationship between UCR and NCS crime rates for personal crimes not characterized by theft may be reflecting embarrassment and definitional problems related to these crimes. The San Jose reverse records check study supports this argument. In officially known cases of rape, aggravated and simple assault victimizations were reported less often to NCS interviewers than cases of all other crimes investigated here. The nature of a personal crime without theft is also harder to define than a crime involving theft, because nothing is taken in crimes without theft.

The strength of the relationship between UCR and NCS victimization rates appears to have depended upon the seriousness of the crime for crimes involving theft. Very strong associations existed for motor vehicle theft and armed robbery. Moderate to strong associations were found for unarmed robbery and burglary. Unarmed robbery and burglary are less serious than armed robbery and motor vehicle theft in that the average dollar loss in burglary is considerably less than the average dollar loss in motor vehicle theft,[7] and unarmed robbery is less life-threatening than armed robbery.

Thus far, the analysis has focused on shortcomings of the NCS interview as one possible explanation of why UCR and NCS rates differ. The next section focuses on how characteristics of the cities were related to differences in UCR and NCS rates. This section is more exploratory in nature.

City Characteristics and Differences in UCR and NCS Rates

Differences between NCS and UCR rates were regressed on several ecological variables thought to be related to either the level of crime or to the chances that crime will be reported to the police. The variables included the city's density, median family income, police expenditure per capita and percentage of black persons. Differences were formed by taking the residual or the regression of standardized NCS rates or "Z scores" on standardized UCR rates for theft crimes and by taking algebraic differences between standardized NCS and UCR rates for personal crimes without theft. Residuals from the regression of NCS on UCR rates were not used for crimes without theft because the regressions were not statistically significant. All rates were transformed into standardized scores so that differences in patterns, rather than differences in the magnitude of relationships, would be measured.

The regressions showed that differences between UCR and NCS crime rates without theft were more closely related to ecological variables than were differences for crimes with theft. Between 32 and 51 percent of the variance in rate differences for crimes not characterized by theft could be accounted for by ecological variables, whereas between zero and 27 percent of the variance in theft crimes could be accounted for by these variables. In general, the stronger the relationship between the UCR and the NCS rate, the less differences between the rates could be accounted for by ecological variables. This suggests that city characteristics were of little consequence in recording the incidence of well-defined and serious crimes, but they did appear to affect the recording of less well-defined personal crimes.

The relationships between each variable and differences in UCR and NCS rates were difficult to summarize because police expenditure was very closely related to percent black and density. A regression analysis of police expenditure on percent black, density, and income showed that over 70 percent of the variance in police expenditure could be accounted for by density and percent black. This high interdependency means that coefficients involving these three variables are likely to appear to be small and to be unusually variable because density and percent black measured largely the same variation as did police expenditure.

Rather than analyzing the relationship between each ecological variable and differences in UCR and NCS rates, it may be more insightful to regress each separate rate on the ecological variables and informally compare regression coefficients. This procedure has the advantage of showing how each variable was separately related to each rate.

The standardized regression coefficients of UCR and NCS rates on the four ecological variables are presented in table 5.1. One of the most interesting and consistent differences in table 5.1 is that police expenditure had negative relationships to NCS rates but positive relationships to UCR rates. This pattern was especially strong for personal crimes of rape, aggravated assault, and unarmed robbery. The coefficients show that opposite conclusions about the relationship of police expenditure and personal crime rates can be reached, depending upon whether UCR or NCS rates are used to measure crime. The NCS rates suggest that personal crime decreased as police expenditure increased, whereas the UCR rates suggest that personal crime increased.

The positive relationship between UCR rates and police expenditure may be due to differences in recording crime. For example, if the quality of recording crimes not characterized by theft depended on the amount of police expenditure, then the crime rate would increase with police expenditure if cities with high police expenditure more accurately recorded crime than cities with low police expenditure. UCR personal crime rates are especially likely to be high for cities in which police departments have special units

Table 5.1.
Standardized Regression Coefficients and Amount of Variance Explained in Seven Types of Crime by Four Ecological Variables for NCS and UCR Crime Rates

Ecological Variable	Crime													
	Rape		Aggravated Assault		Simple Assault		Unarmed Robbery		Armed Robbery		Burglary		Motor Vehicle Theft	
	NCS Rate	UCR Rate	NCS Rate	UCR Rate	NCS Rate	UCR Rate	NCS Rate	UCR Rate	NCS Rate	UCR Rate	NCS Rate	UCR Rate	NCS Rate	UCR Rate
Police expenditure	−.42	.32	−.29	.18	−ᵃ	−.30	−.24	.16	−.30	−.11	−.11	.11	−.12	.06
Percent black	.05	.46	−ᵃ	.24	.52*	.07	.19	.41	.63*	.74*	−.06	.09	−ᵃ	−ᵃ
Density	−.18	−.20	−.24	.09	−.37*	.41	.57	.34	.72*	.43	−.42	−.35	.18	.19
Income	.37	.30	.43	−.36	.40*	−ᵃ	.31	−.12	.06	.11	.24	−.11	.11	−.12
Adjusted R²	.30	.40	.34	.25	.71	−.05	.11	.45	.46	.50	.20	−.04	−.10	−.06

* Significant at the .05 level of significance.
ᵃ This variable was not entered into the model because its partial F-ratio was less than .01.

designed to deal with violent personal crimes, like rape and wife beating. The negative relationship of police expenditure to simple assault, an apparent deviation from the above pattern, could also be due to recording practices if the tendency to record rapes and aggravated assaults as simple assaults was higher in poorly funded police departments than in well-funded departments.

The negative relationship of police expenditure to personal crimes without theft in the NCS data does not necessarily mean that the incidence of personal crimes decreased with increases in police expenditure. Time series data are needed to determine if increases in police expenditure decrease crime rates. Furthermore, if increases in police expenditure reduced personal crime, then theft crimes, which presumably are more affected by the presence or absence of police than personal crimes, should also have decreased with police expenditure. The near-independence of police expenditure with NCS burglary and motor vehicle theft rates suggests that police expenditure did not decrease theft crimes, and by implication, probably did not decrease personal crimes.

The relationship of other ecological variables to UCR and NCS rates depended on the type of crime and were influenced by how police expenditure affected crime rates. For example, percent black had a strong positive relation to UCR rape rates but was un-related to NCS rape rates. If police expenditure had been nega-tively related to rape for UCR rates, then the relationship of percent black and rape would have been more similar in the UCR and the NCS data sets. This can be illustrated by comparing the zero-order correlation of race and UCR rape rates when the regression coefficient of rape on police expenditure equals .32 (the observed coefficient) to the case when it equals − .42 (the coeffi-cient of the regression of NCS rape rates on police expenditure). The correlation equals .52 in the first case and .08 in the second. This shows that the overall relationship of race to rape depended heavily on how police expenditure was related to rape. It also shows that it is difficult to untangle the separate effects of highly interrelated variables. The only consistent relationship of race and crime evident in table 5.2 is that robbery had a positive association with percentage of black persons for both UCR and NCS data sets.

The direction of the relationship of density to crime was the same for all UCR and NCS rates except simple assault. NCS simple assault rates decreased with increases in density but UCR rates increased. However, the positive relationship of density and UCR simple assault is very tentative, because the four ecological variables did not explain any of the variance in UCR simple assault rates. In contrast, these variables explained 71 percent of the variance in NCS simple assault rates. Ignoring UCR assault data, both UCR and NCS rates suggest that the NCS denser cities—primarily older cities and those located in the Northeast and Midwest—tended to be characterized by higher robbery rates; whereas less dense cities—primarily younger cities located in the South and West—tended to be characterized by higher rates of burglary and by slightly higher rates of personal victimization.

Similar to police expenditure, the relationship of income to crime frequently differed for NCS and UCR rates. Table 5.1 shows that income had a positive relation to all NCS rates, whereas it had a positive or negative relation to UCR rates. The positive association between income and NCS crime rates could have arisen if persons living in higher-income cities experienced more crime than persons living in lower-income cities, or if persons living in lower-income cities failed to report victimizations to NCS interviewers more often than persons living in higher-income cities. The latter interpretation seems more plausible and suggests that further research on the reporting of crimes to NCS interviewers by variables related to income should be undertaken.

Thus, differences between NCS and UCR victimization rates were more closely related to ecological characteristics for crimes not characterized by theft than for crimes characterized by theft. The relatively small amount of variance explained in differences between rates for theft crimes suggests that ecological characteristics had little effect on the public's willingness to report such crimes to either NCS or police interviewers, or on the police's willingness to record such crimes. The relatively large amount of variance explained in personal crimes not involving theft suggests that ecological characteristics affected the public's willingness to report such crimes and/or the police's willingness to record them. In general. the weaker the relationship between the NCS and the UCR rates, the more ecological characteristics explained differences in rates.

Comparisons of the effect of each variable on UCR and NCS rates revealed that very different conclusions about determinants of personal crimes can be drawn from NCS and UCR rates. The UCR data suggested that the incidence of personal crimes was positively related to police expenditure whereas the NCS data suggested it was negatively related. Differences in how police expenditure was related to crime rates made it difficult to determine how race and density, two variables closely related to police expenditure, were related to crimes.

NOTES

1. J. Garofalo and M. J. Hindelang, *An Introduction to the National Crime Survey.* Analytic Report SD-VAD-4. Law Enforcement Assistance Administration, National Criminal Justice Information and Statistics Service (Washington, D.C.: U.S. Government Printing Office, 1978).

2. J. Garofalo, *The Police and Public Opinion: An Analysis of Victimization and Attitude Data from 13 American Cities.* Analytic Report SD-VAD-3. Law Enforcement Assistance Administration, National Criminal Justice Information and Statistics Service (Washington D.C.: U.S. Government Printing Office, 1977)

3. Law Enforcement Assistance Administration, *San Jose Methods Test of Known Crime Victims.* Statistics Technical Report no. 1 (Washington, D.C.: U.S. Government Printing Office, 1972).

4. A. L. Schneider, "The Portland Forward Records Check of Crime Victims: Final Report." A report prepared for the National Institute of Law Enforcement and Criminal Justice, Office of Evaluation (Portland, Ore.: Institute of Policy Analysis, 1977). Mimeo.

5. L. R. Murphy and C. D. Cowan, "Effects of Bounding on Telescoping in the National Crime Survey." A paper prepared for presentation at the American Statistical Association Meetings, August 23–26, 1976, Boston, Mass. U.S. Bureau of the Census. Mimeo.

6. F. Shenk and W. McInerney, "Issues from Applications of the National Crime Survey." A paper prepared for presentation at the annual meeting of the Southwestern Political Science Association, Houston, Texas, 1978. U.S. Bureau of the Census.

7. M. L. Blumberg and J. Ranton, "Household Burglary Victimizations: A Descriptive Analysis." Criminal Justice Research Center Working Paper 9; and Blumberg, "Motor Vehicle Theft: A National Analysis." A report prepared for the Law Enforcement Assistance Administration (both Albany, N.Y.: Criminal Justice Research Center, 1978).

࿕ 6 ࿕

Crime, Occupation,
and Economic Specialization

A Consideration of Inter-Metropolitan Patterns

PAUL J. BRANTINGHAM
AND PATRICIA L. BRANTINGHAM

THE FIRST OBSERVATION of systematic research into the nature of crime was that officially recorded crime rates varied remarkably from city to city. This finding emerged from the earliest analyses of conviction statistics in Europe.[1] It was confirmed throughout the nineteenth century and was a major factual base for the theoretical work of the positive school criminologists.[2] It is the longest-lasting and most constantly observed fact about crime: wide-ranging variation in city crime rates is as apparent in the 1980s as it was in the 1820s, and is as obvious in North America as in Europe.

The search for an explanation of this persistent social phenomenon has been directed to its spatial covariation with *other* social statistics. Most researchers have considered gross variables such as "unemployment" or "race." In this paper we explore intermetropolitan crime rates in terms of a more detailed socioeconomic structure: the employment and occupation mixture. Our exploration flows out of three different streams of criminological literature: intermetropolitan ecology, criminal opportunity, criminal motivation. We will deal with each of these briefly.

The Intermetropolitan Ecology of Crime

During the ninteenth century a number of studies examined crime rates in relation to real variations in statistics on poverty and wealth, ignorance and education, sex, age, population density, and such economic specializations as manufacturing, mining, and farming. The general conclusion of these studies was that the variation in official crime rates was a function of real variations in poverty, education, and urban size, and that economic specialization seemed to affect crime rates in urban places.[3]

The collection of more detailed social statistics in the twentieth century has produced a growing interest in this line of research. Ogburn,[4] and Schuessler and Slatin found crime inversely related to work force employed in manufacturing. Schussler and Slatin's results were interpreted as support for a social disorganization model of crime causation in which aggregate criminal motivation (and therefore the crime rate) varies inversely with the ability of a city's social institutions to integrate individuals into the socioeconomic roles and rules of society.[5] In contrast, Ebets and Schwirian found, for Standard Metropolitan Statistical Areas (SMSAs)[6] in 1960, patterns consistent with a relative deprivation theory of criminal motivation. This theory predicts high crime rates in cities where a low-income, low-status minority lives in contact with a high-income, high-status majority. The minority would be motivated to commit crime instrumentally in pursuit of the good life around it, or emotionally in frustration at its inability to obtain the good life enjoyed by the majority.[7] These studies all hint at the need for a more detailed consideration.

A more recent series of studies by Harries has explored the statistical dynamics of interurban crime rate variations and has led to the construction of crime-based typologies.[8] One study using 1970 data found factors labeled "SMSA Size" and "Manufacturing Employment" related to "general crime," while "violent crime" was best explained by factors labeled "Black Population" and "income." A second set of studies explored 1970 crime rates across incorporated municipalities.[9] Harries constructed social indicator typologies[10] of high- and low-crime municipalities and speculated, in passing, than an expanded consideration of employment and occupation patterns might prove useful in understanding crime rate patterns.[11]

There have been a number of other recent efforts of this sort by social scientists.[12] Flango and Sherbenou have used one of the largest city samples. They found that a factor they labeled "economic specialization" helped explain robbery rate variance and auto theft rate patterns in smaller cities.[13]

In sum, this literature suggests that knowledge of the specific economic functions of cities (in the sense of most import/export industries, e.g., manufacturing, insurance, education, government) and of the specific proportions of workers in different occupations, might help us to extend our knowledge about interurban crime rate patterns.

Opportunity and Motivation in Crime

Criminology works with two general elements in seeking understanding of the patterns of criminal events. One element deals with the character of criminal opportunities—the distribution of criminal targets and victims in time and space. The other general element deals with the character of criminal motivation—the origin, strength and persistence of the desire to commit crimes. Contemporary theory assumes that criminal events can best be understood as the results of interactions between these two general elements.[14] Nevertheless, most research deals with one general element or the other.

Crime and Opportunity

Opportunity theory assumes that some people are motivated to commit crimes and seeks to explain the known patterns of criminal events. Why do murders occur in bars on weekends? Why do burglaries occur in the suburbs on weekday afternoons? This understanding is sought in terms of the distribution of targets, victims, witnesses, and police in social space.[15] Of course, the gross number of targets (raw opportunity distribution) has an important impact on the incidence of crimes. But this approach argues that crime rates will vary as social habits and economic fortune cause people and things to move about the physical environment in various temporal cycles and cadences. As victims and targets cluster and disperse, motivated criminals will continue to produce the observed patterns of crime.

This theoretical approach finds empirical support in many recent studies. Sarah Boggs demonstrated how the patterns of known criminal events in St. Louis fit this theory when crime rates were recalculated on a risk-specific base keyed to concentrations of victims and targets rather than standardized numbers of residents.[16] C. R. Jeffery developed the point extensively in *Crime Prevention* Through Environmental Design.[17] Geographers interested in crime trips have shown patterns consistent with this approach.[18] Sociologists interested in auto theft have shown that a complex opportunity model explains the historic patterns of this crime in several countries.[19]

The conceptual bridge between *this* theoretical approach and interurban crime rate variation must be some intraurban phenomenon which differs from place to place. We suggest that *mobility*, a concept advanced by Burgess in his classic article on urban form[20] but strangely ignored by criminologists,[21] might be this bridge. Burgess was not concerned with migration, but with commutation and transport patterns within cities. He was explicit in his argument that these patterns were crucial to shaping many events, including criminal events.[22] The economic and occupational patterns of cities are known shapers of intracity mobility. Different mixtures of industry and occupation influence social networks, business commutation, location and concentration of goods and services, and so forth.[23] Thus we would expect that intercity variations in economic specialization and occupation patterns would help predict intercity variations in crime rates.

Industry, Occupation, and Criminal Motivation

Correctional theory has long been centrally concerned with offender occupation patterns. Most current correctional policies are tied to the idea that improving the occupational skills of offenders will reduce their motivation to commit further crimes.[24] These theories encompass consensus-based models in which legitimate occupational opportunities are denied some individuals through social dysfunctions, so that they are forced to pursue illegitimate occupational opportunities in search of economic and social success. The theories also encompass class conflict models in which crime is the visible consequence of determined power struggles between antithetical economic interests. Mid-range models such as relative deprivation are also included.[25]

Nearly all of the research studies in this theoretical range use occupation as a major index of any given individual's position in the social structure[26] and, for at least some studies, the division of people into different occupations and industrial classifications stands as a significant purpose.[27] Occupation is used as *the* measure of social class, which in turn is seen as a principal component of the social structure.[28] Thus, a measure of the differential occupational mixtures of metropolitan areas may be used as an index of differential class structures which should, in turn, predict differential distributions of criminal motivations among the inhabitants of these areas, and therefore predict differential crime rates.

This Study

In this study we begin to explore mixtures of the economic specialization and occupational distribution in relation to urban crime rates. Such mixtures serve as proxies for the criminogenic opportunity and motivational structure of cities, so that different mixtures ought to associate with different crime rate patterns. But because the behavioral characteristics of different crimes vary markedly, we can infer that the motive-opportunity matrices associated with crimes also vary. In other words, any particular mixture of economic specializations and occupational distributions should relate differently to different crimes, and any particular variable may change its aspects as a variable of opportunity or as a variable of motive with a change in the crime to which it is being related.

We consider the crime rates, economic specializations, occupational distributions, and other census characteristics of those American SMSAs[29] which had 250,000 or more population in 1970. Crime data were drawn from the Uniform Crime

Reports.[30] Each of seven index offenses—murder, aggravated assault, forcible rape, robbery, burglary, larceny over $50, and motor vehicle theft— was examined separately. The economic, occupational, and background (or control) data were taken from the 1970 United States Census and are listed in table 6.1.

Table 6.1.
Census Variables

Employment: Percent Employed in

Manufacturing	MANUF
Government	GOV
Retail and wholesale trade	TRADE
Finance, insurance, real estate	FIRE
Entertainment	FUN
Health	HEALTH
Education (students in college used as proxy)	PCOL

Occupation: Percent Workers Employed as

Professional/Technical workers	TECH
Sales	SALE
Clerical	CLER
Craftsmen	CRAFT
Operatives	OPER
Transportation	TRANS
Service (non-household)	SERVE
Household service	HOUSE

Background Sociodemographic Variables

Percent in-migration in last five years	MIGR
Percent black	BLK
Percent non-black	NBLK
Percent unemployed	UNEMP
Percent females in work force	FEMWK
Median income	INC
Percent in poverty	POV
Mean school years completed—whites	WSCH
Mean school years completed—blacks	BSCH
Percent males in 15–34-year age range	M1534
Log of total population	LPOP

The census data were analyzed against the crime data singly, in derived proportions, and in constructed cross-products on interactions terms. The analysis consisted of three steps: (1) for each crime, zero-order correlations were calculated between the crime rate and the census variables and derived variables;[31] (2) multiple regressions were run for each crime so that a maximum of twelve independent variables were used. Reduced step-wise regression models were than run so that only the better explanatory variables were used, subject to the restriction that independent variables not be highly intercorrelated;[32] (3) the results of these statistical procedures were then examined crime by crime, using an opportunity-motivation matrix conceptual rubric.

Results

The seven index offenses can be assigned to different locations on the opportunity-motivation matrix. Murder and aggravated assault are, principally, motive dependent crimes—emotional explosions at the conclusion of escalating altercations. They are strongly associated with minority ethnicity and poverty measures. Opportunities to murder and assault abound; the opportunity structure constrains these crimes only in the sense of limiting them to well known spatial and temporal positions associated with primary group and leisure interactions.[33] Burglary, larceny, and motor vehicle theft are crimes of opportunity—the spatial and temporal locations of targets appear to constrain the occurrence of these crimes.[34] Rape and robbery are more complex crimes and appear to be strongly influenced by both motive and opportunity.[35] Thus, we expect our economic specialization and occupational distribution data to index the opportunity structure and explain important segments of the variance in intermetropolitan burglary, larceny, and motor vehicle theft. We expect our economic specialization and occupational data to index over motivational patterns and contribute less strongly to an explanation of murder and assault variance. We are unsure whether these variables will explain rape or robbery rate variance.

Table 6.2.

Murder

Correlations: PBLK = .67   POV = .53   HOUSE = .69   NBLK × SCHB = −.70   SCHB = −.52
Full regression model: R^2 = .84
Reduced regression model: R^2 = .72

Variables	R^2 Change	Simple R	Variables	R^2 Change	Simple R
NBLK × SCHB	.49	−.70	FEMWK	.01	.13
HOUSE	.08	.69	TRANS	.015	.22
LPOP	.077	.17	MIGR × POV	−.016	.42
SERVE	.018	−.18	OPER	.016	.11

Assault

Correlations: PBLK = .35   HOUSE = .36   FEMWK × BLK = .34   NBLK × MANUF = −.34   NBLK × INC = −.33
Full regression model: R^2 = .34
Reduced regression model: R^2 = .72

Variables	R^2 Change	Simple R	Variables	R^2 Change	Simple R
HOUSE	.127	.36	MIGR × POV	.02	.32
LPOP	.07	.17	NBLK × INC	.015	−.33

Burglary

Correlations: FUN = .56   MANUF = .52   FUN × FIRE = .59   NBLK × MANUF = −.55   MIGR × POV = .51
Full regression model: R^2 = .64
Reduced regression model: R^2 = .59

Variables	R^2 Change	Simple R	Variables	R^2 Change	Simple R
FUN × FIRE	.347	.59	BLK × CLER × SALES	.01	.16
NBLK × MANUF	.065	−.55	CLER	.03	.32
MIGR × TRANS	.03	.50	POV	.01	.19
LPOP	.02	.25	GOV × FIRE	.01	.35
CLER × SALES × M1534	.02	.046	TECH	.01	.28

Larceny

Correlations: FUN = .51   MANUF = −.52   FUN × FIRE × MIGR = .51   UNEMP × M1534 = .43   UNEMP = .48
Full regression model: R^2 = .58
Reduced regression model: R^2 = .52

Variables	R^2 Change	Simple R	Variables	R^2 Change	Simple R
MANUF	.27	−.52	CRAFT	.04	−.14
UNEMP	.08	.40	GOV × FIRE	.02	.31
FUN × FIRE × MIGR	.06	.51	NBLK × INC	.025	−.002
FEMWK	.02	.03	BLK × TEMWK	.015	.08

Murder and Assault

Murder and assault present similar patterns across the large SMSAs (table 6.2). The variables which appear in these regression models measure the stereotypical urban slum situation: ethnicity, ignorance, recent inmigration, poverty and/or employment at menial occupations. The interaction between a high proportion of black population and low black educational attainment explains about 50 percent of the intermetropolitan variance in murder rates. The log of population adds about 8 percent for both crimes. The employment variables that appear in these models mirror the social conditions classically associated with these crimes. They index the aggregate motivation of a city's population toward commission of these crimes. An urban area's economic specialization—what it does for a living—seems unrelated to its murder and assault rates.

Burglary and Larceny

Burglary and larceny exhibit similar patterns. They vary with economic specialization (table 6.2). Cities which specialize in entertainment and in finance, insurance, and real estate (FIRE), and to a lesser extent, in government and FIRE, have high rates for both crimes. Cities which specialize in manufacturing, consistent with the findings of earlier researchers, have low rates for both crimes. Residential mobility seems to contribute to high rates. Unemployment contributes to known larceny rates, but not to burglary rates.

The explanatory power of economic specialization and occupational variables with respect to these crimes fits an opportunity theory approach to crime. The clear patterns seen here relate well through Burgess' intracity mobility model. FIRE and government cities are often characterized by high levels of office employment in diverse locations and dispersed journey-to-work patterns from bedroom communities. Entertainment cities provide activities which pull people away from home at night and which attract a large number of tourists. Such conditions tend to maximize the opportunities for burglary and theft. Manufacturing cities ar typically very stable with low migration and narrow, middle-range income distributions. They tend to have little poverty, limited shopping, limited entertainment, and fewer government employees. Such conditions tend to minimize the opportunities for burglary and theft.

Robbery and Motor Vehicle Theft

Both of these crimes are associated with the crudest of opportunity measures: target density (table 6.3). Robbery is the only index offense which fits the popular belief that crime rates rise with city size.[36] This is consistent with an opportunity theory model of robbery developed by urban planners and geographers over the past decade.[37] Robbery rates in these SMSAs in 1970 also depended on black unemployment—a motivational condition found in the largest metropolitan areas.

Motor vehicle theft correlates with population, clerical female workers, and mean income. We interpret these findings as showing that economic specialization, occupational distribution, and background social and demographic data act as proxies for some more direct measure of motor vehicle density. To the extent that the specialization and occupation variables matter, a high proportion of female workers may indicate more multicar families and more unattended cars parked in business areas of the city. High income levels may suggest more new, expensive automobiles, multiplying the opportunities for professional car thieves.

Rape

Rape rates vary with a mixture of opportunity and demographic variables (table 6.3).[38] The regression models explain 45 percent of the variance in rape rates across the SMSAs. The cross-product of two economic specializations—FIRE and entertainment—contribute almost half the explained variance. The FIRE industry tends to generate a large number of dispersed journey-to-work patterns by females. Cities which specialize in entertainment provide night-time activities (restaurants, bars, theaters) and increase night-time foot traffic as well as creating social interac-

Table 6.3.

Robbery

Correlations: LPOP = .64   BLK × CLER × SALES = .41   CLER = .36   BLK × UNEMP = .34   INC = .34
Full regression model: R² = .60
Reduced regression model: R² = .51

Variables	R² Change	Simple R	Variables	R² Change	Simple R
LPOP	.415	.64	MIGR × TRANS	.014	.18
BLK × UNEMP	.075	.34	INC	.009	.34

Auto Theft

Correlations: LPOP = .45   CLER = .36   INC = .31
Full regression model: R² = .39
Reduced regression model: R² = .31

Variables	R² Change	Simple R	Variables	R² Change	Simple R
LPOP	.20	.45	SERVE	.02	−.215
CLER	.03	.36	UNEMP × M1534	.02	.07
MIGR	.02	.20	CLER × SALES × M1534	.01	.10

Rape

Correlations: FIRE = .36   FUN = .40   FIRE × FUN = .47   BLK = .34   MIGR × TRANS = .39   TRADE × FIRE = .38
Full regression model: R² = .53
Reduced regression model: R² = .45

Variables	R² Change	Simple R	Variables	R² Change	Simple R
FIRE × FUN	.22	.47	TRANS	.04	.04
BLK	.075	.34	TECH	.02	.30
LPOP	.03	.33	CLER	.02	.29
M1534	.03	.25	MIGR × TRANS	.01	.39

tion settings which may trigger a rape. Thus, the opportunities for stranger-to-stranger rape, and for the far commoner rape between friends or acquaintances, are expanded by these economic specializations.[39] The SMSA analysis shows, in addition, that the percent black, percent young males, high residential mobility, and percent of workers in low-skill occupations also matter. Minority population, youth, high mobility and low-level employment, together with opportunity, are the metropolitan characteristics associated with rape.

Conclusion

Criminal behavior is complex. Analytic studies of criminal behavior have tended to concentrate on motivation *or* opportunity. This study, analyzing crime at the SMSA level, explores crime patterns, using motivation and opportunity concepts concurrently. Economic specialization data were used to index potential opportunity structure; socioeconomic status data were used to index potential motivational structures. At the aggregate level, murder and assault were associated with motivational variables. Burglary and larceny, motor vehicle theft and robbery were associated with opportunity variables. Rape was associated with both opportunity and motivational variables. In general, except for the highly affective crimes of murder and assault, including information about aggregate opportunity structures adds to the analysis of inter-metropolitan crime patterns and makes it possible to see a plausible reason why some types of cities have high (or low) crime rates.

NOTES

1. See, e.g., A. M. Guerry, *Essai sur la statistique morale de la France* (Paris: Chez Crochard, 1833); Thomas Plint, *Crime in England*, (London: Charles Gilpin, 1851).

2. Gabriel Tarde, *Penal Philosophy*, Howell tr. (Boston: Little, Brown, 1912), pp. 338–62; Raffaele Garofalo, *Criminology*, Miller tr. (Boston: Little, Brown, 1914); Enrico Ferri, *Criminal Sociology*, Kelly and Lisle, tr. (Boston: Little, Brown, 1917), pp. 200–01.

3. Terrence Morris, *The Criminal Area* (London: Routledge and Kegan Paul, 1958), pp. 37–64; M. A. Quetelet, *A Treatise on Man* (Edinburgh:Wm. and Robert Chambers, 1842).

4. William F. Ogburn, "Factors in the Variation of Crime Among Cities," *Journal of the American Statistical Association* (1935), 30:12–34.

5. Karl Schuessler and Gerald Slatin, "Sources of Variation in U.S. City Crime, 1950 and 1960," *Journal of Research in Crime and Delinquency* (1964) 1:127–48; Karl Schuessler, "Components of Variation in City Crime Rates," *Social Problems* (1962), 9:314–23.

6. SMSAs are defined by the census to describe urban areas which exceed municipal boundaries, where a core city and its suburban counties together have 50,000 or more population, Kent P. Schwirian, D. G. Bromby, J. P. Gibbs, A. M. Guest, R. M. Jiober, Anthony J. La Greca, W. Michaelson, R. A. Smith, and R. H. Weller, *Contemporary Topics on Urban Sociology* (Morristown, N.J.: General Learning Press, 1977), pp. 248–50.

7. Paul Eberts and Kent P. Schwirian, "Metropolitan Crime Rates and Relative Deprivation," *Criminologica* (1968), 5:43–52.

8. Keith D. Harries, *The Geography of Crime and Justice* (New York: McGraw-Hill, 1974).

9. Harries, "Cities and Crime: A Geographic Model," *Criminology* (1976), 14:369–86.

10. Harries, "A Crime-Based Analysis and Classification of 729 American Cities," *Social Indicators Research* (1976), 2:467–87.

11. Harries, "Cities and Crime," p. 380.

12. Tarald O. Kvalseth, "A Note on the Effects of Population Density and Unemployment on Urban Crime," *Criminology* (1977), 15:105–10; Sheldon Danziger, "Explaining Urban Crime Rates," *Criminology* (1976), 14:291–96; P. E. Spector, "Population Density and Unemployment: The Effects on Violent Crime in the American City," *Criminology* (1975), 12:339–401; G. Swimmer, "The Relationship of Police and Crime," *Criminology* (1974), 12:293–314.

13. Victor Eugene Flango and Edgar L. Sherbenou, "Poverty, Urbanization and Crime," *Criminology* (1976), 14:331–36. Note that Flango and Sherbenou did not mention what fifty-nine variables were used and did not describe the underlying composition of their factors.

14. Paul J. Brantingham and Patricia L. Brantingham, "A Theoretical Model of Crime Site Selection." Paper read at American Society of Criminology annual meetings, Atlanta, Ga., November 18, 1977.

15. *Ibid.* See also John Baldwin, A. E. Bottoms, and Monica Walker, *The Urban Criminal: A Study in Sheffield* (London: Tavistock, 1976), pp. 1–35. The form of social space we have in mind is the complex bend of physical and social environments conceived by the French sociologist P. H. Chombart de Lauwe. See Anne Buttimer, "Social Space in Interdisciplinary Perspective," *Geographical Review* (1969), 59:417–26.

16. Sarah Boggs, "Urban Crime Patterns," *American Sociological Review* (1965), 30:899–908.

17. C. Ray Jeffery, *Crime Prevention Through Environmental Design* (Beverly Hills, Cal.: Sage, 1972).

18. Donald L. Capone and Woodrow W. Nichols, Jr., "Urban Structure and Criminal Mobility," *American Behavioral Scientist* (1976), 20:199–213.

19. Roger Mansfield, Leroy C. Gould, and J. Zvi Namewirth, "A Socio-economic Model for the Prediction of Societal Rates of Property Theft," *Social Forces* (1974), 52:462–72.

20. Ernest W. Burgess, "The Growth of the City," in Robert E. Park, Ernest W. Burgess and Roderick D. McKenzie, *The City* (Chicago: University of Chicago Press, 1925), pp. 47–62.

21. Clifford Shaw and Henry D. McKay, *Juvenile Delinquency and Urban Areas*, rev. ed. (Chicago: University of Chicago Press, 1969); Walter C. Reckless, *The Crime Problem*, 5th ed. (New York: Appleton Century Crofts, 1973); Herman Mannheim, *Comparative Criminology* (London: Routledge and Kegan Paul, 1965) pp. 536–44.

22. Burgess, "Growth of the City," pp. 58–62. In many ways, Burgess is the father of the American opportunity theory of crime. He had argued that opportunity was the key to urban delinquency rates as early as 1916. E. W. Burgess, "Juvenile Delinquency in a Small City," *Journal of the American Institute of Criminal Law and Criminology* (1916), 6:726.

23. See, e.g., P. H. Chombart de Lauwe, *Des Hommes et des villes*, (Paris: Petite Bibliothèque Payot, 1963); *Paris: Essais de sociologie 1952–1964*, (Paris: Les Editions Ouvrières, 1965), pp. 71–101.

24. See, e.g., Martin R. Haskell and Lewis Yablonsky, *Crime and Delinquency* (Chicago: Rand McNally, 1970), p. 390; Harry E. Allen and Clifford E. Simonsen, *Corrections in America: An Introduction* (Beverly Hills, Calif.: Glencoe Press, 1975), pp. 413–15; Home Office, *People in Prison (England and Wales)* (London: H.M.S.O., 1969, CMND. 4214), pp. 36–40.

25. See Gwynn Nettler, *Explaining Crime* (New York: McGraw-Hill, 1974), pp. 136–89; Nanette J. Davis, *Sociological Constructions of Deviance*, (Dubuque, Iowa: Wm. C. Brown, 1975).

26. A. J. Reiss, Jr. and A. L. Rhodes, "The Distribution of Juvenile Delinquency in the Social Class Structure," *American Sociological Review* (1961), 26:pp. 720–32.

27. See, e.g., Eberts and Schwirian, "Metropolitan Crime Rates."

28. Peter Worsley, Ray Fitzhenry, J. Clyde Mitchell, D. H. J. Morgan, Valdo Paris, Bryan Roberts, W. W. Sharrock, and Robin Ward, *Introducing Sociology* (Harmondsworth, England: Penquin Books, 1970), pp. 293–94.

29. The sociological rationale using SMSA data rather than incorporated place data as a measure of urban areas for intermetropolitan crime rate comparisons has recently been developed in Jack P. Gibbs and Maynard L. Erickson, "Crime Rates of American Cities in an Ecological Context," *American Journal of Sociology* (1976), 82:605–20.

30. Federal Bureau of Investigation, *Crime in the United States 1969, 1970, 1971.* (Washington: U.S. Government Printing Office, 1970, 1971, 1972). In each

case, data were from table 5. Rates used in the study represent mean rates for the three years. The rationale for this procedure is developed in Harry A. Scarr, *Patterns of Burglary*, 2d ed. (Washington: Law Enforcement Assistance Administration, 1973), pp. 20–21.

31. The Statistical Package for the Social Sciences (SPSS) was used.

32. In the first cut at the data, step-wise multiple regression was used with minimum inclusion restrictions. Step-wise regression was used because there was no a priori reason for ordering the variables. This part of the analysis produced full models. Next, variable sparing models were produced by using more stringent inclusion requirements. An independent variable had to have an F of 2.0 to be included and have no more than 75 percent of its variance explained by variables already in the equation. More stringent requirements could have been employed but, in an explanatory study, these were considered sufficient.

33. Lynn A. Curtis, *Criminal Violence: National Patterns and Behavior* (Lexington, Mass.: Lexington Books, 1974) pp. 65–79, 147, 181–82.

34. Harold J. Vetter and Ira J. Silverman, *The Nature of Crime* (Philadelphia: W. B. Saunders Co., 1978), pp. 122–53; Boggs, "Urban Crime patterns."

35. Curtis, *Criminal Violence*, pp. 54–61, 87–94, 147–48. Vetter & Silverman, *Nature of Crime*, pp. 81–92, 98–117.

36. James A. Inciardi, *Reflections on Crime* (New York: Holt, Rinehart & Winston, 1978), pp. 67–76.

37. Shlomo Angel, "Discouraging Crime Through City Planning," Working Paper no. 75 (Berkeley: University of California, Center for Planning and Development Research, February 1968); Susan Wilcox, "The Geography of Robbery." *The Prevention and Control of Robbery*, 3, (Davis, Calif.: Center on Administration of Davis, April 1973); Capone and Nicholas, "Urban Structure and Criminal Mobility."

38. Rape data are the most questionable of police statistics. The crime is known to be substantially underreported. Any results based on these statistics must be viewed through a soft-focus lens, at best.

39. Curtis, *Criminal Violence*, pp. 19–43; Vetter and Silverman, *Nature of Crime*, pp. 98–99.

ꙮ 7 ꙮ

Criminogenic Correlates of Intermetropolitan Crime Rates, 1960 and 1970

MARSHALL A. WORDEN

THIS PAPER ASSAYS the causes of intermetropolitan variation in United States crime rates for 1960 and 1970. Ten crime categories, as reported in the *Uniform Crime Reports for the United States*, are considered for each year. That source identifies the amount of total crime and its constituent parts, total violent crime, and total property crime. Violent crime consists of murder, rape, robbery, and assault; property crime includes burglary, larceny, and auto theft.

Explanation for variation in crime rates was sought by utilizing a series of measures that not only captured total metropolitan characteristics but also central-city and outside-central-city attributes. In addition, absolute differences between central-city and outside-central city characteristics were evaluated. To illustrate, the median age of central-city and outside-central-city residents were considered in addition to the absolute difference in median age between the two parts of the city. The major research interest was to monitor the relationship of crime rates in conjunction with: (1) the properties of these ecological units; and (2) the absolute differences between these ecological units. Absolute differences between central-city and outside-central-city proved, except in a few cases, to be singularly unimportant. Thus, the explanation offered in this analysis rests on the concept of relative deprivation or the perception of relative deprivation.

The Sample Data

The sample data for both years are made up of the same 120 Standard Metropolitan Statistical Areas.[1] The ten dependent crime variables consist of rates per 100,000 population for the SMSA. Fifty-two and twenty-four independent variables were utilized for, respectively, 1970 and 1960. Standard SPSS procedures were followed to compute simple correlations and stepwise linear regressions. The results presented are significant to at least the 5 percent level. Simple correlations of less than (.40) are not reported. For parsimonious explanation, the regression models were allowed to accept no more than three independent variables. In no case, however, did the change in R^2 associated with a fourth variable demonstrate significantly improved explanation.

Table 7.1 reports the mean crime rates for the sample cities in 1960 and 1970. Documented here is the frequently noted but nevertheless extraordinary increase in crime rates during these years: a nearly three-fold increase in total crimes and violent crimes. The truly phenomenal increases of approximately 245 percent each in robbery and larceny rates are to be especially noted since they represent higher proportions of total crime by 1970. It is also noteworthy that the proportion of violent crimes has increased less than 1 percent. What explanations or descriptive associations can be offered for these rates? Are macroecological disparities for individual cities associated with these crime rates and are changes in the social ecology of the cities reflected in these increased rates?

The 1960 Evidence

The findings for 1960 are rather limited. Most of the independent variables fail to achieve a (.40) correlation with the various crime categories. Except for murder, the correlations are all rather low but the indicated directions are important. Characteristics of the central city or the area outside the central city per se are seemingly unimportant.

Table 7.1.
Mean Crime Rates per 100,000

Crime Category	1960		1970	
	Rate	% of Total Crime	Rate	% of Total Crime
Total crime	1172.0	100.0	3163.1	100.0
Total violent crime	130.5	11.1	372.1	11.8
Total property crime	1041.5	88.9	2791.0	88.2
Murder	5.5	0.5	8.5	0.3
Rape	8.1	0.7	22.2	0.7
Robbery	47.0	4.0	162.6	5.1
Assault	70.0	6.0	178.9	5.6
Burglary	543.3	46.4	1290.5	40.8
Larceny	297.2	25.4	1034.2	32.7
Auto theft	201.0	17.2	466.5	14.7

Murder rates are correlated with the percent of the SMSA white (−.66), foreign-born (−.55), in sound housing (−.42), black (.76), in housing units with 1.01 or more persons per room (.53), with family incomes under $3,000 (.66), and with median income (−.54). This suggests that high murder rates are found in SMSAs with a relatively large proportion of their population black, with substandard and crowded housing, and with low incomes. Total violent crime is correlated with the percent of the SMSA white (−.41) and black (.50) as is assault (−.44 and .53, respectively). In contrast, none of these variables are important correlates of total crime, property crime, or burglary for which only percent of population increase for the SMSA between 1950 and 1960 is significant (.41, .42, and .41 respectively). Finally, robbery is only correlated with the population rank of the SMSA (−.47), meaning that higher robbery rates are found in larger cities.[2] Two major pathologies are thus evidenced for 1960: one associates violent crimes with SMSA blackness and the other links property crimes with SMSA population growth.

The seven regression models that can be generated for this date have relatively small coefficients of determination. Statistically significant equations could not be derived for rape, assault, or auto theft. All of the equations include some population growth component, with it being the first entered variable for total crime (C_t), property crime (C_p), burglary C_b), and larceny (C_l):

$$C_t = 720 + 5.1X_1 + 47.4X_2 - 4.0X_3 \quad R^2 = .39; \quad (1)$$
$$C_p = 642 + 4.6X_1 + 39.2X_2 - 3.1X_3 \quad R^2 = .37; \quad (2)$$
$$C_b = 290 + 2.5X_1 + 22.5X_x - 1.4X_3 \quad R^2 = .33; \quad (3)$$
$$C_l = 244 + 1.5X_1 - 3.4X_4 + 5.3X_5 \quad R^2 = .25; \quad (4)$$

where

X_1 = Percent SMSA population increase, 1950–1960;

X_2 = Percent SMSA housing units with 1.01 or more persons per room;

X_3 = SMSA population rank;

X_4 = SMSA difference between percent white and nonwhite households that are owner-occupied; and

X_5 = Percent SMSA families with incomes over $10,000.

The growth commonality (X_1) between equations (2), (3), and (4) and equation (1) is not surprising since the former are the major constituent parts of the latter. Population growth explains 17 percent of the variance in total crime, 18 percent in property crime, 17 percent in burglary, and 16 percent in larceny. Crowding and population size variables link burglary and property crimes to total crime. Larceny is somewhat more difficult to interpret because of the negative correlation between X_4 and C_1. This should be interpreted to mean that larceny rates are high when the difference between white and nonwhite owner occupancy is low.[3] While the second loaded variable is somewhat enigmatic, it accomplishes a fine-tuning of the model by explaining an additional 6 percent of the variance. The final element of the larceny equation identifies the positive relationship between relatively high income and larceny rates.

The models for violent crime emphasize somewhat different variables. In the case of robbery (C_r), population rank explains 22 percent of the variance. In addition, population growth outside the central city becomes important, but measures of absolute ecological disparity are unimportant:

$$C_r = 47.5 - .4X_3 + 2X_6 + 1.9X_2 \quad R^2 = .33; \quad (5)$$

where,

X_6 = Percent population increase outside central city, 1950–1960.

This model, in explaining robbery, draws attention to the suburban locus of metropolitan growth as well as to crowding. Murder rates (C_m) are closely predicted by race and poverty conditions:

$$C_m = .135 + .23X_7 + .19X_8 + .25X_1 \qquad R^2 = .69; \qquad (6)$$

where

X_7 = Percent SMSA population black; and

X_8 = Percent SMSA families with incomes under \$3,000.

Percent black alone accounts for 58 percent of the variance and the poverty index explains a further 6 percent. Finally, violent crimes (C_v) as a group are dependent on percent of the SMSA black on population size, and on population growth between 1950 and 1960:

$$C_v = 111 + 4.2X_7 - .7X_3 + .6X_1 \qquad R^2 = .41. \qquad (7)$$

Percent black accounts for 25 percent of the variance while SMSA population rank and growth explain an additional 10 percent and 6 percent.

In general, therefore, the etiology of crime in 1960 encompasses characteristics of population size and change, crowding, income inequality, and percent black.[4] Each of these variables was measured at the SMSA level and intrametropolitan spatial variation in these indexes was statistically insignificant. Only in the case of robbery is ecological variation important and that reflects population growth.

The 1970 Evidence

By 1970, significantly different sorts of observations can be made. In contrast to 1960, a variety of central-city variables are important correlates of total SMSA crime. The percent of black and Spanish-speaking students in central-city high schools is correlated with total crime (.45), all violent crime (.65), murder (.72), rape (.48), robbery (.59), assault (.48), burglary (.42), and auto theft (.45). The absolute size of minority populations in central cities is positively associated with violent crime (.61), robbery (.75), and auto theft (.43). Central-city crowding, as measured by percent of housing units with 1.01 or more persons per room, correlates with SMSA violent crime (.46), murder (.55), and auto theft (.40). Lastly, central-city density is positively related to SMSA robbery rates (.59).

The absolute size of the black and other nonwhite population living outside the central city is positively linked to total crimes (.40), violent crimes (.58), robbery (.65), and auto theft (.46).

Total SMSA characteristics continue to be moderately well correlated with a variety of crimes. The population rank of the SMSA is negatively correlated with violent crime ($-.41$), robbery ($-.53$), and auto theft ($-.52$) while the size of the black and other nonwhite populations is positively related to the same crimes (.62, .76, .45, respectively). The size of the Spanish-speaking population is shown to be important for total crime (.44), violent crime (.46), property crime (.41), and robbery (.46). Finally, in 1970 it is evident that absolute SMSA unemployment is a criminogenic element in the case of violent crime (.53), robbery (.68), and auto theft (.45).

The regression models for 1970 are similarly informative. Most strikingly, for all crime categories, save larceny and auto theft, the percent of youthful minorities in central-city high schools is important; in the case of total crime, violent crime, murder, rape (C_s), assault C_a), and burglary it is the first entered variable:

$$C_t = 2483 + 22X_9 - 250X_{10} + 121X_2 \qquad R^2 = .43; \qquad (8)$$
$$C_v = 60.5 + 6.6X_9 + .1X_{11} + 1.8X_{12} \qquad R^2 = .61; \qquad (9)$$
$$C_m = 2.79 + .21X_9 + .10X_{13} - .32X_{14} \qquad R^2 = .66; \qquad (10)$$
$$C_x = 2.25 + .26X_9 + .22X_{15} + .18X_{12} \qquad R^2 = .43; \qquad (11)$$
$$C_a = 211 + 3.0X_9 - 2.2X_{16} + .6X_{17} \qquad R^2 = .38; \qquad (12)$$
$$C_b = 1097 + 12X_9 + 7X_{18} - 57X_{10} \qquad R^2 = .39; \qquad (13)$$

where

X_9 = Percent black and Spanish-speaking in central city high schools;
X_{10} = Percent SMSA housing units lacking plumbing;
X_{11} = central city population;

X_{12} = Percent of SMSA population in central city;

X_{13} = Percent of black housing units outside central city lacking plumbing;

X_{14} = difference between central-city and outside-central-city density;

X_{15} = Percent SMSA population change, 1960–1970;

X_{16} = Percent SMSA white population outside central city;

X_{17} = Percent difference between population change outside central city and within central city; and

X_{18} = central city population change, 1960–1970.

The concentration of youthful minorities in central cities explains a relatively high percent of the variance in each of these models: 21 percent of total crime, 42 percent of violent crime, 52 percent of murder, 23 percent of rape and assault, and 17 percent of burglary. Besides the dependent role of youthful minority populations in central cities, several other observations should be made regarding the models. The total crime etiology also embodies a negative correlation with substandard housing and a positive correlation with crowding; i.e., SMSAs with relatively good housing stock but with considerable crowding throughout and concentration of youthful minorities in central cities can expect relatively high total crime rates. The "absence of plumbing" variable accounts for an additional 15 percent of the variance and crowding for a further 7 percent. Violent crime is accentuated by the size and level of concentration of population in central cities, with the former explaining 16 percent of the variance. Substandard black housing outside the central city (explaining 12 percent of the variance) and similarity between central-city and outside-central-city density are both criminogenic elements in murder. A population growth variable respectively accounts for 11 percent and 15 percent of the variance in the rape and burglary models. The assault model, through variables X_{16} and X_{17}, identifies the situation where white population is continuing to grow in the central city or is growing relatively less rapid in the suburbs. This explains 15 percent of the variance.

Explanation of robbery rates is found in the size of SMSA minority populations together with the concentration of youthful minorities in the central city:

$$C_r = 74.4 + .26X_{19} + 2.8X_9 - 5.4X_{20} \qquad R^2 = .72; \qquad (14)$$

where

X_{19} = SMSA black and other nonwhite population; and

X_{20} = percent of housing units outside central city lacking plumbing.

Minority population size explains 58 percent of the variance and crowding an additional 10 percent.

While burglary rates primarily reflected youthful minority concentration in central cities, larceny is mainly dependent on SMSA population growth and income level (respectively 20 percent and 6 percent of the variance) and auto theft (C_c) is dependent on SMSA population size, density, and crowding:

$$C_l = 910 + 6X_{15} - 108X_{10} + 45X_{21} \qquad R^2 = .37; \qquad (15)$$
$$C_c = 404 - 2.6X_3 + 78X_{22} + 24X_2 \qquad R^2 = .47; \qquad (16)$$

where

X_{21} = percent of SMSA families with income less than \$5,000; and

X_{22} = SMSA density.

SMSA rank explains 28 percent of the auto theft variance, density another 11 percent, and crowding a final 8 percent.

These various property crime components are then rolled together in an overall property crime model that shows a dependent relationship with the size of the Spanish-speaking population in the SMSA, SMSA population growth, and youthful minority concentration in the central city:

$$C_p = 1889 + 1.8X_{23} + 20X_{15} + 15X_9 \qquad R^2 = .36; \qquad (17)$$

where,

X_{23} = SMSA Spanish-speaking population.

These variables account for 17 percent, 12 percent, and 7 percent of the variance.

From equations (8) through (17), it is evident that violent crimes are better modeled by using central city measurements while property crimes are better described by using SMSA characteristics. Population growth or decline are relatively important in the case of property crime and its components, burglary and larceny, in addition to rape. Finally, violent crime, murder, rape, and assaults are partly explained by measures that contrast the central city with either the entire SMSA or with the area outside the central city.[5]

Evaluation

Comparison of the 1960 and 1970 crime models reveals that substantially different variables have predictive value for each year. In 1960, SMSA population growth, crowding, and population rank were the best predictors of total crime, property crime, and burglary. Ten years later, the concentration of youthful minorities in the central city and the size of the Spanish-speaking population in SMSA's emerged as critical predictors for the same crimes. The major correlates of larceny changed very little, with SMSA population growth remaining a major attribute. In the case of robbery, variables representing SMSA population rank, outside-central-city population growth, and crowding are replaced by the size of nonwhite populations in the SMSA and the level of concentration of youthful minorities in central cities. And, finally, for the murder and violent crime models, the size of the SMSA black population is replaced by the concentration of high-school-age minorities in the central city. These sundry shifts in independent variables may identify some of the root causes of the dramatic increase in crime rates during the 1960s.

In all of these models, measures of absolute difference between central city and outside central city proved highly unimportant. Yet for most of the models there are suggestions in the structure of the variables that differences between the central city and the rest of the SMSA are of some significance. While not directly measured through this analysis, the concept that seems applicable here is that of the perception of relative deprivation as opposed to absolute deprivation.

Robbery in 1970, equation (14), serves as an example. The model indicates that robbery is positively correlated with the size of the SMSA black and other nonwhite populations and the proportion of black and Spanish-speaking students in central-city high schools, and negatively associated with housing units outside the central city that lack plumbing. We might expect, therefore, high robbery rates in SMSAs with large minority populations concentrated in central cities surrounded by relatively affluent suburbs. The 1970 burglary model, equation (13), relies on a similar logic in that relatively satisfactory housing conditions are linked to crime rates. Finally, in the model for total crime in 1970, equation (8), the hypothesis of relative or absolute deprivation, would lead us to expect a positive relationship between inadequate plumbing and crime. Instead, we find the opposite. Theoretically, in each of these cases, the perception of difference, not the actual difference, is what propels this criminogenic relationship. Chester has argued this before in discussing property crime:

> Absolute poverty, however, has been shown to be far less criminogenic than relative poverty. Therefore, lower-class crime against the middle and upper classes occurs most often where access to perceived middle-class values and lifestyles is most pronounced: in areas where large numbers of the relatively rich live near the relatively poor, or in areas of high media penetration, where more affluent lifestyles are constantly and widely depicted.[6]

Chester's conclusions have merit, but violent crimes should also be included with property crime. The argument concerning relative deprivation does not seem to apply as well in 1960 as it does in 1970. I interpret the several models in this essay to mean that by 1970, coincident with phenomenal increases in crime rates, perceived relative deprivation became a truly significant cause of levels of United States crime rates. This is not to say that perceived relative deprivation was not previously a causal factor but it appears to me to represent a dominant force by 1970. If we are to understand this phenomenon, we must examine the macro-ecological reorganizations that occurred in the city during the 1960s.[7] This is a critical issue that geographers, criminologists, and other policy planners need to address.

To what extent are the other findings of this paper consistent with or divergent from some other recent analyses? The evidence on crowding and density is mixed, partly because the two concepts are frequently confused or incorrectly used as interchangeable terms. Booth, Welch, and Johnson conclude that dwelling units per square mile is more related to property crimes than to violent crimes, but household crowding is not well correlated with either in large cities.[8] Their measure of areal density has not been utilized in the present analysis, but density, as measured by people per square mile, appears to be particularly unimportant in my 1960 analysis, with the highest correlation being between central-city density and robbery (.25). In contrast, in 1970, SMSA density correlates with robbery (.50) as does central-city density (.59). The only other meaningful correlation is between SMSA density and auto theft (.48). Furthermore, equations (1), (2), (3), (5), (8), and (16) identify crowding as a criminogenic variable.[9] The analyses of this report provide no support for the conclusions of Booth and his associates. Unfortunately, most of our understanding of crowding and density relies on intracity studies and that knowledge is not always directly transferable to intermetropolitan analysis.[10]

Harries, in a study of incorporated cities for 1970, correlates robbery and total crime with a vector incorporating the percent black, police per capita, and high density.[11] For SMSA rates, equations (8) and (14) enter black and other nonwhite variables but with the emphasis placed on the magnitude of central-city concentration. For total crime, a crowding measure emerges rather than a density measure.[12] Comparison with 1960 shows an important shift in explanation. In that year, population size and growth were most important in explaining robbery, equation (5), and total crime, equation (1); crowding entered as a secondary variable. Harries associates a second vector with burglary. "Cities with relatively stable residential population and high manufacturing employment tend to score low on the burglary vector."[13] His variables do not appear in my model, equation (13), but since growth of the central city population was slowing and in some cases declining, the second entered variable may encompass Harries' stability factor. In contradistinction, equation (3) explains burglary in 1960 in terms of population growth.

In addition, Harries identifies high assault rate cities with lower than average black population and below average income levels. The assault model, equation (12), curiously embodies some of Harries's findings. Central-city youthful minority populations are emphasized but, at the same time, the percent of the white population outside the central city is negatively associated with assault. In other words, some degree of mixing is necessary to the equation and, in this regard, the concept of perceived relative deprivation is useful.

Finally, McCarthy, Galle, and Zimmern review assault and homicide for cities between 1950 and 1970.[14] For 1970, they identify percent nonwhite, percent poor, and crowding as highly associated with homicide and percent nonwhite and crowding as highly associated with assault. They are able to identify regional differences as well. Similar findings for 1950 are also recorded. But McCarthy and his colleagues further analyze changes over time in the mean values for their dependent and independent variables. They conclude:[15]

> The trends for most of the independent variables which are strongly related to homicide and assault rates . . . are in the wrong direction to be consistent with a hypothesis of a *direct causal relationship* with increasing rates of interpersonal violence. Looking at the southern region illustrates the problem dramatically. There the percentage of the population which is non-white does not change appreciably between 1950 and 1970, and the percentage who live in crowded circumstances declines.

Nevertheless, during that same period homicide and assault increased dramatically. This, therefore, is further direct evidence in support of the thesis that perceived relative deprivation emerged as a most relevant criminogenic element during the 1960s.

NOTES

1. The data analyzed in this paper are drawn from U.S. Department of Commerce, Bureau of the Census, *Statistical Abstract of the United States*, 1969 and 1972, Section 33; and U.S. Federal Bureau of Investigation, *Uniform Crime Reports for the United States*, 1960 and 1970.

2. Throughout this essay it should be remembered that populations were ranked in descending order, and thus the largest SMSA received a rank of 1. On that scalar, a negative correlation in this instance would indicate that large population is associated with high robbery rates.

3. This variable, X_4, is moderately well but negatively correlated with the percent of nonwhite households that are owner-occupied ($-.67$) and weakly cor-

related with percent of white households that are owner-occupied (.35). A criminogenic environment for larceny may be one where white home ownership is relatively low and nonwhite home ownership is particularly high.

4. Modeling crime rates with racial variables raises serious ideological and ethical questions. Their use here seems acceptable, since in 1960 blacks accounted for 50 percent of arrestees for murder and 58.5 percent of arrestees for violent crime.

5. Arrestee data during 1970 provide substantiation for the logic of these models. In 1970, blacks under 18 constituted 5.1 percent of the United States urban population. In that year, this age and race cohort accounted for considerably inflated percentages of urban arrestees: 7.2 percent of murder, 13.7 percent of rape, 23.2 percent of robbery, 8.7 percent of assault, 19.0 percent of burglary, 15.0 percent of larceny, 20.0 percent of auto theft, 14.3 percent of violent crime, 16.6 percent of property crime, and 16.2 percent of total crime. The comparable white cohort accounted for 27.8 percent of the urban population and 3.2 percent of murder, 6.8 percent of rape, 7.3 percent of robbery, 6.9 percent of assault, 30.3 percent of burglary, 31.8 percent of larceny, 34.0 percent of auto theft, 6.8 percent of violent crime, 31.7 percent of property crime, and 27.2 percent of total crime. With regard to equation (14), blacks accounted for 68.2 percent of the urban robbery arrestees.

6. C. Ronald Chester, "Perceived Relative Deprivation as a Cause of Property Crime," *Crime and Delinquency* (1976), 22:17–30.

7. For support of the notion that absolute ecological disparities are less important in the 1960s, see Marjorie Cahn Brazer, "Economic and Social Disparities Between Central Cities and Their Suburbs," *Land Economics* (1967), 43:294–302. For further discussion of the relationship of changing social ecology and crime, see Wesley G. Skogan, "The Changing Distribution of Big-City Crime. A Multi-City Time Series Analysis," *Urban Affairs Quarterly* (1977), 13:33–48.

8. Alan Booth, Susan Welch, and David Richard Johnson, "Crowding and Urban Crime Rates," *Urban Affairs Quarterly* (1976), 11:291–307.

9. The crowding measure is itself correlated with a variety of other deprivational measures, but not with areal density. Thus, in 1960, SMSA crowding was correlated with percent of SMSA population that was white (−.62), percent of SMSA population that was black (.50), percent of SMSA families with income below $3,000 (.60), and with the SMSA's median family income (−.50). In 1970, SMSA crowding correlated with percent of SMSA families below the low income level (.70), percent of black and Spanish-speaking students in high school (.44), with SMSA median black income (−.44), and percent of SMSA families with income below $5,000 (.58).

10. For an example of the violence that can be done to the concept of density, see Allen Blitstein, "Population Densities and Urban Crime," *Arizona Review* (August–September 1974), 23:8–11. For a thoughtful review of these various intracity studies, see Dennis W. Roncek, "Density and Crime. A Methodological Critique," *American Behavioral Scientist* (1975), 18:843–60.

11. Keith D. Harries, "Cities and Crime: A Geographic Model," *Criminology* (1976), 14:369–86.

12. It may be that the present analysis has not utilized a sufficiently sensitive measure of density. For a potentially useful alternative, see Robin M. Haynes, "Crime Rates and City Size in America," *Area* (1973), 5:162–65.

13. Harries "Cities and Crime," p. 380, fn. 7.

14. John D. McCarthy, Omer R. Galle, and William Zimmern, "Population Density, Social Structure, and Interpersonal Violence: An Intermetropolitan Test of Competing Models," *American Behavioral Scientist* (1975), 18:771–91.

15. *Ibid.*, pp. 783 and 785.

INTRAURBAN

The five papers in this section consitute a considerable variety of approaches to intraurban analysis. There is a combination of methodological innovation, originality in substantive topics, and treatment of topics of timely current interest.

The first paper, by Christopher Dunn, treats social areas in a suburban county of New York. Traditional approaches to this type of analysis have been correlational. Dunn's paper represents an attempt to overcome what he refers to as the "blurring" that can occur when variables reflecting crime and social area characteristics are aggregated spatially. Although Dunn's technique is founded in a correlation matrix including measures of income, education, housing, and demographic characteristics, he turns to cluster analysis and methods derived from it rather than to the traditional reliance on linear regression models. Some readers will see some similiarities with factorial ecological classification techniques, but Dunn's approach, labeled "differential typological prediction," not only indentifies homogeneous social area types, but also incorporates crime rates for each social area. Furthermore, it enables the calculation of a set of probabilities giving an indication of whether the crime rates observed for particular social area types differ with respect to the overall rate for the county. The importance of Dunn's contribution lies not only in his attempt to get away from the traditional methological directions, but also in his substantive finding that there is, at least in Westchester County, New York, no direct linear relationship between levels of crime and what may be broadly defined as socioeconomic status by neighborhoods. Many criminal justice researchers have acknowledged that the relationships that are dealt with in crime analysis are nonlinear, but the overwhelming majority of research continues to utilize techniques that are based in assumptions of linearity. Dunn's approach represents a refreshing departure from this mold, one that may encourage other criminal justice researchers to experiment further with models that avoid the linearity assumption.

The increasing sophistication of police information systems, including the possibilities of merging crime data and census data, followed by the production of computer maps (all in a relatively short space of time and with considerable precision), provides the potential for a display of information about crime that has never been accomplished previously. Indeed, it would seem that our ability to display information has in many cases outrun our ability to describe the distribution that appears, or to explain that distribution in any depth. Larry Stephenson's paper on the centrographic analysis of crime is a contribution to the description of distributions, either at one point in time or on the basis of change through time. Centrography may be thought of as the application of central tendency statistics to spatial distributions. Just as the mean provides an indication of central tendency in a data series, so the mean center of a set of spatially distributed points provides an indication of the spatial center of that distribution. In cities, the development of new neighborhoods and the transition of old neighborhoods generally means that crime distributions are changing over time. Centrographic techniques provides bases for describing such changes in crime distributions. In a case study of Phoenix, Arizona, Stephenson points out that there were substantial differences between the mean centers of offense locations by ethnic group, and he shows that offense locations of Anglos were more dispersed compared to blacks, Mexican-Americans, or American Indians. Stephenson suggests that the measures that he discusses could be used for testing hypotheses about offender movements between place of residence and place of offense. Theoretically, formulations about the spatial behavior of specific types of offenders could be evaluated through the application of centrographic methodologies including the analysis of movement patterns cross-classified with demographic characteristics.

Although not based on the use of centrographic techniques, Woodrow Nichols's paper, dealing with criminal mobility and social characteristics, approaches the same problem previously outlined by Stephenson. Nichols suggests that in many criminal activities there is an element of spatial planning. The criminal will at some point search what is, in effect, his mental map of his territory in order to evaluate the possible crime site and come up with the most efficient route to and from the place of offense. Nichols refers to this as the "action space" which is conceptualized as a subset of the criminal's mental map. Nichols reviews the relationships between age, sex, and race with respect to crime, and then presents an analysis of the journey to crime based on cleared arrest files from the Miami SMSA, involving 498 robbery trips selected at random. Based on a division at age 20, it was found that there was a significant difference in the mean distances traveled, with those

20 years of age or older traveling significantly further than those under 20. Whites traveled further than blacks and males traveled further than females. When robberies were dichotomized into armed and unarmed categories, significant differences again emerged with respect to age and race, but with respect to sex. Similarly, analysis based on a breakdown of types of premises showed significant differences by age and race but not by sex. These findings assist in developing our understanding of criminal decision-making processes. As Nichols himself suggests, the analysis should ideally be corroborated by additional analyses in other places and involving other crime categories.

The next paper, by Phillip Phillips, provides some of the corroboration that Nichols was hoping for. Phillips used data for 872 offenses involving juvenile crime in the jurisdiction of the Lexington-Fayette police department in Kentucky. Ten offense categories were included in the study, and fifteen data items were compiled for each offense. Phillips points to the similarity between the distance decay function calculated for Lexington and the curve found by Capone and Nichols in an earlier phase of the Miami study. Phillips corroborates Nichols' finding that journey-to-crime distance increases with age. Although Phillips was dealing with a juvenile population, the younger juveniles traveled shorter distances than the older ones. Phillips and Nichols are also in agreement on the question of differences in distances on a racial basis. Phillips found white juveniles had longer journeys to crime than blacks. There is some disagreement with respect to differentials in trip length based on sex. Nichols found that males traveled significantly further than females, but Phillips discovered that females had a mean journey length some 40 percent longer than males. Phillips points out that the explanation for this may lie in the fact that many female juveniles are actually arrested while with adults or with older juveniles. Inherent differences in the age structure of Phillips' sample as compared to Nichols' should not be overlooked. Phillips also develops a typology of journeys to crime and, like Nichols, suggests that further research in other geographic areas and utilizing various demographic controls would be appropriate.

The final chapter constitutes an empirical case study of homicide. The frequency of homicides in retail and commercial locations means that this is a timely topic. Robert Swartz points out that homicide in businesses can influence the pattern of investment in specific neighborhoods and can, in the long run, contribute to the blight and general decline of neighborhoods. Detroit, a city that periodically leads the nation in homicide rate, is an appropriate site for the Swartz case study. In recent years, about 20 percent of Detroit's homicides have been at retail/commercial locations. Of the 20 percent (based in 1974 on a total of 801 homicides in the city of Detroit), some 90 percent are in retail stores. Of the retail homicides, just a few functions—bars, liquor stores, groceries or supermarkets, restaurants, and gas stations—accounted for the majority of homicides. The patterns discussed by Swartz convey the key finding that retail/commercial homicide exhibits a pattern of migration outward from the center of the city toward the suburbs, in the years 1968 through 1974.

࿕ 8 ࿕

The Social Area Structure
of Suburban Crime

CHRISTOPHER S. DUNN

THIS CHAPTER EXAMINES the distribution of rates of four officially recorded offenses (aggravated assault, robbery, burglary, and vehicle theft) among types of social areas in a large northeastern suburban county.[1] The analysis employs differential typological prediction methods, in contrast to the sole use of correlational procedures or factor analytic designs typically found in crime area research.[2] The findings reported here are mainly illustrative of the general research design of differential typological prediction. Considerations of space prohibit any detailed substantive interpretation, but nevertheless, some important substantive criminological and social ecological questions are addressed. Among these are:

1. Is the social area structure of suburban metropolitan counties similar to that of urban places?
2. Is the ecological distribution of crime in suburban places similar to that of urban places?
3. Are patterns of association of contingencies among elements of suburban social area structure and crime distribution similar to or different from those associations or contingencies found in urban places?
4. In view of recent trends indicating the "urbanization" of suburban places, what criminogenic or ecological forces can be identified that may require more intensive analysis, prevention, or remediation?[3]

Such questions are important referents for the type of data and analytic strategy described here, and hopefully the findings reported will serve to stimulate direct comparative studies of urban and suburban places.[4] However, the discussion of findings concentrates upon the capacity of differential typological prediction to identify true ekistical or cross-level effects.

Differential Typological Prediction

Most crime area research utilizes procedures which involve an assumption of concomitant variation in the distributions of crime and social variables. Consequently, the statistical findings, although accurate and appropriate to levels of measurement employed, may not fully reflect the geographical and ecological diversity of the patterns of crime and related social phenomena. As Polk has argued:

> The explanatory power of an ecological frame of reference is obscured by the use of a method of statistical analysis which does not permit examination of characteristics within various types of urban social areas. The "mosaic" nature of the organization of urban life is hopelessly blurred by product-moment correlations of census tract variables, and this blurring becomes especially confounded when higher order correlation terms such as partial correlation or standardized coefficients are employed.[5]

In contrast, the strategy of differential typological prediction overcomes the "blurring" that may be incurred by lumping together crime and social area variables on the basis of an assumption of concomitant variation. In the present use, differential typological prediction refers to a three-stage procedure involving (1) the identification of homogeneous social area types within the county, (2) the identification of rates of reported crime within each social area type and the comparison of rates across area types, and (3) the stochastic assessment of area type crime rates, specifically, determination of the probability that the observed rates for area types differ from the overall county rate. Thus, differential typological prediction does not depend upon assumptions of linearity, but allows one to stochastically assess the observed

configuration of social area attributes and crime rates or patterns
for specific types, as well as how likely it is that criterion differences among types are related to different patterns of predictor
(social area) attributes.[6] Furthermore, the form of such findings
lends itself to interpretation in terms of contingent control relationships and conditional probability. These latter "explanatory"
constructs would appear to be more intuitively appealing in
explaining true ecological effects, i.e., cross-level, than are linear
regression-based results.[7]

The Social Area Typology

The empirical construction of nine homogeneous types of social
areas to represent the social, cultural, economic, and geographic
diversity in the county involved a two-stage analysis. First, four
general dimensions of social area attributes were empirically
identified from patterns of intercorrelations among thirty social
indicator variables such as income, education, housing conditions,
population distribution, social problems, and age and sex structure, (N = 202 census tracts).[8] Each of the four resultant area attribute dimensions (housing structure/household size, social problems, sex composition, and socioeconomic status) was then used in
the definition of nine unique social area types. Each area type
named in table 8.1 is an empirical grouping of census tracts having
similar characteristics in terms of the four area attribute dimensions, each type also reflecting a different pattern of attributes
across the four dimensions. The methods of data analysis that
were employed in the construction of this typology were the techniques of "variable" and "object" cluster analysis as described by
R. C. Tryon and D. E. Bailey in their book, *Cluster Analysis*.

Table 8.1 (left side) presents the results of the procedures
described above. It shows that the largest number of census tracts,
54 (approximately one-fourth of all tracts), are in a type that is
moderate on all four dimensions. This particular type was
designated WORKSUB, reflecting that it has the characteristics of
lower-middle- and working-class suburban neighborhoods. Other
specific types that are like WORKSUB in most ways, but differ

Table 8.1.
Social Area Types and Offense Rate Predictions,

| | | Social Area Types | | | | | Rates of Reported Crime per 1,000 Persons | | | |
| | | Area Attribute Dimensions | | | | | Aggravated Assault | | | |
Social Area Type	Number of Census Tracts	Housing Structure—Household Size	Social Problems	Sex Composition	Socioeconomic Status	Area Homogeneity[a]	Mean Rate	Significance Level (Proportion of random samples)	Homogeneity[a]	Significance Level (Proportion of random samples)
CENTRAL	29	Low	Med	Med	Med	.92	0.7259	.497	.80	.453
ETHMIX	13	Med	Med	Low	Med	.84	0.7457	.543	.78	.633
WORKSUB	54	Med	Med	Med	Med	.93	0.5101	.010*	.94	.000*
MEDSUBURB	23	Med-Hi	Med	Med	High	.94	0.3697	.013*	.98	.000*
HIWEALTH	11	High	Med-Low	Med	High	.93	0.5367	.220	.91	.230
COUNTRY	28	High	Med	Med	Med	.93	0.3693	.007*	.93	.037*
SINGLEMAN	8	High	Med	High	Med	.95	0.1030	.003*	.99	.013*
MEDPROB	19	Med	High	Med	Low	.90	1.6394	.030*	.46	.817
HIPROB	13	Med	High	Low	Low	.87	3.5668	.000*	−2.65	.080
WESTCHESTER COUNTY	202[b]	—	—	—	—	—	0.8048	—	—	—

[a] See footnotes 9 and 11 in the text.
[b] See footnote 8 in the text.
* Statistically significant at < .05.

slightly in racial composition or housing, are ETHMIX, a type in which the percentage of black/other population is somewhat higher than in WORKSUB (which is mainly white), and CENTRAL, which has lower-middle- or working-class population characteristics but central-city-like housing characteristics (apartments and multifamily dwellings).

Table 8.1 also indicates that a substantial number of census tracts in Westchester County (specifically 32) are low socioeconomic status, high social problem tracts, namely those in social areas HIPROB and MEDPROB. Thus, approximately one-sixth of the

Westchester County, New York, 1970

Rates of Reported Crime per 1,000 Persons

Robbery				Burglary				Vehicle Theft			
Mean Rate	Significance Level (Proportion of random samples)	Homogeneity[a]	Significance Level (Proportion of random samples)	Mean Rate	Significance Level (Proportion of random samples)	Homogeneity[a]	Significance Level (Proportion of random samples)	Mean Rate	Significance Level (Proportion of random samples)	Homogeneity[a]	Significance Level (Proportion of random samples)
0.8668	.373	.80	.307	6.8820	.137	.89	.037*	5.4897	.007*	.55	.610
0.7896	.333	.95	.113	5.0597	.017*	.94	.040*	2.7522	.277	.87	.113
0.7383	.080	.88	.043*	6.7240	.017*	.74	.080	4.0535	.140	−.98	.163
0.1433	.000*	.99	.000*	6.0646	.017*	.95	.003*	1.4217	.000*	.91	.003*
0.3226	.033*	.96	.127	7.5235	.453	.86	.317	1.3199	.007*	.97	.003*
0.2463	.000*	.98	.000*	7.1202	.193	.68	.337	0.8304	.000*	.97	.000*
0.5544	.277	.97	.153	8.5575	.360	.76	.537	2.2411	.137	.75	.460
2.6961	.003*	−.80	.230	14.2645	.000*	−1.43	.110	5.5478	.030*	.82	.143
4.4478	.000*	−1.94	.007*	18.0794	.000*	−1.05	.090	5.9301	.060	.72	.400
1.0445	—	—	—	8.2651	—	—	—	3.4884	—	—	—

tracts are decidedly disadvantaged in relation to the others. In fact, the two specific types that fulfill that definition constitute the second largest group of census tracts in the county.

The stereotype usually associated with Westchester County— upper- and upper-middle-class suburbia—is represented by two specific types listed in table 8.1. These are HIWEALTH and MEDSUBURB. Particular mention should be made of COUNTRY and SINGLEMAN, two specific types with housing and social status characteristics similar to, but somewhat less well-to-do than HIWEALTH and MEDSUBURB. SINGLEMAN is a somewhat difficult type to explain because its predominant differentiating characteristics is its "high" value on the sex composition dimension. This value reflects a population that is more male than female and has higher proportions of males who are single. The 8 tracts that comprise this type are otherwise very much like those in COUNTRY, which are tracts that are in the relatively more rural portions of the county.

Table 8.1 also presents a statistic called the "homogeneity" of each type. It is a measure of how similar, across all four attribute dimensions, the census tracts in any specific type are in relation to all the census tracts.[9] The measure typically varies from 0 to 1.00. If a homogeneity approaches 1.00, this means that there is no variation of individual census tracts in a social area type. In other words, each census tract of the type is almost exactly like every other census tract of the type. In fact, if the homogeneity is 1.00, the members are identical in their score profiles on the attribute dimensions. If the homogeneity approaches zero, this indicates that the census tracts of a particular type are quite dissimilar on their score profiles. As table 8.1 shows, the homogeneity of each social area type across the attribute dimensions is quite high. In other words, each of the nine specific social area types is composed of census tracts that have quite similar patterns of score profiles on the attribute dimensions.

Although not presented here (but see Dunn),[10] a map of the social area types indicates that the census tracts comprising the types are by no means randomly distributed throughout the county. In other words, census tracts with similar patterns of scores on attribute dimensions not only form social area clusters; they also are, in many cases, geographically adjacent. In some cases, there even appear to be concentric or graded patterns to the geographic distribution of social area types. Thus, the social area types appear to be spatially distinct constructs as well, even though an area type may be found in more than one locale or site in the county. To recall Polk's point, it is exactly this kind of "mosaic" that the sole use of correlational methods may blur or mask, particularly if there are differences in crime that occur in different spatial expressions of the same social area type.

Offense Rates of Social Areas and
Differential Typological Prediction:
Aggravated Assault

In addition to the thirty variables used as raw data in describing the social area structure of the 202 census tracts, rates of aggravated assault, robbery, burglary, and vehicle theft (per 1000 persons) were also available for each tract. These rates were originally computed from records of offenses reported to all police agencies in the county (municipal, county-wide, and the State Police).[11]

Mean offense rates of each social area type (n = number of tracts in each type) and of the entire county (N = 202 census tracts) are also reported in table 8.1 (right side). Also shown are the homogeneities of each of the social area types vis-a-vis offense rates.[12] The above data are provided by a subroutine known as 4CAST. This subroutine allows an analyst to evaluate, for any set of object types (in the present instance the nine social area types), the position or value of the types on *predicted* variables, i.e., single variables or variable clusters *not* used in the definition of the object types. In using this subroutine, the analyst is not only provided with information about the actual means, standard deviations, and homogeneities of offense rates in the nine social area types. Information is also provided that permits the stochastic assessment of these observed values, and thereby, an assessment can be made of how likely it is that differences among types in predicted variables (viz., differences in offense rate means, standard deviations, and homogeneities) are related to differences among patterns of social area attributes.

In general, these analytic procedures utilize a series of random samples from the full set of scores (N = 202) on a predicted variable (for example, census tract rates of aggravated assault). For each area type and predicted variable used, a series of random samples is drawn, the number of cases in each random sample equaling the number of census tracts comprising each social area type. For example, for the social area type CENTRAL which is comprised of 29 specific census tracts, 300 samples of scores (n = 29) on the predicted variable, aggravated assault rate, are drawn randomly from the pool of aggravated assault rate scores of all 202 census tracts in the county.[13]

Collectively, the statistics calculated on each of the 300 random samples of aggravated assault rates constitute sampling distributions. In other words, the actual mean aggravated assault rate of the 29 specific census tracts which comprise the social area type CENTRAL can be compared with a distribution of aggravated assault rate means obtained from successive independent random samples drawn from all 202 census tract aggravated assault rate scores. Also computed and summarized in similar fashion are standard deviations and homogeneities of the 300 random samples of aggravated assault rates. This process is repeated for each combination of predicted variable and O-type (see note 9) which an analyst may wish to use as a predictor. In the present analysis, there were four offense rates used as predicted variables, nine social area types used as predictors, and 300 random samples for each of the thirty-six combinations, resulting in a total of 10,800 random samples and seventy-two separate sampling distributions, one each for an observed mean, and for the standard deviation and homogeneity of that mean.

In table 8.1 (right side), each of the nine actual social area type mean assault rates is compared to the distribution of its respective randomly generated sampling distribution of mean rates, and similarly, so are the actual homogeneities. For example, for social area CENTRAL, 49.7 percent of the random sample means of aggravated assault rates were below the actual mean assault rate and 50.3 percent were above. For social area MEDPROB in contrast, 97 percent of the random samples (a different set than that used for CENTRAL) had assault rate means lower than the actual mean assault rate, while only 3 percent of the random samples had means that exceeded the actual mean.

These proportions of means of random samples above and below actual means in each social area type are interpreted as probability estimates for the actual means; similar probability interpretations apply to the comparison of random sample homogeneities with actual homogeneity values.[14] The proportions are used to establish estimates of the statistical significance of the actual means and homogeneities.[15] If the actual *mean* is *less than* the overall county mean, the level of significance is given by the proportion of random sample means *below* the actual mean; for CENTRAL, the level of significance shown in table 8.1 is thus .497. If the actual mean is *greater than* the overall county mean, the level of significance is given by the proportion of random sample means *above* the actual mean; for MEDPROB, the level of significance shown in table 8.1 is thus .03. The same interpretation applies to the proportion of random sample standard deviations above and below the actual standard deviation (not shown in table 8.1). For the homogeneity, the proportions of random sample homogeneities above and below the actual homogeneity are simply the reverse of the standard deviation proportions, since the homogeneity calculations are based on a comparision of within-type variance to total variance, and hence the greater the homogeneity).

The data in table 8.1 show that, according to conventional levels of statistical significance, WORKSUB, MEDSUBURB, COUNTRY, and SINGLEMAN have significantly lower mean rates of aggravated assault, and HIPROB and MEDPROB have significantly higher mean rates of aggravated assault than the overall mean for the county. All the social areas with significantly low mean rates of aggravated assault also have statistically significant homogeneities, thereby allowing one to reject the hypothesis that low within-type variance in low rates is due to chance factors. In contrast, the homogeneities for the high rate areas HIPROB and MEDPROB have negative or very low positive values indicating a large within-type variance in rates at the upper end of the distribution. In other words, even though these areas are very similar in terms of defining social characteristics, and have significantly high mean assault rates, variance in assault rates within these area types is great (compared to overall variance in the county).

Distribution of Robbery

The same procedures were used to analyze the distribution of robbery, burglary, and vehicle theft among the nine social area types. The results for robbery (shown in table 8.1) indicate that five of the nine social area types have mean robbery rates per 1,000 residents which differ significantly from the overall mean robbery rate. These areas are social areas MEDSUBURB, HIWEALTH, COUNTRY, MEDPROB, and HIPROB. Mean robbery rates in areas MEDSUBURB, HIWEALTH, and COUNTRY are significantly lower than the overall mean robbery rate. Mean robbery rates in HIPROB and MEDPROB are significantly higher than the overall mean robbery rate.

The data in table 8.1 also show that of the social areas with significant mean robbery rates (either high or low), three of the five also have significant homogeneities. Of these three, MEDSUBURB and COUNTRY (which have low robbery rates) have high homogeneities, .99 and .98 respectively. In other words, the low mean robbery rates characterizing those social areas are also typically low in each of the census tracts comprising the social areas. In contrast, the significance of the negative homogeneity of the high mean robbery rate in HIPROB indicates that the within-type variance represents actual large differences among census tracts comprising the area type, relative to the differences throughout the county. We can be fairly confident that the relatively large variation in high robbery rates in HIPROB is due to more than chance factors; a similar interpretation cannot, however, be made for MEDPROB. The data in table 8.1 also indicate that although WORKSUB has a mean robbery rate that only approaches statistical significance, the relatively high homogeneity (0.88) is significant, thereby allowing one to infer that the within-type similarity of average robbery rates is due to more than chance factors alone.

Distribution of Burglary

The distribution of burglary among the social areas of Westchester County is somewhat similar to the distributions of assault and robbery. As was the case with robbery, five of the nine social areas have mean burglary rates which differ significantly from the overall mean rate in the county of about 8.3 burglaries per 1,000 residents (see table 8.1). However, these areas are not exactly the same areas as the five for robbery. Social areas HIPROB and MEDPROB have mean burglary rates which are significantly higher than the overall mean burglary rate. These areas also had mean rates of assault and robbery which were higher than the respective overall county means. On the other hand, areas which have significantly low mean rates of burglary (ETHMIX, WORKSUB, and MEDSUBURB) differ from those having low mean rates of robbery. Of these three areas, only MEDSUBURB had a mean robbery rate which was significantly lower than the overall county mean for robbery. All five areas have homogeneities that are significant at or approach the .05 level.

As was the case with assault and robbery, both HIPROB and MEDPROB (which have significantly high mean burglary rates) have negative homogeneities, thereby indicating relatively large within-type variation in rates. In addition, CENTRAL (which has a mean burglary rate of about 6.9 per 1,000 persons, not significantly different from the overall county average of about 8.3 per 1,000 persons) has a homogeneity of about .89, significant at the .04 level. In being fairly confident of this low within-type variance of burglary rates in CENTRAL, we can conclude that the configuration of social area attributes is associated with about average rates of burglary, since these average rates are consistent throughout the tracts comprising CENTRAL.

One difference in the pattern of burglary rates is the smaller proportionate difference between high and low rate areas, compared to aggravated assault and robbery. Although not shown in tabular form here, ratios of high mean rate to low mean rate were calculated. For assault, this ratio is about 35:1; for robbery, it is about 31:1. For burglary, in contrast, even though actual rates are much higher, the relative difference between the high mean rate area and the low mean rate area is about 3.5:1.

Distribution of Vehicle Theft

The distribution of vehicle theft among the social areas exhibits some interesting differences from the distribution of the other three offenses. The major difference is the identification of another social area, besides HIPROB and MEDPROB, as an area having an offense rate *significantly higher* than the overall county average. Another difference is the absence of a very high level of statistical significance associated with the mean vehicle theft rate of HIPROB, the area with the highest mean vehicle theft rate. A third difference is the relative equity of the distribution of vehicle theft rates across all social areas; the relative difference ratio is about 7 : 1.

The data in table 8.1 show that five of the nine social areas have mean vehicle theft rates which are significantly different at the .05 level from the overall county mean of about 4.5 per 1,000 residents. Noticeably absent from this group is the social area with the highest mean rate of vehicle theft, HIPROB (with a mean rate of about 5.9). However, its significance level (.06) approaches conventional levels, and this area is therefore included in the set of social area types whose mean vehicle theft rates are substantially higher than the overall county mean.[16]

Also joining HIPROB and MEDPROB as a high vehicle theft rate area is CENTRAL. The mean rate for CENTRAL is only slightly less than that of MEDPROB, 5.48 versus 5.54. Thus, three empirically different kinds of social areas have high auto theft rates. A summary of the attribute dimensions of these three social areas[17] indicates that none have especially similar patterns of social attributes. Even though HIPROB and MEDPROB differ qualitatively only on one dimension (the sex compositon dimension), substantial quantitative differences between these two areas are also found on the social problems dimension, such that social problem levels are much higher in HIPROB.

In regard to the homogeneity of vehicle theft rates within types, the high rate areas, CENTRAL, HIPROB, and MEDPROB, have the lowest homogeneities. However, those for HIPROB (.72) and for MEDPROB (.82) are considerably higher than the negative homogeneities observed in each area type for the other three offenses. Moreover, variation in CENTRAL is slightly higher, since the homogeneity (.55) is lower than in HIPROB or MEDPROB. In other words, it is possible that in CENTRAL a few tracts may be particularly high rate tracts, thereby accounting for the high mean rate for the area type as a whole. Finally, the negative homogeneity characterizing the moderate mean vehicle theft rate in *WORKSUB* indicates that the moderate mean is actually a product of relatively low and relatively high rates in the census tracts comprising WORKSUB.

Discussion

The data for vehicle theft provide the best example of the value of the differential typological prediction approach employed in the present analysis. The data in table 1 indicated that comparably high mean vehicle theft rates were found in three different social area types. Without specific evidence, one would be hesitant to infer behavioral variation among social areas with different configurations of structural attributes.[18] Yet such evidence is not altogether lacking in the current study. Certainly, the general differences among social areas in the frequency of reported offenses are indicative of differences in the quantity of reported criminal behavior; evidence from other studies (e.g., of urban-rural differences between CENTRAL and COUNTRY highly plausible. Thus, given equally high rates of vehicle theft and differences in the configuration of ecological attributes, one might reasonably deduce qualitative variation in the nature of vehicle theft among the three social areas.

Data about site of vehicle theft[19] provides evidence that such variation does in fact occur. It was found that in the three high vehicle theft rate areas (CENTRAL versus HIPROB/MEDPROB combined) considerable difference existed between the two most frequent sites of occurrence, namely, "parking lots and public garages" and "street." For example, in CENTRAL, 35.2 percent ($n = 50$) of the vehicle thefts occurred from parking lots and public garages and 64.8 percent ($n = 92$) were stolen from the street, whereas in HIPROB and MEDPROB (when combined), only 16.5 percent ($n = 10$) occurred from parking lots and public garages but 83.5 percent ($n = 101$, total N $= 263$) were stolen from the street. Thus, the relative conditional frequency of vehicle theft from parking lots and public garages in CENTRAL is more than twice that in HIPROB and MEDPROB (Chi-square $= 16.1$, df $= 1$, $p < 0.001$; Yule's Q $= 0.47$).

It might be concluded that one particular reason for such a difference would be the greater number of vehicles available to be stolen from parking lots or public garages in CENTRAL, and that such differences in availability would probably occur as a function of the differences in general attributes of the two area types. That is, since CENTRAL has concentrations of business, commercial, or light industrial land usage (as was suggested above), then it would probably have larger numbers of and more frequently utilized parking lots and public garages than adjacent urbanized, lower-class residential neighborhood areas such as HIPROB or MEDPROB. Thus, the evidence provided by examining the social area distribution of qualitative characteristics of auto theft lends credence to the characterization of CENTRAL as somewhat more business- or commercially-oriented than the focal variables originally indicated. Moreover, without specifying the social area types prior to analyzing incident characteristics (or behavior patterns if such relevant information were to be available), it would have been extremely likely to have overlooked or mistakenly interpreted incident-level (or individual-level) patterns of criminal behavior. Stated differently, the value of the typological approach is that in specifying social areas, it becomes possible to discuss some apparent reasons as to how rates of crime which are similar among social areas may actually reflect different patterns of occurrence or etiology.

In general, these patterns of association between the qualitative aspects of crime occurrence and structural attributes of social area identified on the basis of differential typological prediction methods are perhaps most fittingly interpreted as *contingent control relations*.[20] Such relationships are described as those in which characteristics of the setting or environment place limits upon, or provide opportunities for, the occurrence or existence of certain entities. Such relationships are not causal, in the sense that (A) is a direct and immediate cause of (B). Rather, contingent control refers more appropriately to the influence which a particular structure of the environment has in creating or facilitating conditions under which behaviors or activities such as particular kinds or patterns of offenses occur. For example, elsewhere it was shown that the ecological association between variables (e.g., percent black and rate of crime) was consistent with, or even facilitated (i.e., evidenced more strongly) the proportionate involvement of blacks in crime (in specific area types).[21]

These instances (as illustrated above by the vehicle theft site and black involvement in crime examples), in which the ecological pattern resulted in consistent and even contributory effects upon the nature of individual or incident-level patterns, are no longer regarded merely as "trivial" or as ammunition for critics invoking "fallacy of the wrong level."[22] In fact, as Hannan demonstrates,[23] there is a major renascent concern with the extension of existing methodological techniques in analyzing data (and hence, concepts and constructs) from different levels of analysis. The importance of different levels of analysis is, of course, that these represent different realms of causal processes (e.g., psychological, social, environmental).

Contingent control relations are only one example of such cross-level variables or effects. In the health sciences, the processes and operation of such variables across ekistical levels (e.g., from environment to social to behavioral to individual, and vice versa) is one major focus of the epidemiologic perspective.[24] It is not argued on the basis of the data presented here that analogous cross-level contingent control effects of environment on criminal behavior operate in ways similar to the epidemiology of certain diseases (or, more emphatically, that criminal behavior is a disease!). Instead, the proper and important empirical point is that differential typological prediction is a potentially important strategy for identifying cross-level effects in regard to the spatial analysis of crime and behavior. Additional evidence for the utility of this analytic strategy is found in the recent theoretical and methodological work of English geographers, epidemiologists, and statisticians.[25] Mollison shows, for example, that

a wide variety of phenomena of geographical spread can be described in terms of a mechanism of "growth" (e.g. birth, infection) and a "contact distribution" which describes how the locations of individuals involved in a migratory move, or infection at a distance, are spatially related.[26]

Such a general analytical model appears to be directly germane to recent theoretical formulations by Felson and Cohen[27] that direct contact predatory violations (of the sort analyzed herein) can be explained in terms of "routine social activity" patterns. In their theory, Felson and Cohen point out that the factors facilitating commission of a criminal offense extend beyond the sole variable of offender inclination and include such variables as target availability, victim proximity, and guardian or protective behavior. Their important contribution is then to show that all of these may be a function of the pace and rhythm of routine social activities (family life, work, transit, recreation, and the like). Although present tests of Felson and Cohen's theory are limited to macrosocial trends over a twenty-five-year period (1947–1972), it takes little imagination to note that such social activities as family life, work, transit, recreation, and the like, which place potential offenders, victims, and guardians at risk, are also spatially organized and constrained. Consequently, the application of Mollison's work with "contact distributions" within the framework of empirically defined social activity areas would seem to be especially appealing for specifying the contingencies among social geography, routine activity patterns, and crime occurrence.

NOTES

1. The data analyzed in this chapter are from Westchester County, New York. The author is especially indebted to Lawrence E. Fine of the Westchester Community Service Council, Inc., for providing these data for secondary analysis. The analysis reported here was originally supported under LEAA Grant No. 72-SS-99-6006, awarded to the Criminal Justice Research Center, Inc., by the Statistics Division, National Criminal Justice Information and Statistics Service, Law Enforcement Assistance Administration, U.S. Department of Justice. Points of view or opinions stated in this document are those of the author and do not represent the official policies or positions of any of the above-named organizations or the National Institute of Mental Health, U.S. Department of Health, Education, and Welfare, where the author is currently employed.

2. For a more detailed discussion of the problems inherent in the sole use of correlational methods for ecological analyses, see K. Polk, "Urban Social Areas and Delinquency," *Social Problems* 14:320–25; and C.S. Dunn, "The Analysis of Environmental Attribute/Crime Incident Characteristic Interrelationships," Ph.D. dissertation, State University of New York, Albany (1974).

3. See, for example, J. O. Kasarda and G. V. Redfearn, "Differential Patterns of City and Suburban Growth in the United States," *Journal of Urban History* 2:43–66; or B. Schwartz, ed., *The Changing Face of the Suburbs* (Chicago: University of Chicago Press, 1976); or A. M. Guest, "Suburban Social Status: Persistence or Evolution?" *American Sociological Review* 43:251–64.

4. See H. S. Scarr, *Patterns of Burglary*, 2d ed. U.S. Department of Justice, National Institute of Law Enforcement and Criminal Justice, Law Enforcement Assistance Administration (June 1973); or W. G. Skogan, "The Changing Distribution of Big-City Crime: A Multi-City Time-Series Analysis," *Urban Affairs Quarterly* (1977), 13:33–48.

5. Polk, "Urban Social Areas and Delinquency," pp. 321–22.

6. Specific details of the methodological procedures and techniques are explained or cited below.

7. See discussion, *infra*, and J. Besag, "Spatial Interaction and the Statistical Analysis of Lattice Systems, " *Journal of the Royal Statistical Society* B:36 (1974), B36:192–236; A. D. Cliff and J. K. Ord, "Model Building and the Analysis of Spatial Pattern in Human Geography," *Journal of the Royal Statistical Society* B37:297–348; and J. K. Ord, "An Alternative Approach to Modelling Linear Systems," Research report, University of Warwick, England, 1976. In particular, these explanatory constructs tend to reflect the basic idea of spatial and temporal *interdependence*, a tenet central to geographic analysis and some forms of econometric analysis. For example, Cliff and Ord note:

> In econometrics, temporal autocorrelation among observations on economic variables is the norm rather than the exception. Similarly, spatial dependence among geographic data is usual. . . . What is the effect of spatially autocorrelated observations upon tests of influence? The consequences in some cases are well known. Thus, standard applications of the t and F statistics for the comparison of means or construction of confidence intervals require spatial independence. . . . The same assumption is necessary for the error terms in regression analysis if the ordinary least squares estimators are to be BLU (best linear unbiased)(pp. 300–1).

8. For an extended discussion of these methods and their application in the current example, the reader is referred to Dunn, "The Analysis of Environmental Attribute"; Dunn, *The Patterns and Distribution of Assault Incident Characteristics Among Social Areas* and *Patterns of Robbery Characteristics and Their Occurrence Among Social Areas*. U.S. Department of Justice, Law Enforcement Assistance Administration, National Criminal Justice Information and Statistics Service, Utilization of Criminal Justice Statistics Analytic Reports 14 and 15 (1976); and to R. E. Tryon and D. E. Bailey, *Cluster Analysis* (New York: McGraw-Hill, 1970) for the development and description of the techniques of cluster analysis. In 1970, there was a total of 205 census tracts in Westchester County. However, 3 were deemed as inappropriate for inclusion in the analysis. These 3 were special use census tracts. One was the New York State Correctional Facility at Ossining (Sing-Sing Prison). Another was a Veterans's Administration Hospital, and the third was an uninhabited island. The number of tracts actually used in the analysis was thus 202. In the course of the empirical assignment of

tracts to types, some tracts may have attribute patterns so unique that an empirical type cannot be formed according to the statistical criteria. In the present analyses, there were 4 such tracts; thus the sum of tracts that are type members is 198, but the total used was 202.

9. The homogeneity (H) is a measure of the "tightness" of the cases comprising an O-type. For a particular type, one determines the overall homogeneity by averaging the homogeneities of the type on each dimension or variable which is used in defining the type. The homogeneity of an O-type on a particular dimension is equal to the square root of the quantity one minus the ratio of the variance of the cluster scores of type member cases to the variance of cluster scores of all cases (in other words, one minus the ratio of within-type variance on a dimension to total variance on the dimension). See Tryon and Bailey, *Cluster Analysis*, pp. 261–62.

10. Dunn, "The analysis of Environmental Attribute" p. 179.

11. These offense data were compiled in a separate research project conducted by the Westchester Community Service Council (WCSC) from 1971 to 1973. Information regarding offenses reported to police was sought from thirty-nine municipal police jurisdictions, the Westchester County Parkway Police, and New York State Police, who had sole jurisdication in five towns in the northern part of the county (WCSC, 1973a, *Individuals in Conflict with the Law*, I:3). Information tallied for each reported offense included the address of the location of its occurrence. Subsequently, rates of reported offenses were computed for each census tract and were available in WCSC, 1973b, *Crime in Westchester*, vol. 2. Additional information concerning the characteristics of reported offenses was compiled in the WCSC study. Random samples of reported offenses (50 percent of aggravated assaults and robberies, 25 percent of burglaries and vehicle thefts) were selected about which detailed information from police offense reports about the nature, site, time, participants, and victims was recorded and coded for the WCSC study. The distribution of these incident characteristics among social area types was analyzed in detail (Dunn, "Analysis of Environmental Attribute"; *Patterns and Distribution of Assault Incident Characteristics*; and *Patterns of Robbery Characteristics*).

12. See note 9 above for the general definition of homogeneity. The homogeneity of an 0-type (social area type) on a predicted variable (a crime rate) is simply the square root of the quantity one minus the ratio of the within-type variance on the predicted variable to the total variance of the predicted variable across all cases. As the ratio of V^2_w / V^2_T approaches 1, the homogeneity value approaches 0. If the ratio exceeds 1 (i.e., if $V^2_w > V^2_T$), then the quantity under the radical will be negative, and the homogeneity is the negative of the absolute value of the square root, thus indicating that the within-type variance on the predicted variable is greater than the total variance of the predicted variable across all cases. See Tryon and Bailey, *Cluster Analysis*, pp. 217–51, for a complete descripton of 4CAST procedures.

13. The number of random samples for each area type/crime rate prediction was 300, the standard option in using the 4CAST subroutine. Sampling distribu-

tion means and standard deviations typically converge with an *n* of random samples of less than 300; thus the proportion of means and standard deviations above and below the overall mean and standard deviation of a predicted variable would not be materially changed with a larger number of random samples. See Tryon and Bailey, *Cluster Analysis*, pp. 217–51.

14. Tryon and Bailey, *Cluster Analysis*, p. 224.

15. *Ibid.*

16. Concerning the arbitrary nature of .05 as a criterion for statistical significance, see J. K. Skipper, A. L. Guenther, and G. Nass, "The Sacredness of .05: A note Concerning the Use of Statistical Levels of Significance in Social Science," *The American Sociologist* 2 (1967), pp. 16–18; or T. Hirschi and H. D. Selvin, *Delinquency Research: An Appraisal of Analytic Research* (New York: Free Press, 1967), p. 218.

17. Dunn, "Analysis of Environmental Attribute," pp. 222–24, 479.

18. See Dunn's earlier essay in this book for a discussion of the problems in making valid behavioral or ecological process inferences from area attribute data.

19. Dunn, "Analysis of Environmental Attribute," p. 478.

20. See D. S. Cartwright, "Ecological Variables," in E. F. Borgatta, ed., *Sociological Methodology* (San Francisco: Josey-Bass, 1960), p. 204.

21. Dunn, "Analysis of Environmental Attribute"; *Patterns and Distribution of Assault Incident Characteristics*; and *Patterns of Robbery Characteristics*.

22. J. Galtung, *Theory and Methods of Social Research* (New York: Columbia University Press, 1967).

23. M. T. Hannan, "Problems of Aggregation," in H. M. Blalock, Jr., ed., *Causal Models in the Social Sciences* (Chicago: Aldine-Atherton, 1971), pp. 473–508.

24. M. Susser, *Causal Thinking in the Health Sciences: Concepts and Strategies of Epidemiology* (New York: Oxford University Press, 1973).

25. E.g., Besag, "Spatial Interaction"; Cliff and Ord, "Model Building"; C. Chatfield, "Some Recent Developments in Time-series Analysis." *Journal of the Royal Statistical Society* (1977), A 140:492–510; and especially D. Mollison, "Spatial Contact Models for Ecological and Epidemic Spread." *Journal of the Royal Statistical Society* (1977), B 39:283–326.

26. Mollison, "Spatial Contact Models," p. 283.

27. M. K. Felson and L. E. Cohen, "Social Change and Criminal Activity: A Routine Activity Approach." Paper delivered to the Annual Meeting of the Population Association of America, Atlanta, Georgia (April 1978).

↻ 9 ↻

Centrographic Analysis of Crime

LARRY K. STEPHENSON

SPATIAL ASPECTS of urban crime and delinquency have attracted the attention of a variety of scholars whose basic research objective has been to discern the spatial organization of this type of social disorganization. Studies of spatial distributions of criminal activities and related variables have been frequent and applications have been made of a variety of statistical and associational measures. Despite numerous studies there is still lack of agreement about the interpretation of these areal associations.[1]

Some problems of interpretation may result from the use of different sets of languages.[2] Much social research is carried out utilizing substance or property languages in which individuals are defined by specifying a set of properties associated with each individual. Spatially oriented research, on the other hand, utilizes space-time languages in which the definition of an individual "depends upon specifying the location of an object within a coordinate structure which represents space and time."[3] Ideally, sociospatial research into crime patterns should make use of some combinational language which is a merger of a property language and a space-time language. Unfortunately, the realities of present research often involve the use of the two separate languages simultaneously.

Rather than suggesting a solution to this problem of interpretation, this chapter is concerned with presenting centrography as an alternative spatial methodology, one which is capable of providing

The author is grateful to Lloyd Haring for comments made on an earlier draft of this essay.

information regarding the morphological nature of intraurban criminal distributions and movements. Measures of centrography represent a relatively pure spatial-temporal language, yet they are capable of specifying a variety of important and interesting attributes of social properties of groups. Thus, centrography can be viewed as a spatial methodology which lends itself especially well to the analysis of areal criminal distributions. Examination of spatial series by centrographic techniques may provide clues for the development of new theories of urban crime and criminal behavior.

Mean Center and Standard Distance

Data concerning intraurban criminal activity represents a voluminous mass of observations and generally requires the imposition of some outside order if any meaningful analysis and evaluation are to be made. Centrography aids in this respect by transforming the data into succinct summary spatial statements which can be more easily understood and which allow certain regularities in crime patterns to be isolated.

The most basic centrographic measure is that of mean center. If a set of points is considered to represent some phenomenon in two-dimensional space,[4] these points can be defined with reference to an arbitrarily established set of orthogonal axes and these points identified by pairs of coordinates (X_i, Y_i). The mean center of such a distribution is defined by the pair of coordinates $(\bar{X}, \bar{Y})$, where

$$\bar{X} = \frac{\sum_{i=1}^{N} X_i}{N} \quad \text{and} \quad \bar{Y} = \frac{\sum_{i=1}^{N} Y_i}{N}$$

and N is the number of points in the distribution. The mean center is thus a synthetic point representing the average location of some phenomenon. Mean centers of various types of spatially distributed criminal activities (e.g., various offense types) may be easily computed, providing the basis for some initial comparisons. One potential use of mean centers could be in tracing the movement over space and through time of various criminal activities, perhaps through the application of the concept of velocity,[5] which can be defined as

$$V = \frac{S}{T}$$

where S is the distance separating the mean centers of crime distribution for two time periods, and T is the interval of time between the two periods. Velocity, thus defined, is a measure of the rate of change of aggregate position with time. Knowledge of the direction and velocities of crime types in urban areas could be an important dimension supplementing the more common information concerning the changing rates of occurrence through time.

Another common centrographic measure is that of standard distance, defined as the quadratic mean of distances between any point in a distribution and the mean center of that distribution.[6] A leading proponent of standard distance says that it

> appears to be the simplest measure of geographical dispersion to be associated with the [mean] center . . . it enables one, *inter alia*, to describe synthetically the actual dispersion of a phenomenon, to compare it with the dispersion of other phenomena.[7]

Though capable of being defined in a variety of ways, perhaps the simplest operational definition of standard distance is

$$D = \sigma_X^2 + \sigma_y^2$$

where σ_X^2 and σ_Y^2 are the variances of longitude and latitude, measured from a set of arbitrarily established orthogonal axes. Standard distance, analogous to a two-dimensional standard deviation, can thus provide a quantitative statement about the dispersion (or concentration) of a spatially distributed criminal activity. Neft has developed a normal probability surface for use with standard distance values which, assuming a normal distribution, allows for assessment of the number of points within any given radius from the mean center.[8]

The mean centers and standard distances for various particular offense categories of juvenile delinquency in Phoenix, Arizona, for

1968 have been computed (table 9.1). Both offense locations and residence locations were analyzed.[9]

There was greater variation among the mean centers of the offense locations of the nine offense categories in a north-south direction than in an east-west direction, while the dispersions of the respective offense groups varied slightly. There were only slight differences in the mean centers and standard distance values between male and female delinquents regarding offense locations. The dispersion values for delinquent offense locations arrayed to ethnic group, however, displayed wide variability. Greatest differences in mean center locations were in the north-south direction, where there was a range of 3.77 miles between Anglos in the northern part of the city and blacks in the southern part. Standard distance values revealed that Anglos were the most dispersed, blacks and Mexican-Americans least dispersed, and American Indians in an intermediate position. The sharp differences among ethnic delinquent groups with regard to mean center and standard distance were indications of distinct locational patterns of offenses committed. Black and Mexican-American delinquents generally committed offenses in a more restricted space than Anglos.

Comparison of the mean center components of residential locations arrayed by offense type revealed that variation was greatest in the north-south direction, with simple assault located significantly further south of the composite mean center, and curfew violations located significantly further north of it. Dispersion of the residences was similar, all within a 0.47 mile range. There appeared to be a slight difference between the mean centers of residences of male and female delinquents in a north-south direction. The dispersion of residences of male and female delinquents was approximately the same.

As with offense locations, the residence locations of the ethnic groups of delinquents showed wide variability in terms of both mean centers and dispersion values. Differences in the mean centers of residences of the respective ethnic groups tended to reflect the general spatial distribution of the population of Phoenix, for the vast majority of Mexican-American and black residents lived in the southern portion of the city, while Anglos tended to reside in the northern portions. The mean center for

Table 9.1.
Centrographic Values for Delinquent Offense and Residence Locations

Delinquent Group	Frequency	Mean Center (E-W)	(N-S)	Standard Distance (miles)
All Delinquent Offenses	*10,831*	*8.96*	*11.76*	*4.49*
Offense type				
Burglary	1,149	8.94	11.34	4.55
Larceny over $50	202	9.11	11.33	4.38
Larceny under $50	2,772	9.19	11.68	4.37
Auto theft	490	9.42	11.23	4.31
Simple assault	316	8.72	11.00	4.40
Vandalism	965	8.85	11.78	4.72
Liquor violations	584	9.02	11.55	4.14
Curfew violations	1,495	9.11	12.40	4.37
Runaway	2,858	8.80	11.84	4.65
Sex				
Male	7,561	8.94	11.67	4.48
Female	3,270	8.94	11.90	4.47
Ethnic Group				
Anglos	7,356	8.69	12.78	4.63
Mexican-Americans	1,902	9.32	9.61	3.13
Blacks	1,231	9.91	9.01	2.79
American Indians	202	9.43	11.91	3.47
All Delinquent Residences	*10,831*	*8.92*	*11.70*	*4.69*
Offense type				
Burglary	1,149	8.92	11.34	4.59
Larceny over $50	202	9.17	11.20	4.32
Larceny under $50	2,772	9.02	11.47	4.73
Auto theft	490	9.21	11.14	4.39
Simple assault	316	8.60	10.60	4.58
Vandalism	965	8.79	11.71	4.79
Liquor violations	584	9.08	11.85	4.67
Curfew	1,495	8.98	12.34	4.70
Runaway	2,858	8.61	11.92	4.70
Sex				
Male	7,561	8.87	11.58	4.63
Female	3,270	8.74	11.99	4.71
Ethnic Group				
Anglos	7,356	8.51	12.85	4.83
Mexican-Americans	1,902	9.27	9.40	3.03
Blacks	1,231	10.09	8.51	2.51
American Indians	202	9.34	11.90	3.91

American Indians reflected the large concentration of Indian youths residing at a Bureau of Indian Affairs boarding high school.

The standard distances of the residence locations of ethnic-grouped delinquents were indicative of distinct patterns of dispersion. Anglos were the most widely dispersed group, followed by American Indians, Mexican-Americans, and blacks. The rather low dispersions of the residences of Mexican-American and black delinquents seemed to indicate that these groups lived in fairly homogeneous areas (such as barrios or ghettos).

Standard Deviational Ellipse

In addition to knowledge about average location and dispersion provided by the mean center and standard distance, another important spatial property of criminal distributions which can be derived from centrography is that of directionality or alignment of the aggregate distribution.[10] By rotating the original reference axes (from which the measurements for mean center and standard distance were made), it is possible to establish a new set of axes, along one of which the variance of the X_is or Y_is is maximized, and along the other the variance minimized. These two axes represent the major and minor axes, respectively, of an ellipse which is focused on the mean center. Computation of this standard deviational ellipse will yield added information about the spatial distribution of intraurban criminal activities. Comparison could be made, for example, among the alignments of various criminal distributions by utilizing the coefficient of circularity, which is defined simply as the ratio of the major axis of the ellipse to the minor axis. The coefficient of circularity ranges from zero for a perfectly linear alignment to one for a perfectly circular distribution.

Criminal Movements

An area of interest in the study of intraurban criminal behavior is the movement of offenders from their places of residence to places of offense. Such a movement can, of course, be viewed in an origin-destination framework, and any one of a variety of flow methodologies could be applied to analyze movement patterns. Bachi, however, has suggested some easily computed centrographic indices which can be used to assess the aggregate spatial movements of criminals.[11] For example, the quadratic average of actual distances between residence and offense locations of criminals can be found by

$$D^2_{Act} = (\overline{X}_R - \overline{X}_O)^2 + (\overline{Y}_R - \overline{Y}_O)^2 + D^2_R + D^2_O - 2(r_x \sigma_{R_X} \sigma_{O_X} + r_Y \sigma_{R_Y} \sigma_{O_Y})$$

where

$(\overline{X}_R, \overline{Y}_R)$ and $(\overline{X}_O, \overline{Y}_O)$ are the mean centers of residence and offense locations,

D^2_R and D^2_O are the standard distances of residence and offense locations,

σ_{R_X}, σ_{R_Y} and σ_{O_X}, σ_{O_Y} are the standard deviations of the respective locational coordinates, and r_X and r_Y are the correlation coefficients of the paired points of the residence and offense location sets.

If each point in the origin set of residences is associated with a point in the destination set of offense locations in such a way as to minimize the sum of the squares of the distances, a minimum quadratic average of distances may be found.[12] The value of this minimum quadratic average may be approximated by

$$D^2_{Min} = (\overline{X}_R - \overline{X}_O)^2 + (\overline{Y}_R - \overline{Y}_O)^2 + (\sigma_{R_X} - \sigma_{O_X})^2 + (\sigma_{R_Y} - \sigma_{O_Y})^2$$

where

$(\overline{X}_R, \overline{Y}_R)$ and $(\overline{X}_O, \overline{Y}_O)$ are the mean centers of residence and offense locations, and

σ_{R_X}, σ_{R_Y} and σ_{O_X}, σ_{O_Y} are the standard deviations of the residence and offense locational coordinates.

If points of origin of criminal activity are associated at random with offense locations, the quadratic average of random distances can be found by

$$D^2_{Ran} = (\overline{X}_R - \overline{X}_O)^2 + (\overline{Y}_R - \overline{Y}_O)^2 + D^2_R + D^2_O$$

where

$(\overline{X}_R, \overline{Y}_R)$ and $(\overline{X}_O, \overline{Y}_O)$ are the mean centers of residence and offense locations, and

D^2_R and D^2_O are the standard distances of residence and offense locations,

An index of proximity between residence locations and offense locations can also be established:

$$I_P = \frac{D^2_{Ran} - D^2_{Min}}{D^2_{Ran}}$$

This index of proximity ranges from one when the paired points of the origin and destination sets coincide to zero with increasing distances between mean centers and dereasing standard distance values.

Utilization of the above discussed measures can be made in testing hypotheses of random movements of offenders between residence and offense locations; or of "efficient" movement of offenders in a distance minimization context. Empirical testing of such hypotheses could help determine the extent to which criminal offenders tend to exhibit spatial behavior similar to that postulated by social and/or economic geographic location theory.

Brown and Holmes have utilized centrographic measures to study the morphology of migration in an intraurban setting.[13] Their methodology could easily be applied to study movements of groups of offenders from residence to offense locations. The methodology consists of two phases. First, the mapped movement vectors are transformed to a spatial distribution by rotation and translation of the reference axes, a procedure which retains the distance and directional bias of the movements relative to an orientation node. Secondly, centrographic techniques such as mean center, standard distance, standard deviational ellipse, and coefficient of circularity are applied to the transformed spatial distribution, yielding information about movement morphology. One potential application of this two-stage methodology would be in the delimitation of various crime activity spaces. For example, it is possible to delimit and compare the movement spaces of offenders grouped by, say, offense type, age, or sex. Temporal trends in the changes of these movements could then also be monitored.

Caveats

As with many of the other methodologies used to analyze spatial distributions, centrography is not entirely without problems in its application to empirical data. The mean center of a distribution is a synthetic point having no real counterpart in the landscape. Thus it can be found outside a distribution, depending upon the general geometric layout of the individual distribution. If, for example, a certain type of criminal behavior in an urban area were concentrated along two major thoroughfares perpendicular to one another, the mean center of such an L-shaped distribution might be somewhat removed from actual crime locations. In cases where the criminal distribution is multimodal as, for example, in the residential locations of larceny offenders around shopping centers, the study area might have to be redefined so as to compute centrographic measures for separate distributions. Some knowledge of the general form of the distribution to be analyzed is helpful in the resolution of problems associated with the application of centrographic techniques.

Conclusion

There have been recent indications that centrography, once shunned as a spatial methodology, is again an acceptable means of analyzing spatial series: there are computer programs currently available which provide as output a variety of centrographic measures.[14] To geographers and others interested in the spatial aspects of criminal activity, centrography offers a useful complementary tool to traditional associational techniques. The particular methods and examples presented here are intended to be suggestive of a possible avenue of research which could be imaginatively pursued.

NOTES

1. R. A. Gordon, "Issues in the Ecological Study of Delinquency," *American Sociological Review* (1967), 32:927–944.

2. This section draws on the excellent methodological discussion by D. Harvey, "Social Processes and Spatial Form: An Analysis of the Conceptual Problems of Urban Planning," *Papers of the Regional Science Association* (1970), 25:47–69.

3. *Ibid.*, pp. 60–61.

4. The extension from consideration of punctiform to areal distributions is easily made for the various centrographic measures by simple weighting procedures.

5. See D. G. Janelle, "Surface Motions: A Key to Isolating Changes in Urban Land Use," *Proceedings of the Association of American Geographers* (1971), 3:86–90.

6. This measure has been called by a variety of terms, including standard radius by D. B. Lee, *Analysis and Description of Residential Segregation* (Ithaca: Cornell/University Center for Housing and Environmental Studies, 1967); standard distance deviation by D. S. Neft, *Statistical Analysis for Areal Distributions* (Philadelphia: Regional Science Research Institute, 1966); and dynamical radius by J. Q. Stewart and W. Warntz, "Macrogeography and Social Science," *Geographical Review* (1958), 48:167–84. The use of the term standard distance and its definition follows R. Bachi, "Standard Distance Measures and Related Methods for Spatial Analysis," *Papers of the Regional Science Association* (1963), 10:83–132.

7. Bachi, "Standard Distance Measures," p. 103.

8. Neft, *Statistical Analysis for Areal Distributions.*

9. For a detailed discussion of delinquency in Phoenix, see L. K. Stephenson, "Spatial Dispersion of Intra-Urban Juvenile Delinquency," *Journal of Geography* (1974), 73:20–26.

10. This property was first noted by D. W. Lefever, "Measuring Geographical Concentration by Means of a Standard Deviational Ellipse," *American Journal of Sociology* (1962), 32:89–94.

11. Bachi, "Standard Distance Measures."

12. See *ibid.* for a discussion of the problem of calculating D^2_{MIN}.

13. L. A. Brown and J. Holmes, "Intra-Urban Migrant Lifelines: A Spatial View," *Demography* (1971), 8:103–22; and "Search Behavior in an Intra-Urban Migration Context: A Spatial Perspective." *Environment and Planning* (1971), 3:307–26.

14. For example, W. R. Tobler, "Plotting of Bivariate Deviations (ELIPS)," in W. R. Tobler, ed. *Selected Computer Programs*, (Ann Arbor: Michigan Geographical Publication, 1970); and J. Hultiquist, J. Holmes, and L. A. Brown, "CENTRO: A Program for Centrographic Measures," Discussion Paper 21, Ohio State University, Department of Geography, 1972.

࿋ 10 ࿋

Mental Maps, Social Characteristics, and Criminal Mobility

Woodrow W. Nichols, Jr.

THE MOVEMENT OF criminals is often planned, and it is logical for one to assume that perpetrators of crimes such as robbery, burglary, auto theft, and others have knowledge or the willingness and ability to search geographic space for locations that offer opportunities to commit an offense. In other words, after the offender decides to commit a crime, there is a search and evaluation of possible sites within the subconscious mind on what can be called a *mental map*. Such maps provide the outer limits of potential *action space* or that area containing the majority of the destinations of a particular offender. Action space is a subspace within the mental map and is often discontinuous because unknown or undesirable sites probably exist between certain preferred locations. The spatial boundaries of action spaces are delimited by the movement patterns of offenders, who have well-marked distance and directional biases from points of origin of their crime trips. There are many reasons why offenders may travel certain distances and directions to commit crimes; included are such factors as urban structure and/or individual psychological, cultural, economic, and social variations. The primary objective of this study is to investigate the relationship between criminal offender movements and their social characteristics. The research problem is one of determining how age, sex, and race influence the mental maps and resulting action spaces of robbery offenders.

Age, Sex, Race, and Crime in Review

Crime statistics and published research have consistently reported and concluded that the younger age groups commit violations of criminal law more frequently than older ones. For example, in 1976 57.4 percent of all persons arrested in U.S. cities were under 25 years of age and 37.4 percent were under 20 years of age. The evidence also indicates that most of the crimes against property involve a younger age group than the ones against persons.[1] Also in 1976, 42.6 percent of all persons arrested for homicide and 57.2 percent of those arrested for rape were under 25 years of age. In addition to those arrested for homicide and rape, 9.2 and 17.3 percent respectively were under 18 years of age.[2] Likewise, of those arrested for burglary and larceny, the percentages were 84.3 and 73.8 for offenders under 25 years of age, and 51.5 and 43.0 for those under 18 years, respectively.

Many studies have concluded that a relationship exists between age and criminal behavior. Reckless observed that the age of the criminal offender varies by type of crime in that older (adult) offenders are involved more frequently with crimes such as gambling, fraud, embezzlement, and vagrancy.[3] In addition to the above crimes, other reports have included homicide as a crime occurring more frequently among older offenders, while offenses such as auto theft, burglary, and robbery were thought to be more frequent among youth offenders.[4] Allison, in a study of crime in Chicago, concluded that of a large number of suspected crime-producing variables, age (15–24 years) ranked high in importance.[5] It should be pointed out, however, that many observers feel that young offenders are probably overrepresented in the arrest statistics because they are more susceptible to arrest.[6]

In 1976, 80.2 percent of all persons arrested for serious crimes were male and 19.8 percent were female.[7] In terms of criminal behavior and sex of offender, it has been observed that certain crimes are much more typically male than female. For example, burglary, auto theft, manslaughter, and gambling are generally "male" crimes; comparatively, crimes such as fraud, embezzlement, and larceny are more frequently committed by females.[8] Connor[9] and Mays[10] indicated that delinquency is more frequent

among males; Allison found that the difference between the proportion of males and females in Chicago was an important variable influencing crime;[11] and Wolfgang concluded that sex and
crime are related, especially in homicide.[12] One should be aware
that there are some crimes that are legally defined in such a way
that they are the sole domain of females—for example, prostitution. Also, empirical evidence lends support to the idea that as the
social roles of men and women become more alike, crime rates for
the two groups also become more alike. In recent years, the difference between the crime rates for men and women has been
decreasing.[13]

In 1976, the arrest rate for black Americans for serious crimes
was 24.2 per 1,000, while that of the white population was 5.9 per
1,000.[14] Pyle has discussed two major areas of concern with
respect to such differences in crime rates:

> This discrepancy throughout recent years has produced two very disparate
> schools of thought concerning the Negro and crime. One position maintains
> that a high black crime rate is in fact deceptive; it represents the results of
> either imcomplete data and/or faulty statistical analyses, or the discrimina-
> tory practices involved in law enforcement procedures. The opposite position
> upholds a high black crime rate and endeavors to identify or explain the un-
> derlying causes.[15]

Those who maintain the first position point out that young,
male, and low-income blacks are more likely to be arrested,
prosecuted, and convicted than whites, because blacks dispropor-
tionately commit crimes (crimes against persons) for which there
is a high clearance rate.[16] For example, in 1976 the clearance rate
for offenses against persons was 45.5 percent, while that of
property crimes was only 18.0 percent. Also, black crime rates are
highest among urban, poorer, less educated, and younger blacks.
The highest crime rates have been consistently concentrated
among poor urban sectors of the population, regardless of race.[17]
Thus, the answer to a question about the possibility of a cause and
effect relationship between race and crime must surely indicate
that race does not determine crime rates.

The other school of thought has focused on an explanation of
the tendency for blacks to manifest higher crime rates than whites.

Most allude to such factors as social disorganization or the effects of the environment, discrimination, or cultural differences.[18] Few researchers still contend that crimes by blacks are a result of biological differences.

The data show that some crimes are more typically black and others more typically white. In 1976 the black arrest rate for murder was approximately 9.3 times that of whites; but the rate of black arrests for burglary was only about 3.3 times that of whites.[19]

Offender Behavior in Space: The Problem

It can be gleaned from the above discussion that criminal behavior varies in terms of age, sex, and race; that is, younger age groups commit more property crimes than older ones; females have a tendency to commit to so-called "white collar" crimes more than others, and blacks tend to commit more crimes against persons compared to whites. Such observations engender additional questions about the social characteristics of criminal offenders and their behavior. One such question relates to movement patterns; that is, what is the relationship between age, sex, and race and the action spaces of offenders? To date, only a few studies have examined the movement behavior of offenders in an effort to gain some insight into individual offender decision-making and spatial preferences.[20] For example, in a study of robbery offender movement in the Miami SMSA, Capone and Nichols observed that: (1) the frequency of robbery trips in geographic space declines with increasing distance from the residential location of offenders (assumed to be the origin of the trip); (2) there is a significant difference in the mean lengths of armed and unarmed trips (armed trips were longer); and, (3) the subjective evaluation of locations (mental mapping) by robbery offenders produced differences in distances traveled to different types of premises.[21] Thus the authors concluded that type of robbery and type of premise were significant factors explaining the distance biases of robbery offenders' action spaces. In view of such findings this study attempts to answer the following questions:

1. Is there a significant difference in the robbery trip distance, robbery type, and premise selection between youthful and robbery offenders?
2. Do male robbery offenders differ significantly from female robbery offenders in terms of robbery trip distance, robbery type, and premise selection?
3. Are robbery trips for blacks significantly different from those of whites in terms of distance, robbery type, and premise selection?

Data and Methodology

The data used in this analysis were obtained from the cleared arrest files of the Dade County Public Safety Department of the Miami SMSA. They consist of 498 randomly selected robbery trips that took place in the unincorporated area in 1975. The trip distances were calculated for each trip by first plotting the origin (location of residence) and the destination (location of occurrence) on a detailed street map and then converting these to coordinate (x and y) locations; trip distances were computed by applying the following formula:

$$D = \sqrt{(x_2 - x_1)^2} + \sqrt{(y_2 - y_1)^2}$$

Robbery type is measured in terms of armed or unarmed offenses. Robbery is defined as the felonious and forcible taking of the property of another, against one's will, by violence or by putting the person in fear. It differs from larceny in that it is aggravated by the element of force or the threat of force. If the offense includes the use of a weapon such as a firearm, knife, or some other dangerous weapon, the robbery is referred to as an armed robbery. However, where no weapon is used but strong-arm tactics are employed with the hands, fists, feet, etc., the robbery is an unarmed robbery.[22]

Robberies occur at locations (streets, parking lots, highways, vacant lots) which are relatively ubiquitous on the landscape, and at others (convenience stores, restaurants, gas stations, etc.) that are not as widespread but generally conform to an orderly pattern of commercial or some other type of land use. Given this knowledge, premise selection can be thought of as a surrogate measure of direction, because a potential offender plots the locations of potential targets (or premises) on a mental map in relation to some known point. The type of premise selected by an offender is used here because it is thought to be a more relevant and revealing measure of criminal behavior in space than the vector measurement of direction.

Distance of Robbery Trips

The relationship between the average distance traveled to commit a robbery and social attributes of offenders appears to be highly significant in terms of age and race, and less so for sex. The sample of trips revealed that 49.8 percent of the robberies were committed by persons less tha 20 years old and 50.2 percent were older than 19 years of age. The average distance traveled by the older offenders was significantly more than twice that of the younger ones—4.98 and 2.02 miles respectively (table 10.1). Even though blacks committed more than 2.6 time the number of robberies than did whites (361 and 137 respectively), whites traveled greater distances; blacks averaged 2.29 miles per robbery trip, whites averaged 6.67 miles (table 10.2). Males committed 94.18 percent of the total robbery trips and averaged 3.56 miles per trip; females averaged 2.45 miles in only twenty-nine trips, a difference that is significant at an alpha level of less than 0.032 with 44 degrees of freedom (table 10.3). Based on these observations, age, race, and sex are significant variables influencing the distance criminal offenders travel to commit a robbery. However, age and race are more important than sex.

Armed and Unarmed Robberies

Age and race also appear to be significant factors influencing the type of robbery committed by offenders. In the sample of offenders, older ones committed a significantly greater proportion of armed robberies and a smaller proportion of unarmed robberies compared to offenders less than 20 years of age (table 10.4). The influence of sex on robbery type does not appear to be very significant (table 10.5). Table 10.6 indicates that a significant difference also exists between race and type of robbery; blacks committed more armed and unarmed robberies than whites, with the difference being greater with respect to unarmed offenses.

Premise Selections

Again, with respect to the type of premise robbed, age and race are important variables. Older offenders showed a preference for open space sites, convenience stores, miscellaneous businesses, and residences. Younger offenders preferred open spaces, convenience stores, gas stations, and miscellaneous businesses (table 10.7). The influence of sex on premise selection was not found to be a significant variable (table 10.8). Black offenders robbed more frequently than did whites at all types of premises except convenience stores (table 10.9). The greatest disparity in the selection of robbery premises by race was in the open space category where, of 288 robberies, blacks committed 240 (83.3 percent).

Table 10.1.
Mean Robbery Trip Distances and Age of Offenders

Age	Sample Size	Mean Distance	t-Value	F-Value
< 20 years old	250	2.02	7.29*	4.81
≥ 20 years old	248	4.98		

* Significance = 0.00 with 345 degrees of freedom.

Table 10.2.
Mean Robbery Trip Distances and Race of Offenders

Race	Sample Size	Mean Distance	t-Value	F-Value
Black	361	2.29	−7.46*	4.66
White	137	6.67		

* Significance = 0.00 with 158.68 degrees of freedom.

Table 10.3.
Mean Robbery Trip Distances and Sex of Offenders

Sex	Sample Size	Mean Distance	t-Value	F-Value
Male	469	3.56	2.22*	4.08
Female	29	2.45		

* Significance = 0.032 with 43.74 degrees of freedom.

Table 10.4.
Robbery Type and Age of Offenders

Age	Armed	%	Unarmed	%	Total
<20 years	119	23.89	131	26.31	250
>20 years	178	35.74	70	14.06	248
Total	297	59.63	201	40.37	498

Chi-square = 30.23 with 1 degree of freedom; significance = 0.00.

Table 10.5.
Robbery Type and Sex of Offenders

Sex	Armed	%	Unarmed	%	Total
Male	283	56.8	186	37.3	469
Female	14	2.8	15	3.0	29
Total	297	59.6	201	40.3	498

Chi-square = 1.19 with 1 degree of freedom; significance = 0.28.

Table 10.6.
Robbery Type and Race of Offenders

Race	Armed	%	Unarmed	%	Total
Black	191	38.4	170	34.1	361
White	106	21.3	31	6.2	137
Total	297	59.7	201	40.3	498

Chi-square = 23.69 with 1 degree of freedom; significance = 0.00.

Table 10.7.
Premise Type and Age of Offenders

Premise	<20 years old	%	>20 years old	%	Total
Convenience Store	25	5.0	46	9.3	71
Open Space	177	35.5	111	22.3	288
Residence	12	2.4	25	5.0	37
Restaurant	9	1.8	15	3.0	24
Gas Station	13	2.6	9	1.8	22
Other Businesses	13	2.6	40	8.0	53
Other	1	0.2	2	0.4	3
Total	250	50.2	248	49.8	498

Chi-square = 42.21 with 6 degrees of freedom; significance = 0.00.

Table 10.8.
Premise Type and Sex of Offenders

Premise	Male	%	Female	%	Total
Convenience	69	13.9	2	0.4	71
Open Space	269	54.0	19	3.8	288
Residence	33	6.6	4	0.8	37
Restaurant	24	4.8	0	0.0	24
Gas Station	21	4.2	1	0.2	22
Other Businesses	50	10.0	3	0.6	53
Other	3	0.6	0	0.0	3
Total	469	94.2	29	5.8	498

Chi-square = 4.90 with 6 degrees of freedom; significance = 0.56.

Table 10.9.
Premise Type and Race of Offenders

Premise	Black	%	White	%	Total
Convenience	32	6.4	39	7.8	71
Open Space	240	48.2	48	9.6	288
Residence	22	4.4	15	3.0	37
Restaurant	13	2.6	11	2.2	24
Gas Station	13	2.6	9	1.8	22
Other Businesses	38	7.6	15	3.0	53
Other	3	0.6	0	0.0	3
Total	361	72.5	137	27.5	498

Chi-square = 54.07 with 6 degrees of freedom; significance = 0.00.

Conclusions

This study has sought to determine the relationship between offender social characteristics—age, sex, race—and criminal mobility. The data suggest that age and race are significant variables influencing the distance an offender travels, the type of offense, and premise selected in committing robberies in Dade County, Florida. These findings are consistent with other research reports that have concluded that social characteristics of criminal offenders influence criminal behavior. Sex of offender, however, was not found to be highly significant in terms of distance traveled and insignificant in influencing the selection of type of robbery and premise. Subsequent analyses, where females constitute a greater proportion of the sampled robberies, may result in different conclusions.

The above conclusions have broader conceptual implications for the behavioral scientist and spatial analyst. For the former they shed additional light on the decision-making process of criminal offenders; that is, mental mapping and the determination of resulting action spaces. The data should also help to make the mapping of aggregate social variables more meaningful to the spatial analyst, simply because age, sex, and race distributions in a region can be thought of as partial predictors of robbery movement behavior. The obvious shortcoming of the analysis is the lack of corroboration from studies in other locations and with other types of crimes.

NOTES

1. Federal Bureau of Investigation, *Crime in the United States, Uniform Crime Reports*, (Washington, D.C.: U.S. Government Printing Office, 1976). pp. 181–82.
2. *Ibid.*
3. Walter Reckless, *The Crime Problem*, 4th ed., (New York: Appleton-Century-Crofts, 1967), p. 102.
4. Gerald F. Pyle et al., *The Spatial Dynamics of Crime*, University of Chicago, Department of Geography, Research Paper no. 159, 1974), pp. 22–23.
5. John P. Allison, "Economic Factors and the Rate of Crime," *Land Economics* (1972) 68(2):pp. 193–96.

6. Yong Hyo Cho, *Public Policy and Big City Crime*, (Akron, Ohio: Center for Urban Studies, University of Akron, 1972).

7. Federal Bureau of Investigation, *Crime in the United States*, p. 178.

8. Pyle, et al., *Spatial Dynamics of Crime*, p. 23.

9. Walter D. Connor, "Juvenile Delinquency in the U.S.S.R.: Some Quantitative and Qualitative Indicators," *American Sociological Review* (1970), 35(2):283–97.

10. John B. Mays, *Crime and Social Structure* (London: Faber and Faber, 1963).

11. Allison, "Economic Factors and the Rate of Crime."

12. Marvin E. Wolfgang, "A Sociological Analysis of Criminal Homicide," in B. Cohen, ed., *Crime in America* (Itasca, Ill.: F. E. Peacock, 1970), pp. 52–60.

13. *Encyclopedia of Sociology*, (Guilford, Conn.: Dushkin Publishing 1974), p. 63.

14. These figures were calculated according to the following method using the *Uniform Crime Reports*:

$$\frac{561,912 \text{ (total black arrest rate for Index crimes)}}{23,189 \text{ (total 1973 black population/1,000)}} = 24.2$$

$$\frac{1,064,038 \text{ (total white arrest rate for Index crimes)}}{179,574 \text{ (total 1973 white population/1,000)}} = 5.9$$

15. Pyle, et al., *Spatial Dynamics of Crime*, p. 25.

16. Edwin M. Schur, *Our Criminal Society: The Social and Legal Sources of Crime in America* (Englewood Cliffs, N.J.: Prentice-Hall, 1969).

17. *Ibid.*

18. Sterling Tucker, "The Ghetto, The Ghettoized, and Crime," *Federal Probation* 33(3):5–10.

19. Federal Bureau of Investigation, *Crime in the United States*, p. 185.

20. D. L. Capone and W. W. Nichols, Jr., "Crime and Distance: An Analysis of Offender Behavior in Space," *Proceedings, Association of American Geographers* (1975), 7:45–49; "The Journey to Crime: A Preliminary Analysis of Robbery Trips in Dade County," Paper presented at the Meetings of the Association of American Geographers, Southeastern Division (1974); "Urban Structure and Criminal Mobility," *American Behavioral Scientist* (1976), 20:199–213; "robbery Opportunity Structure, Target Premises, and Trip Distance in Dade County, Florida: 1971 and 1975, unpublished paper (1977).

21. Capone and Nichols, "Urban Structure and Criminal Mobility," pp. 206–11.

22. *Ibid.* Capone and Nichols found "type of robbery" to be related to the movement patterns of offenders.

⛭ 11 ⛭

Characteristics and Typology
of the Journey to Crime

PHILLIP D. PHILLIPS

ECOLOGICAL STUDIES of crime and delinquency have traditionally focused on social and economic characteristics of areas with high numbers of offenses or offenders' residences. While differing as to the precise relationships between crime and population characteristics, ecological studies have generally concluded that high crime areas are typified by low levels of socioeconomic status, crowded living conditions and substandard housing, high population mobility, and large proportions of minority groups.[1] These characteristics have been related to many theoretical formulations of delinquent and criminal behavior, including anomie, delinquent subcultures, differential association, value conflict, and societal role typology.[2]

A small but growing number of researchers, however, have directed their work away from static ecological correlations between socioeconomic characteristics and point residence or occurrence data toward a more dynamic view of crime within the context of the "journey to crime" that links the place of criminal residence and crime occurrence.[3] The study of this dynamic link promises to provide a better integration between ecological and behavioral criminology and a sounder interpretation of ecological data.[4] Studies of the journey to crime also promise to help overcome conceptual difficulties resulting from the fact that "occurrence rates cannot be explained by the same factors that account for the prevalence of offenders."[5] Residence patterns reflect criminogenic factors influencing individuals, while occurrence patterns reflect target opportunity structure and the perceptions of criminals.[6]

Though the previous literature is sparse, several important characteristics of the journey to crime have already been investigated and described. All researchers have reported finding a distance-decay relationship, in which the number of offenses declines with increasing distance from the residence of the offender both on an absolute and a per-unit basis. This distance-decay pattern results from the friction of distance, the cost in money, time, or energy of overcoming distance. Those reporting this form of relationship were Bullock, in a study of homicide in Houston,[7] Turner, in a study of journey to juvenile offenses in Philadelphia,[8] Capone and Nichols, in a study of robbery trips in Dade County (suburban Miami),[9] and Baldwin and Bottoms, in a study of crimes known to the police in Sheffield.[10] Turner reported a generally linear relationship between distance from the offender's residence and the number of offenses committed on a per unit area basis. The only exception Turner found was a slightly smaller than expected number of offenses within very close proximity to the offender's residence, which was hypothesized to result from the offender's desire to go far enough from his home to avoid being recognized while committing the offense. Capone and Nichols found that the number of robberies, not transformed to area rates, declined with distance following a Pareto-exponential curve, which they believed indicated that both purposeful and accidental trips were involved.

A number of authors have calculated mean distances of the journey to crime, and a number have calculated mean distances for subgroups of specific crime classifications. All of these studies have found relatively short mean journeys and have obtained very similar results for similar crime classifications. For example, White found a mean travel distance of 1.66 miles for all felons in Indianapolis and 2.14 miles for those committing robbery.[11] Pyle found a mean travel distance of 1.77 miles for a wide range of crimes in Akron with a mean of 2.1 miles for unarmed robbery and 2.2 miles for armed robbery.[12] The coincidence of these studies is remarkable, given that they were conducted over four decades apart.

Mean journey to crime distances do show considerable variation among offense types according to most previous studies. White found averages ranging from 0.11 miles for manslaughter to 3.73 miles for auto banditry and concluded that crimes against persons generally had shorter journey distances than crimes against property. Pyle found much the same patterns in Akron. Capone and Nichols found relatively wide differences in journey length for various types of robbery and concluded that armed robberies involved longer journeys than strong-armed robberies and that the greater the degree of planning, the longer the journey.[13] Turner, in contrast to these studies, found no differences in mean distances traveled by delinquents by crime type.[14]

A four-part typology of journey to crime patterns was developed by Boggs, based on a study of incidence and residence patterns of crime in St. Louis, though she had no direct information concerning journeys between specific residences and specific places of offense.[15] Boggs hypothesized the following journey types:

1. Homicide and assault—high incidence in offender residence areas.
2. Business robbery, nonresidential burglary, auto theft and grand larceny—high incidence in high social rank areas adjacent to low social rank areas where offenders lived.
3. Rape and miscellaneous crimes—no residence-offense locational association.
4. Miscellaneous robbery and highway robbery—high occurrence rates in high offender residence areas, but not necessarily the same area in which the offender lives.

Carter and Hill, in the "Criminal's Image of the City and Urban Crime Patterns," provided an explicit link between ecological and social psychological perspectives by studying the journey to crime. Their study examined how criminals evaluated these same areas, and how the evaluations of criminals related to their choice of places for offense commission. Carter and Hill found similar perceptions of areas by white criminals, black criminals, white noncriminals, and black noncriminals. Most significant, perceptual factors were found to account for three-quarters of the variation in crime commission by both blacks and whites, indicating a close link between perception, the journey to crime, and the victimization of targets.

Overall, previous studies have provided a relatively consistent picture of the journey to crime in many respects. Average journey lengths are generally short, with a rapid decline in the number of offenses on an absolute and per-unit area basis as distance from the offender's residence increases. Previous studies, with the notable exception of Turner, have also indicated substantial variation in the average distance traveled with the nature of the offense and the target. These studies have not, however, attempted to measure differences in the length of the journey to crime based on age, sex, race, or area of residence in the city, nor have they attempted to determine how much of the observed variation in journey length by type of offense might actually be the result of systematic differences in these offender characteristics.

Data and Research Design

The data used in this study are a sample of 872 offenses drawn from an original set of 3,837 offenses. The larger data set included all juvenile arrests made by the Lexington-Fayette Urban County (Kentucky) Police Department from January 1, 1974 to June 30, 1975. Juvenile offenses were chosen for this study because of the complete range of data available on individual juveniles and the pertinence of age as a factor in the journey patterns of those under 18. The large number and varied nature of the cases necessitated the selection of a smaller sample for this study. The offense and residence location for each crime included in the study (1,744 points) was located on a city map. Each point was assigned X and Y location coordinates for use in determining distances. Because one important aspect of this study was the comparison of various offense types, many offenses which included only a small number of cases were eliminated from the sample. An arbitrary lower limit of fifty cases was used as a minimum for a particular offense category to be included. Also, many status offenses, such as truancy and "waywardness," were eliminated from consideration because they reflect a behavior pattern rather than behavior at a specific offense location.

Lexington as a study area is somewhat different from those in previous studies. The city is relatively small, with a population of about 200,000. Inner sections of the city display many of the complex patterns of an older southern city. Whites and blacks are jumbled in a jigsaw puzzle of residential areas, with whites along the major thoroughfares and blacks in back alleys and almost invisible "towns." Around this core is a large, newer city resulting from rapid growth that has tripled population since World War II. The newer city is largely middle-class and consists of tracts of suburban housing developments liberally sprinkled with apartment complexes and shopping malls. The dichotomy of the old and new in Lexington, and the complexity of the older city, combined with its small size, bring the poor residents of the inner city within a relatively short distances of suburbia.[16]

A peculiarity of Lexington's political structure has a significant impact on the nature of the data used in this study. In 1973, the city of Lexington and surrounding Fayette County became an "urban county" with a completely consolidated government, including police functions. As a result, there is no problem of interjurisdictional differences in reporting practices within the urbanized area, nor are there large numbers of interjurisdictional journeys with significant directional bias. Over 90 percent of the juveniles arrested by the Lexington-Fayette Urban County Police Department are residents of the county. The remaining few percent generally represent clearly intermetropolitan and long-distance flows, primarily from Louisville and Cincinnati, which are about eighty miles distant, and from the Appalachian section of Kentucky. Within the county the maximum possible distance of journey to crime is about twenty miles, but few journeys extend beyond the urbanized area, which has a diameter of about eight miles. The small and socially complex nature of the Lexington area may have significant effects of the journey to offense by reducing the possible journey length and by exposing the juvenile to a wider range of social and morphological areas of the city within the extent of his mental map of familiar area.

Ten common offense categories were chosen for study (table 11.1). These categories represent a wide range of severity, ranging from assault, which can be a class-B felony requiring a ten-to-twenty-year sentence, to loitering, a misdemeanor which can only result in a fine but not imprisonment. A random sample of individual offenses was chosen from each category. In developing the sample, several types of cases found in the official records had to be eliminated. These were:

1. Juveniles whose residence is out of county. These cases represent inter- rather than intraurban travel patterns and would hopelessly bias any average distance measures.
2. Cases where the offense address was missing or ambiguous.
3. Cases where the residence address was missing, incomplete, or nonexistent.

A total of fifteen items of data were compiled about each offense. Some items, such as name of offender and date of offense, were used primarily in obtaining a "clean" file of unduplicated data from police records. Eight items were obtained directly from police data, four locational variables were generated by plotting each offense and residence as paired points, while three distance

Table 11.1.
Sample Offenses and Data Obtained for Each Offense

Sample Offenses	Number of Cases
Assault	67
Burglary	100
Drug-related offenses	108
Auto theft	92
Grand larceny	99
Petty larceny	100
Vandalism	53
Public intoxication	55
Disorderly conduct	100
Loitering	98

measures were computer-generated from grid coordinate pairs for offense and residence addresses and a coordinate location for the CBD.[7] Unlike Turner's study of Philadelphia, no attempt was made to measure a shortest street distance because: (1) there is no reason to assume that the shortest street distance measured from a map has any relation to actual travel routes, which may be by more direct, nonstreet routes or may be by circuitous street routes; and (2) making such measurements of street distance is very time consuming and produces results very similar to straight line distances between grid coordinates.

The overall characteristics of the sample offenses are very similar to total arrests in age, sex, and race composition. The youngest arrest was at age 7. Arrests increased regularly with age to reach 224 at age 17. About 85 percent of the offenders were male and over two-thirds were white. Though blacks are over-represented in comparison to the approximate 20 percent of the juvenile population they represent, the preponderance of white offenders was contrary to what police department and court officials believed. The data used here are superior to those used in some other studies because they refer to specific, paired residence and offense locations and to the characteristics of the individual offender. Also, unlike some studies such as Spence, point locations rather than data aggregated by census tract are used.

Journey Characteristics

Journeys to commit delinquent acts in Lexington followed a distance decay pattern. A steep gradient of decline was found in the absolute number of offenses (and in the number of offenses adjusted to a per-square-mile basis) from 0 to 10,000 feet from the home of the offender. The number of offenses remained at a relatively stable, low number from 10,000 to 20,000 feet from the residence of the offender and became sporadic beyond 20,000 feet. Very few offenses were committed beyond 30,000 feet (a little less than six miles) from the offender's residence.

The decline in offenses with distance in Lexington very closely parallels the Pareto-exponential curve found by Capone and

Nichols in Miami, rather than the linear decine found by Turner in Philadelphia. More detailed analysis of cases in the 0–1000 foot range indicated a high number of offenses at the residence of the juvenile, a rapid drop to 1000 feet from the residence (approximately Turner's finding in Philadelphia), and then a slight rise in number of offenses. The peak of offenses at the residence included a large number of assaults, while the dip in the under-1000-foot range is primarily in petty larceny, bearing out Turner's hypothesis that juveniles do not commit property crimes in their immediate home areas to avoid recognition.

Distances from residence to CBD showed a considerably different pattern than distances from offense to CBD. Offenders' residences reached a peak in inner-city areas on the edge of the CBD, with the largest absolute and per-square-mile concentrations of offenses being in the 3,000-to-10,000-foot range.[18] An inward journey to the CBD by many juveniles was indicated by the concentration of 13.3 percent of all offenses, versus 6.7 percent of all offenders' residences within 3,000 feet of the CBD. Juveniles also moved from the inner city to suburban areas, as indicated by the concentration of 49.1 percent of offenses more than 10,000 feet from the CBD, but with only 40.8 percent of offenders' residences more than 10,000 feet from the CBD. Thus a net total of 15.7 percent of all juvenile offenses were "exported" from an inner-city zone 3,000 to 10,000 feet from the CBD both to the suburbs and the CBD itself. This net flow away from high offender residence areas probably represents a movement toward greater perceived opportunity to commit property crimes in downtown and suburban areas.

The average distance traveled for the entire sample of offenses was 1.43 miles (table 11.2). This is similar to, though slightly longer than, the 1.18 mile average distance found by Turner but slightly less than the 1.66 mile average found by White, 1.77 miles found by Pyle, and 3.35 miles for robberies found by Capone and Nichols. The longer distances found by White, Pyle, and Capone and Nichols may result from the fact that they were dealing with all offenders, not just juveniles. The probability that the shorter distance results from the use of juvenile offenders is reflected by the fact that the 17-year-old age group has an average journey

Table 11.2.
Mean Distances by Characteristics of Offenders and Category
of Offense

By Age of Offender	Mean Distance in Miles	Distance in Feet
7, 8 or 9	0.95	5,000
10	1.50	7,909
11	0.61	3,233
12	1.13	5,989
13	1.12	5,903
14	1.30	6,846
15	1.36	7,156
16	1.53	8,079
17	1.72	9,067
Race of Offender		
White	1.48	7,792
Black	1.34	7,070
Sex of Offender		
Male	1.36	7,162
Female	1.86	9,827
Offense Category		
Assault	0.70	3,694
Burglary	1.05	5,520
Drug related	1.93	10,194
Auto theft	1.15	6,076
Grand larceny	1.31	6,914
Petty larceny	2.46	12,995
Vandalism	1.31	6,943
Public intoxication	1.37	7,247
Disorderly conduct	1.06	5,580
Loitering	1.65	8,689
All Offenses	1.43	7,568

length of 1.72 miles, nearly identical to the distance Pyle found for
all offenders in Akron.

Differences in mean distance of the journey to crime by age,
race, sex, and offense category reveal many interesting patterns
(table 11.2). As would be expected, journey length generally
increases with age. Thus, a regular increase occurred from age 11,
with a journey length of 3,233 feet, to age 17, with a journey

length of 9,067 feet. This increase in distance with age undoubtedly reflects two factors. First, as age increases juveniles develop a more widely dispersed set of acquaintences as they move from grade to junior high to high school. Also, as juveniles grow older they attain greater mobility as they, or their friends, reach driving age and obtain greater access to automobiles. Both of these factors undoubtedly widen the range of a juvenile's mental map. The longer journey distances under age 11 may reflect small numbers of cases, only eight in the 7- to 9-year-old category, or the possibility that young juveniles, who were often arrested for petty larceny, were with their parents at the time of the offense.

White juveniles had somewhat longer journeys to crime than black juveniles, 7,792 feet versus 7,070 feet (table 11.2). This small difference seems to confirm the conclusion by Ladd that little or nothing in juveniles' mental maps of internal urban structure is related to race.[19] Also, the relatively small interracial difference in journey length may reflect the small size of Lexington, which does not place many suburban areas beyond the mental maps of blacks, or it may represent limited mental maps characteristic of lower-class youth who predominate among both black and white offenders.[20]

Sex differentials in the length of the journey to crime (table 11.2) present an unexpected result. It was originally believed that males would travel farther than females, but females actually have an average journey length about 40 percent longer than males. While no completely satisfactory explanation can be given for the greater journey length of females, it is possible that many female juveniles are arrested while with older juvenile or adult males.

It was believed that suburban juveniles would travel further to crime than inner-city juveniles because of higher social status, which is associated with more extensive mental maps and greater physical mobility, and because of the less dense opportunity structure in suburban areas. The distance of the residence of the juvenile from the CBD had no apparent relationship, however, to journey length. Part of the explanation for the comparable length of trips by inner-city juveniles may be provided by the relative frequency with which they are arrested for petty larceny at suburban shopping centers served by bus routes.

Mean journey length varied nearly four-fold with the type of offense, from 3,694 feet for assault to 12,995 feet for petty larceny (table 11.2). This variability of journey length with offense confirms the findings of White, Pyle, and Capone and Nichols that journey length varies with offense rather than those of Turner that journey length does not vary with offense. Assault, the only crime against persons with a sufficient number of cases to be included in the sample, had by far the shortest journey length, supporting previous conclusions of White and Pyle that crimes against persons are characterized by short journey lengths. No systematic differences could be found in journey length for different levels of crime severity, in contrast to Capone and Nichols' finding that robberies involving larger dollar amounts had longer journey lengths. In fact, the mean journey length for petty larceny (12,995 feet) was nearly twice as long as for grand larceny (6,914 feet).

Variability of age, sex, and race characteristics of offenders among offense categories suggested the strong possibility of interrelationships among these attributes. In order to measure the independence of these characteristics in their relationship to journey length, an analysis of variance was performed using offense category, sex, age, race, and residence to CBD distance as independent variables and journey to offense distance as the dependent variable. Two variables, offense category and sex, achieved F ratios significant at the .001 level, and age was significant at the .018 level. Neither race nor residence to CBD distance showed F ratios significant even to the .20 level. Two-way interactions between variables did not prove to be significant. This analysis supports the hypothesis that both the category of offense committed and the personal characteristics of the offender have an important impact on the journey to crime.

A Typology of Journey Patterns

The importance of offense category in the variability of the length of the journey to crime suggested further investigation of differences among categories in journey length and orientation. Journey paths for each category were mapped and various length and orientation measures for journeys were computed. Four distinct types of journey patterns were revealed: (1) *assault*, characterized by concentrated residences and offenses and short journey lengths; (2) *vandalism*, with disposed residences and offenses and short-to-medium journey length; (3) *petty larceny*, with long journey lengths and high target specificity; and (4) *drug offenses*, with disposed residences and offenses and long journey length.

This typology confirms White's hypothesis that crimes against persons involve shorter journeys than crimes against property. No support was found for Capone and Nichols's finding that property crimes involving a higher value of "payoff" had longer journeys. In fact, petty larceny had the longest journey of any crime category. The extraordinarily long journeys for petty larceny may merely reflect reporting biases, however.

This typology of journey patterns does not closely parallel Boggs' typology based purely on incidence and residence data. Part of the difference may result from differing crime categories and part from the age of offenders. It does appear that assault occurs mainly among low-status-area residents, as she hypothesized, but not always in the same area. Robbery, burglary, auto theft, and grand larceny did not have the low-status to adjacent high-status journey pattern proposed by Boggs. Rather, both offenders' residences and places of offense were primarily in low-status areas of the inner city and CBD.

Conclusions

This study indicates that juvenile journey to crime follows a classic distance-decay pattern in the length of journeys. A significant proportion of juveniles move out of high offender residence areas in the inner city to the CBD and suburban areas. Mean journey lengths vary by offense category, age, sex, and race. An analysis of variance indicated that offense category, sex, and age were important factors in the variation in journey to crime length, but that race and distance of residence from the CBD are not important determinants.

Several areas of further research into the journey to crime are suggested by this study. Additional work utilizing similar methodology and age, sex, race, and offense variables needs to be conducted both for adult offenders and for larger metropolitan as well as rural or small-town areas. Variability in offense length by character of offender and offense should be further investigated through interview studies with sample delinquents or adult criminals, to determine both how personal characteristics alter mental maps and target selection processes as well as how differences in offense category alter target selection. Self-reporting studies of all juveniles, and not just those arrested, should also be conducted. Further study is also needed to determine why racial differences have so little impact on the journey to crime.

NOTES

1. R. W. Beasley and G. E. Antunes, "The Etiology of Urban Crime," *Criminology* (February 1974), 11:439–61; C. K. Shaw and H. D. McKay, *Juvenile Delinquency in Urban Areas*, rev. ed. (Chicago: University of Chicago Press, 1969); and E. H. Sutherland and D. R. Cressey, *Criminology*, 9th ed. (Philadelphia: Lippincott, 1974).

2. Sutherland and Cressey; A. K. Cohen, *Delinquent Boys: The Culture of the Gang* (Glencoe, Ill.: Free Press, 1955); S. Kobrin, "The Conflict of Values in Delinquency Areas," *American Sociological Review* (October 1951), 16:653–61; and R. C. Merton, *Social Theory and Social Structure* (Glencoe, Ill.: Free Press, 1957).

3. P. D. Phillips, "A Prologue to the Geography of Crime," *Proceedings of the Association of American Geographers* (1972), 4:86–90.

4. R. L. Carter and K. Q. Hill, "The Criminal's Image of the City and Urban Crime Patterns," *Social Science Quarterly* (December 1976), 57:597–607.

5. S. L. Boggs, "Urban Crime Patterns," *American Sociological Review* (December 1966), 30:899–908.

6. D. L. Capone and W. W. Nichols, "An Analysis of Offender Behavior in Space," *Proceedings of the Association of American Geographers* (1976), 7:45–49.

7. H. A. Bullock, "Urban Homicide in Theory and Fact," *Journal of Criminal Law, Criminology, and Police Science* (December 1955), 45:565–75.

8. S. Turner, "Delinquency and Distance," in T. Sellin and M. Wolfgang, eds., *Delinquency: Selected Studies*, pp. 11–26 (New York: Wiley, 1969).

9. Capone and Nichols, "An Analysis of Offender Behavior."

10. J. Baldwin and A. E. Bottoms, *The Urban Criminal: A Study in Sheffield*, (London: Tavistock, 1976).

11. R. C. White, "The Relation of Felonies to Environmental Factors in Indianapolis." *Social Forces* (May 1932), pp. 498–509.

12. G. F. Pyle et al., "The Spatial Dynamics of Crime." University of Chicago Department of Geography, Research Paper no. 159 (1974).

13. Capone and Nichols, "An Analysis of Offender Behavior."

14. Turner, "Delinquency and Distance."

15. Boggs, "Urban Crime Patterns."

16. The relationship of criminal and delinquent residences to social areas in Lexington, Kentucky, was described by R. Quinney in "Crime, Delinquency, and Social Areas," *Journal of Research in Crime and Delinquency* (July 1964), 1:149–54.

17. The CBD was defined as a prominent downtown street intersection. Movement of this point to another location in the core of the CBD would have had minimal effect of the results of the study.

18. For the purpose of this study, the area from 0 to 3,000 feet is termed the CBD; from 3,000 to 10,000 feet, the inner city; and greater than 10,000 feet, suburbia.

19. F. C. Ladd, "Black Youths View Their Environments: Neighborhood Maps," *Environment and Behavior* (June 1970), 2:74–79.

20. R. D. Garst, "Influences of Social Structure and Action Space on Cognitive Maps: Images of Louisville, Kentucky," *Southeastern Geographer* (November 1976), 16:113–26.

ꙮ 12 ꙮ

A Spatial Analysis of Retail/Commercial Homicides in Detroit: 1968–1974

ROBERT D. SWARTZ

IN BOTH the applied store location literature and related urban morphological material there is essentially no reference to crime, especially violent crime, as a component of retail sales potential or retail location. However, the variation of crime within an urban area—perceived or actual—is a frequently voiced rationale for explaining store closings, relocations, shopping preferences, and commercial investment in office developments.[1] In a survey of major Detroit area investors, developers, and realtors, crime was mentioned more than twice as often as any other factor in rationalizing failure to invest in the northwestern part of the city.[2] If store owners, managers, and others are right—that differences in the concentration of violent and serious crime directly affect the performance and longevity of retail facilities—then the crime parameter should be included in commercial location studies.

Homicide, the most severe of violent crimes, is also most complete in police or criminal justice records. However, there is very little material that specifically separates the retail/commercial portion of homicides from the general homicide classification.[3] Insofar as commercial homicides usually result from robbery or

Funding for this study was partially provided by the Center for Urban Studies, Wayne State University. The excellent assistance of Marilyn Swisher, a graduate student in Wayne's Geography Department at the time, is gratefully acknowledged. The assistance and cooperation of the Detroit Police Department is also most appreciatively noted.

intended robbery, a potential for homicide exists in some retail/commercial armed robberies.

Detroit—Selecting a Case Study Area

The relatively high homicide rate in Detroit compared to other major urban areas suggests the appropriateness of the selection of this city for an analysis of serious and violent commercial crime. In a study of 1972 criminal victimization in the nation's five largest urban centers—New York, Los Angeles, Chicago, Philadelphia and Detroit—commercial burglary and robbery rates for Detroit were almost double those in the other cities. The number of robberies and burglaries in Detroit's retail units (as separated from all other commercial facilities), averaged more than one incident per store during the year.[4]

While major concern here is with the spatial distribution of retail/commercial homicides, several other matters are so pertinent to this type of crime that they are necessarily included. In particular, the very nature of the commercial homicide classification and the possibilities of misleading raw data warrants review. The figures on victim/defendant characteristics are also inherently worth noting, especially to indicate the sizeable proportion of victims responsible for initiating crimes. That is, based on the 1968–1974 Detroit experience, a substantial percentage of homicide victims at retail/commercial locations were those attempting robbery and armed robbery.

Overview of Retail/Commercial Homicides

In 1974, the most recent year included in the study, Detroit had 801 homicides (including justifiable homicide and non-negligent manslaughter), the highest annual number ever recorded, climaxing increases in each successive year encompassed by the study. Of those 801 homicides, police files indicate that 149 (resulting from 135 incidents), or 19 percent, were at commercial locations. In fact, less than half of these 149 victims died as a result of actions against them because of their business relationship to the establishment as owners or employees or customers. What is true of 1974 is essentially true for other years. As indicated by table 12.1, the actual retail/commercial homicide percentages range from a low of 32 percent (1973) to a high of 60 percent (1970).

Explanations for this marked difference are based on several rationales. For example:

1. If an argument between acquaintances (or others) reaches a violent and ultimately homicidal conclusion in a bar or restaurant, it will be recorded as commercial although the business location had no significance *per se* in the homicide.
2. If a homicide victim is taken from the location of the crime to, say, a parking lot of a business and the body is found there, it will be entered as a homicide at a commercial location.
3. If a victim is pursued into or found in a bar or other retail facility, or staggers into the doorway of a store, the homicide will be recorded as commercial although the commercial nature of the location was essentially irrelevant to the crime.

There are instances where it is not possible to ascertain whether a homicide falls into the retail/commercial classification as defined above, and only those identifiable from case descriptions were allocated to the category and used in this study. Generally, if the record did not indicate a retail/commercial involvement (e.g., armed robbery of a store as opposed to simply an argument in a retail facility which ended with a homicide) the homicide was excluded.

Concentrations of Retail/Commercial Homicides by Business Types

More than 90 percent of the retail/commercial homicides (as defined in this analysis) occurring in Detroit during each year of the 1968 through 1974 period were in retail stores. Very few were in manufacturing or warehousing locations. In only one year, 1972, did the percentage in industrial facilities exceed 7 percent of all retail/commercial homicides (table 12.2). Of the several dozen retail types found in shopping centers and commercial strips of

Table 12.1.
Homicides at Retail/Commercial Locations and Homicides Verified to Result from Retail/Commercial Operations in Detroit, 1968–1974

Year	Total homicides	Homicides at Retail/Commercial Locations			Homicides Verified to be Retail/Commercial in Nature	
		No. of incidents	No. of victims	% of total homicides	No. of victims	% at retail/ commercial locations
1974	801	135	149	18.6	66	44.3
1973	672	141	153	22.8	49	32.0
1972	601	83	88	14.6	46	52.3
1971	577	89	94	16.3	55	58.5
1970	495	85	91	18.4	55	60.4
1969	439	89	90	20.5	41	45.6
1968	389	66	68	17.5	35	51.5
			Mean:	18.4	Mean:	49.2

Table 12.2.
Retail/Commercial Facilities with the Highest Number of Homicides in Detroit 1968–1974

Year	No. of incidents	No. of victims	Facilities with Highest Number of Homicides												
			Bars		Liquor Stores		Grocery-Supermkts		Restaurants		Gas Stations		Total		Industrial	
			No.	%	No.	%	No.	%	No.	%	No.	%	No.	%	No.	%
1974	59	66	22	33.3	6	9.1	4	6.1	5	7.6	3	4.5	40	60.6	3	4.5
1973	47	49	12	24.5	5	10.2	7	14.3	6	12.2	3	6.1	33	67.3	3	6.1
1972	42	46	11	23.9	3	6.5	10	21.9	2	4.3	3	6.5	29	63.1	4	8.7
1971	49	55	6	10.9	5	9.1	15	27.3	6	10.9	7	12.7	39	70.9	1	1.8
1970	52	55	14	25.5	6	10.9	14	25.5	1	1.8	1	1.8	36	65.5	3	5.5
1969	40	41	12	29.3	4	9.8	5	12.2	3	7.3	4	9.8	28	68.4	2	4.9
1968	33	35	8	22.9	—	—	8	22.9	4	11.4	2	5.7	22	62.9	—	—

Detroit, only a few account for the majority of incidents. Five retail functions—bars, liquor stores, groceries or supermarkets, restaurants, and gas stations consistently had 60 to 70 percent of the retail/commercial homicides in each year of study period. In all but one year the number of homicides in bars equaled or exceeded those in any type of business.[5]

Victim Classification

Victims of retail/commercial homicides were initially grouped into five classifications according to their relationship to the establishment in which the crime occurred. These five groups were: (1) employees; (2) owners/managers; (3) patrons; (4) offenders; and (5) others. The last category, "others," results primarily from instances in which the relationship of the victim to the establishment or its personnel could not be determined. It also includes police officers (less than 1 percent of the total).

Among the five classifications, "offenders" constituted the largest proportion of retail/commercial homicide victims. Employees, owners, and managers, accounted for an average of some 48 percent of victims for the seven-year period (table 12.3). However, criminals engaged in armed robbery or attempted armed robbery were a close second, averaging 39 percent of the victims. It appears that in recent years a substantial portion of Detroit's retail personnel in stores likely to be victimized by armed criminals are armed to meet the challenge of potential violence.

The Location and Changing Spatial Pattern of Retail/Commercial Homicides in the City of Detroit 1968–1974

Retail/commercial homicides in the City of Detroit are, as indicated, nearly all retail store incidents. Consequently, their location is largely limited to the many commercially-zoned strips throughout the city. Many of the homicides have occurred on

Table 12.3.
Retail/Commercial Homicides in Detroit
(Percentages in major victim classifications, 1968–1974)

Year	Owners/Managers and Employees	Patrons	Criminals
	Victim Classification		
1974	46.5	10.3	43.1
1973	53.4	11.1	35.6
1972	45.4	13.6	40.9
1971	49.0	5.9	45.1
1970	50.0	7.7	42.3
1969	57.5	10.0	32.5
1968	33.3	27.2	39.4
Means:	47.9	12.3	39.4

NOTES: Percentages are based on the totals of classifications used in the table. In several instances the victim category was not clear and in a very few instances the victim was a police officer. In all but two years 95 percent of victims were in the above categories. Row totals may not equal 100 due to rounding.

arterials with increasing vacancy rates.[6] For purposes of spatial analysis, this linear characteristic of retail locations is awkward, and amalgamation by zones or regions is expedient. Each zone used in the analysis is coincident with city divisions recognized by the city planning department. These essentially concentric areas are called the inner, middle, and outer zones.[7] They reflect generalized social and physical conditions as well as sequence of historical development. With the exception of the Central Business District (CBD) and some renewal areas, the progression from inner to outer zone is coincident with a progression toward less deterioration.

The CBD, technically a part of the inner zone, was analyzed separately. Moreover, as a result of the separation of Detroit's CBD functions into two foci, the traditional CBD and the fifty-year-old New Center area, these two areas were also treated separately. In Detroit this combined area is referred to as the Central Functions Area (CFA) and includes major cultural facilities between the two foci (e.g., Wayne State University, The Detroit Art Institute, the Main Branch of the Public Library, the

Detroit Historical Museum and a vast complex of medical facilities). Details for these areas as well as an east side/west side tabulation are shown in table 12.4.

During the entire seven-year period, only two retail/commercial homicides occurred in Detroit's CBD. This figure is less than 1 percent of the slightly more than 300 retail/commercial homicides recorded during the period using criteria of this study. Both were in bars, at locations that are peripheral to the downtown concentration of stores.

The Central Functions Area outside the CBD had many times the number of retail/commercial homicides experienced within the CBD. However, the total number was still a small proportion (only 5 percent) of city-wide figures. In every instance the locations of the CFA homicides were away from the major concentration of retail traffic; there were no office building occurrences. Moreover, on no occasion did a store dependent on the sale of merchandise to the metropolitan trading area have an incident. Only one service unit which might depend on the regional attraction of a CFA location, a fast-food operation, experienced a homicide—at two o'clock in the morning. In brief, the CBD and CFA have not recorded a retail/commercial homicide during normal shopping hours in retail or service establishments with regional or CBD trading areas.

The percentage distribution of retail/commercial homicides has tended to vary for the three zones in the seven-year study period, although fluctuations have been within a moderate range (approximately 10 to 20 percent).[8] In general, the shift has been from the middle zone to the outer zone, with percentages for the inner zone remaining stable. The percentage of incidents in the middle zone was lower in the later years of the study than in the earlier years. In the outer zone the percentage of incidents was higher in each of the later than in the earlier years.

Although seven years may be a modest period from which to infer trends in so volatile an issue as retail/commercial homicides, the overall data indicate that this category of crime, like several other negative features of retail business (particularly high vacancy rates), is moving outward and reaching into city segments that are adjacent to suburban communities. If the retail/commercial

Table 12.4.
Retail/Commerical Homicide Incidents in Detroit
by Major City Zone 1968–1974

	Inner Zone							Middle Zone		Outer Zone		East		West	
	CBD		CFA		Total										
Year	No.	%	No.	%	No.	%	No.	%	No.	%	No.	%	No.	%	
1974	0	—	2	3.4	11	18.6	29	49.2	19	32.2	23	39.0	36	61.0	
1973	0	—	1	2.2	9	19.6	25	54.3	12	26.1	22	47.8	24	52.2	
1972	1	2.4	1	2.4	8	19.5	22	53.7	11	26.8	13	31.7	28	68.3	
1971	1	2.1	2	4.3	15	31.9	23	48.9	9	19.1	15	31.9	32	68.1	
1970	0	—	7	13.2	15	28.3	33	62.3	5	9.4	19	35.8	34	64.2	
1969	0	—	2	5.0	6	15.0	26	65.0	8	20.0	20	50.0	20	50.0	
1968	0	—	0	—	6	18.8	19	59.4	7	21.9	19	59.4	13	40.6	

NOTE: Based on commercial homicides for which the location of the incident was clearly identifiable. In some instances incidents occurring in border locations were adjusted to split approximately evenly into the two zones on each side of the border. Data peculiarities or omissions result in minor discrepancies with other study calculations, usually the alteration by a single case in the above catagories.

blight, high vacancy rates and rising homicide rates prevalent in these peripheral areas cannot be curtailed, it appears that nearby suburban areas will be the next locales for increasing percentages of retail homicides. Prospects for the penetration of commercial blight into Detroit's near suburbs have already been noted in the literature, and the long-term ineffectiveness of city borders in resisting transition diffusing from the center of Detroit has also been documented.[9] Although it may be premature to conclude, without qualification, that retail/commercial homicide in the peripheral portions of the City of Detroit will continue to increase as a percentage of the total, and that nearby suburban areas may be similarly affected, it is clear that this is a reasonable extrapolation.

NOTES

1. Walter A. Kleinschord, "Southfield, Michigan: Life in 'Office City,'" *Administrative Management* (July 1970), 31(7):36. See also Don Tschirhart "Business Against Crime," *Detroit News*, (November 13, 1974), P. 1G; "Sad Ending for a Bookstore: Owner Has Had It with Detroit," *Detroit News*, (Sep-

tember 12, 1975), p. 4A; "Grocer Who Fled City Is Slain in Suburbs." *Detroit News* (January 25, 1975), p. 2A; "Attendant Wants Out After Two Holdups in Day," *Detroit News* (November 13, 1974), p. 6A; "Fed Up. Shop Owner Fleeing Detroit - He's Had His Fill of Crime," *Detroit News* (June 7, 1974), p. 1A. The listing here is only a sampling of relevant articles from Detroit's largest-circulation newspaper.

2. Robert D. Swartz, "Retail Development," *Commercial Land Utilization Study* (Detroit: Office of Industrial and Commercial Development, Community Development Commission, 1974), 2:102-3.

3. In the following works, all from the U.S. Department of Commerce, Domestic and International Business Administration, Bureau of Domestic Commerce, retail/commercial homicide is essentially omitted: *Crime Against Business*; proceedings of a seminar held in Cincinnati, Ohio, 1975; *The Cost of Crime Against Business*, rev., January 1976; *Crime Against Business: A Management Perspective*. proceedings of a seminar held in Los Angeles and San Francisco, California, 1976.

4. U.S. Department of Justice, Law Enforcement Assistance Administration, National Criminal Justice Information and Statistics Service, *Crime in the Nation's Five Largest Cities* (Washington, D.C.: U.S. Department of Justice, 1974), pp. 4, 9, table 1; p. 24, table 7G.

5. Based on surveys of residents in two communities in Detroit—the area where the 1967 riot was focused and a much larger twelve square-mile area in northwest Detroit—bars are the least-desired retail facilities. See Robert D. Swartz, "Past and Future Shopping Facilities in a Riot Area," in: Robert D. Swartz, John M. Ball, Fred E. Dohrs, and Merrill K. Ridd, eds., *Metropolitan America: Geographic Perspectives and Teaching Strategies* (Oak Park, Ill.: National Council for Geographic Education, 1972), p. 75, and *Commercial Land Utilization*, p. 100.

6. Robert D. Swartz, "Retail Development," pp. 89–97, especially table II (Number of Retail Establishments: 1965–1972).

7. Homer Hall, "Commercial Shopping Strips in Detroit," in Robert D. Swartz *Metropolitan America*, p. 157-60, especially fig. 1, p. 158.

8. Plotting data for several years indicates fewer incidents than appear in table 12.2 because locations for some homicides were not clear from data available.

9. Robert D. Swartz, "The Retail Outlook in Northwest Detroit." *Michigan Academician* (Fall 1972), 5:185–92; and John H. Haake, "Political Fragmentation and the Growth of Black Residential Areas: The Case of Highland Park," in Robert D. Swartz et al., *Metropolitan America*, pp. 199–215.

PSYCHOSPATIAL

This section posits the belief that the public, or more precisely certain sectors of the public, labor under faulty perceptions of the relative danger and safety within the different neighborhoods within the urban mosaic of the city. Authors in this section note that such factors as age, race, income, and residential location appear to be correlated with misconceptions of site-specific crime rates. It is also noted that criminals weigh a number of site and situational factors before committing certain acts of criminality. Specifically, Carter and Hill examine the utility of studying urban crime from a perspective based on the criminal's perception of the urban milieu. They discuss the rationale for such an approach by studying: (a) problems inherent in other, more traditional research perspectives on crime (biological, sociological, ecological); and (b) the conceptual background for an area-image and behavior perspective. The latter material indicates how criminal behavior can be seen as a special form of general human behavior in its relationship to specific aspects of the urban geographic and physical setting.

Second, the authors review the existing empirical evidence which supports the importance of this "image and behavior" approach. The bulk of this evidence is in the authors' own prior research, but supporting material in other studies is discussed as well. Finally, the authors discuss the theoretical and policy implications of the image and behavior perspective on crime. Much of this discussion addresses the implications of this perspective for the impact of environmental design efforts on crime occurrence.

Smith and Patterson argue for the potential usefulness of cognitive mapping procedures in the spatial study of criminal behavior. They contend that a cognitive map is a mental representation of a phenomenon, which in many instances bears little or no resemblance to the objective reality of the phenomenon. For example, ideas about which city streets are thought to be dangerous are based in part on the resident's knowledge of the facts (the objective geography), and in part on a complex mix of personal attributes and perceptions (the subjective geography). The authors believe that the importance of studying cognitive maps of crime is that attitudes and action are influenced at least as much, if not more, by what people believe or think are the facts than by the facts themselves.

Smith and Patterson point out that cognitive maps can be applied to the spatial study of crime in two major ways. One application involves the relationship between criminal events and the physical environment. They state that in recent years it has become fashionable to argue that crime and the fear of crime can be manipulated and prevented by changes in a) environmental design; and b) the way residents individually or collectively exercise sovereignty over their territorial rights in their neighborhoods. They then describe how studies of perception and cognitive maps can be useful in both these contexts.

Smith and Patterson also note that a second application involves studying the "subjective geographies" of the major actors in criminal events: the offenders, the public (actual and potential victims), and law enforcement officers. To illustrate this application, the authors report on some preliminary findings from their ongoing studies of the perceived and actual locations of rapes, burglaries, and street crimes.

Pyle offers an interesting analysis of systematic sociospatial variations in perceptions of crime location and severity. He finds that many suburbanites have exaggerated perceptions of crime within the central city of Akron, Ohio. He also contends that a person's perceptions of crime as manifested within specific areas of the city appear to vary in terms of sex, age, and income cohorts. In closing he notes that false perceptions of crime may affect use and investment patterns within the milieu of the central city as well as the suburbs.

卐 13 卐

Area-Images and Behavior:
An Alternative Perspective for Understanding
Urban Crime

RONALD L. CARTER AND KIM QUAILE HILL

Conceptual Models of the Criminal's
Environment-Behavior System

BOTH Carter and Brantingham and Brantingham have offered quite similar conceptual models which describe the network of environment-behavior relationships which might account for the property criminal's choice of locales for crimes.[1] Each author assumes that the motivations for choosing crime as a life path are diverse—possibly a combination of environmental, sociological, biological, and psychological factors. Moving away from the criminogenesis issue, however, the model maintains that the criminal interacts with and receives stimuli from the environment in terms of cues (as does the non-criminal) which influence in a probabilistic manner the ultimate location of his crimes. In other words, there exists more than a random association between the environmental image and behavior in terms of urban crime patterns. Figure 13.1, from Carter's "Criminal Image of the City," is one such conceptualization of the general process.

In this model perceived needs and perceived environmental offerings to meet these needs converge to form the criminal's perceptions.[2] These perceptions are not only used for general assessments of one's personal situation, but also guide, at another level, human spatial behavior. Brantingham and Brantingham (1977) refer to

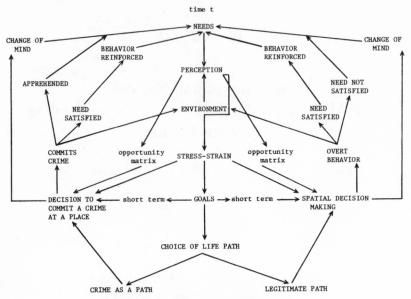

Figure 13.1. Model of Criminal Behavior

this level of perception as a template which is used to guide the criminal through time and space. Scarr (1973) refers instead to an opportunity matrix formed from the general and site specific characteristics of urban areas.[3] These conceptualizations all, therefore, assume that the template or matrix is used by the criminal to select an area within a city and then a specific site within the area. Criminals' macro-scale perceptions are thought by most to consist of vague intuitive feelings about some areas and more precise feelings about others. The criminal, in other words, is thought to possess a Gestalt-type image of an area as a whole. This image has a meaning different from the one that would derive from the separate images of the area characteristics taken separately.

Given that criminal behavior is relevant not to an objective environment, but to a perceived one, how is the opportunity matrix or template constructed and how does the criminal go about evaluating his environment in terms of his particular goals? In other words, where are the areas in his environment which might provide suitable opportunities? A partial answer is that it depends on his level of information about his environment gained either through his own experiences or from associates. Through such information the criminal becomes aware of differential environmental opportunities. The environment (which provides information for both the criminal and noncriminal) has been conceived by several researchers, most notably Wolpert (1965), Horton and Reynolds, and Brown and Moore,[4] as a set of "behavior spaces." The most common division of these behavior spaces is into "action spaces" and "activity spaces." It is through his behavior spaces that the criminal receives the information necessary for purposeful spatial mobility. It is generally assumed in this approach that knowledge of spatial opportunities decreases by some function of distance. This is analogous to what some have termed an "information field." If this is true, then the lengths of the criminal's trips to commit crimes would be biased toward familiar locations. This would be reflected by the aggregate patterns of some crimes being concentrated in close proximity to the offender's home. Distance bias could be manifested in another way, however, if the criminal is aware of "marks" at a greater distance, all marks in between are intervening opportunities which may be perceived as containing greater utility. Information available to the criminal, thus, is a critical factor in his decision process and should affect the outcome of the process.

The criminal, in possession of varying amounts of information about his environment, searches for an area and a specific mark. This is illustrated by Letkemann in terms of "casing":

> The concept of casing, usually thought of as preparation for a specific caper may be broadened to include the more general observations the criminal makes that bear on his work. The criminal's mentality consists in part of a complicated rating system that includes countries, states, provinces, cities, suburbs, down to specific companies and businesses . . . the criminal, like the tourist, the farmer, or the potential resident, makes evaluations on the basis of factors relevant to his interests.[5]

The criminal thus looks at the city in terms of his specific goals. Scarr supports this proposition of a rating system, stating: "Ecological studies—including our own—strongly suggest that burglars perceive specific areas of the city as providing a greater opportunity for their crimes than others."[6] The criteria for establishing this rating system are based on a consistent use and organization of sensory cues from the environment—the opportunity matrix and template. The criminal's search behavior is guided by this matrix. When planning a crime, the rating attached to each element is determined by both strategic and tactical considerations. Strategy, as used here, concerns the broader aspects of the problem such as the area to select, while tactics involve a very short term plan required to surmount or neutralize site deterrents.[7]

The criminal's environmental image, based on the above, is transformed via a complex evaluative process into a potential reaction surface. This surface will indicate a measure of the probability that he will commit a crime at a particular place within a particular area of the city. It will affect his personal assessment of the probable outcome of his crime. The criminal, thus, builds a differentiative predictive field which is used in the search for a mark, one which is multiscale in composition. This implies that he anticipates differential satisfaction of his needs in the accomplishment of his goals in various areas, that is, differential spatial opportunities.

After the individual has made his decision and has actually committed the crime, both his mental image and his environment are affected. His mental image is affected because the outcome is either as expected, which confirms his feelings and adds to his learning—or the outcome was unexpected, which also contributes to his learning about the area. Confirmed expectations are likely to increase the probability that he will go to the area in the future, while unconfirmed expectations decrease the probability.

The environment is also immediately affected by the addition of one more crime occurrence. The actions of several offenders, thus, result in the spatial patterning of crime within the city. This represents a feedback effect of human behavior on spatial structure and is one way in which the individual's actions influence his environment.

Rather than reaching equilibrium with his environment, the criminal probably continues to learn and perceive new meanings which in turn affect his interaction with the environment. With repeated behavior there is a decreased uncertainty of behavioral outcomes. Time has expanded his experience, thus changing his image of the city. He has repeatedly confirmed and rejected hypotheses concerning perceived relationships by actual behavior or through the acquisition of relevant information regarding the location of new opportunities or new deterrents. Over time, learning is a multistage process as suggested by Burnett when she says that "Decision makers continually improve their knowledge in selection of alternatives."[8]

It is also important to emphasize that the criminal's environmental evaluations may develop with little conscious effort. Letkemann has described this process in a fashion that accords with anecdotal studies of criminal life styles:

> Respondents agreed that perception increases with experience, yet, the degree of consciousness while casing diminishes. [The experienced criminal] seems to come upon his 'victims' by accident; he seldom can account for the factors that led to his discovery. He does not deliberately look for a score—he just "spots" them. Although experienced criminals may be relatively unconscious of the casing procedures in which they are engaged, the dimensions of what seems to be intuitive can be documented.[9]

In summary, this model suggests that there is a strong probabilistic relationship between the criminal's mental image of the differential opportunity structure of the city and his eventual criminal activity patterns. In the next section we examine the evidence currently available to support this model.

Evidence to Support the Environment-Behavior Model

To this point, little systematic scholarship exists which directly addresses the adequacy of the conceptual approach outlined above. There are, however, threads of supportive evidence in some past scholarship and the present authors are engaged in the preparation of an extended analysis of some aspects of this approach.[10] In this section we wish to review the existing evidence and its implications. There are three broad categories of research which offer such evidence.

First, some support for the environmental approach arises from the large number of ecological analyses of crimes within cities. From the earliest to the most recent of such studies, a common finding has been that crime occurrences are patterned rather than randomized within individual cities.[11] Whatever the specific motivations of criminals (whether for access, for familiarity, for expected gain, or for relative safety) some areas must be recognized as more suitable for burglary or robbery by those in the trade.

As noted earlier, as well, there is often considerable divergence between the locations of criminals' home neighborhoods and the areas where they commit their offenses. Criminals are not, therefore, restricted in their behavior to highly familiar areas. These spatial patterning studies suggest, instead, that some more complex decision-making process is involved. There is evidence here for the argument that criminals recognize differential environmental opportunities and that they evaluate such opportunities in terms of more than one criterion.

A second source for at least some evidence that criminals are influenced by environmental perceptions is "autobiographical" and "life style" reports on criminals.

David's in-depth interviews with five conventional criminals (only one of whom might be termed highly professionalized) indicated that all of them employed certain well-developed routines in the choice of a target and the approach for accessing it. David comments "The successful burglar is an up-to-date urban psychologist. He knows very well when and how to strike."[12]

Similar conclusions arise from Letkemann's interviews and conversations with some forty-five burglars and robbers in Canada (only a portion of which are clearly highly professionalized). In an intriguing chapter on "casing," Letkemann describes the process of choosing a particular target. His discussion is in terms precisely related to the "area image" conceptual model described earlier. He notes: "In addition to the required technical skills . . . a criminal must possess a variety of perceptual skills relevant to his trade. . . .The criminal must be able to recognize opportunities"; and, as quoted previously, "The criminal's mentality consists in part of a complicated rating system that includes countries, states, provinces, cities, suburbs, down to specific companies and businesses."[13]

Additional evidence on this matter is available in an interview-based study of the criminal careers of forty-nine incarcerated conventional criminals by Petersilia, Greenwood, and Lavin.[14] When the authors queried the respondents about their pre-crime *planning*—in terms of a rather extensive set of rigid-response possibilities—they discovered little of such activity. The respondents did, nonetheless, engage in certain kinds of *premeditative* activities related to choosing and observing the crime target. These locale-selection contemplative activities were simply not the kind of planning behaviors which the authors had anticipated.

In addition to the preceding general evidence on criminal decision-making, there is material in several research reports which suggests that the criminal's use of systematic procedures and his interaction with environmental cues increase with experience. Some of these latter studies also suggest ethnicity-specific variations in the criminal's opportunities to respond to environmental cues. Many anecdotal reports emphasize, for example, that criminals seek and recognize areas of differential opportunity in terms of expected "take." Reppetto's (1974) interviews with ninety-seven burglars support this view,[15] as do those of Petersilia et al. Reppetto's over-age-25 respondents indicated that the apparent affluence of areas was "the prime factor in their choice of targets." His younger respondents generally chose multi-family dwellings instead because they rated ease of access over likely take.

On other age-related matters, Reppetto, Baldwin and Bottoms, and Petersilia et al. all report that younger criminals were more likely to work their home neighborhoods than were older ones. This observation should be coupled with the additional one by Reppetto and by Petersilia et al. that precrime planning increased with experience. Taken together, these results suggest that with age and experience the criminal increases in confidence, and begins to respond to environmental cues of opportunity at large in his community rather than continuing to rely upon targets close to home.

Reppetto also reports some interesting variation depending on the race of the criminal. Nonwhites of all ages were more likely to thieve close to home, even though they preferred white areas because of greater affluence. On the other hand, whites preferred to avoid nonwhite areas for fear of violence. Even more interesting was the finding that blacks were more likely to be deterred by police patrols. All these findings, some of which are not very surprising, do indicate that criminals' perceptions of opportunities in their spatial milieu vary by age, experience, and race. Those perceptions do exhibit patterning, but it is a patterning shaped not only by the objective reality of the environment but also by the social attributes of individual criminals. This evidence clearly indicates, therefore, the necessity of linking information on individual criminals with ecological or environmental information in order to account for criminal behavior patterns.

There is a third body of evidence which lends support to the adequacy of an environment-behavior model for explaining patterns of urban property crime. This last evidence arises from the present authors' own on-going empirical research on this topic. Early reports on our work are now available, but the complete explication of our research activities is only now nearing completion.[16]

The distinguishing characteristic of this research is that it has attempted to examine directly the utility of the environment-behavior model described earlier in this chapter. Based on the study of interview data from eighty-three property criminals from Oklahoma City, we have found that criminals' images of discrete areas of the city can be summarized into a small number of "dimensions of evaluation" which are themselves patterned in ways consonant with some theoretical expectations. For example, separate evaluative dimensions of familiarity and strategy emerge.

We have also found that criminals' images of areas differ from those of noncriminals in some important ways. The divergences are not extreme, but they are systematic and appear explainable in terms related to the social positions of criminals and noncriminals. For example, many of the differences in area image seem to be a product of the criminals' more "work oriented" involvement with crime. Some of the other differences appear to result from the "nonconventional" aspirations and modes of fulfilling aspirations of criminals. As an example, both criminals and noncriminals recognize clear social status and wealth variations among areas of the city. Yet, the criminal connotes "status" and "livability," whereas the noncriminals can more easily distinguish the two. Evidently the social and economic aspirations of the criminals were less realistic than those of the non-criminals—who seem to accept a more conventional view of their position in the city's social hierarchy as well as of the behavior appropriate for altering their position.

We have also found that components of the area image matrix are systematically related to criminals' choices of locales for crimes. Interestingly, these relationships are ethnicity specific. Black criminals' crime patterns were predominately influenced by familiarity evaluations, whereas whites were influenced about equally be perceived ease of committing offenses in given areas and familiarity with areas. For the whites, these two criteria constituted independent dimensions of area evaluation.

Our research should not be seen as confirming completely the adequacy of the environment-behavior model for criminal activity. Much more work will be necessary, focusing on several issues we were unable to address and filling in many important details. Our findings do provide important support, nonetheless, for the area-images perspective. The two other classes of evidence we have summarized also provide *indirect* support for this analytic perspective. Our own work was intended to address at least some of the issues *directly*, and the findings are highly encouraging.

Policy Relevance of the Area-Images Approach

The policy relevance of this approach is, of course, in helping both criminal justice professionals and citizens understand better why crimes are committed where they are. Individual citizens and groups of citizens could draw upon such information so as to improve private efforts to reduce neighborhood crimes. Criminal justice officials might also draw upon such knowledge in a variety of ways to fashion crime prevention programs.

Unfortunately, the approach is still too new and too little developed to offer specific policy recommendations. If, however,

specific aspects of areas which criminals perceive as inviting or repelling are isolated, perhaps the inviting ones can be modified and
the repelling ones introduced in other areas.

There has been a certain amount of research on the possibilities
of modifying site-specific characteristics of businesses or
residences to create crime-repelling images of individual *sites*. The
work of Oscar Newman on site-specific architectural design criteria,[17] and the related work of Duffala, Jefferey, and Phelan,[18]
have explored the effect of site characteristics on target selection
by conventional criminals. This approach is not without its
critics,[19] and later research does not always support Newman's
specific contentions. Even this approach to understanding crime
patterns, while more studied than the strict area-images approach,
is still in a very early stage of both hypothesis formulation and
testing. Much more systematic research is required to explore its
utility. Yet, the primary insights which lie behind the site-specific
approach are quite similar to those which we have explicated in
this paper. Ultimately, it will probably be necessary to merge information on specific sites and on broad areas such as neighborhoods so as to develop a complete understanding of criminals'
area images.

Whichever of the two foregoing approaches is employed, they
both share some common assumptions. One of these is that areas
of a city take on a meaning to the individual that is greater than
the sum of their physical characteristics. Physical attributes are
important in the image, but the socioeconomic and behavioral "at-
mosphere" is equally important. In attempting to understand the
criminals' area image or in attempting to modify areas to deter
criminals, this fact should be kept in mind. The manipulation of
physical characteristics alone may be insufficient to achieve the
desired results.

At the same time, urban designers should consider the implications of site- and area-form for criminal behavior and for resident
behavior which might have crime-deterring effects. Certain
physical attributes may impede the operation of important social
behaviors which enhance territoriality and facilitate surveillance.

We are still at an early stage in the development of a satisfactory area images model to explain the patterning of urban crime.

More research will be required to isolate fully the relevant aspects of areas and sites and the extent to which they can be suitably altered. The present paper had addressed the promise of this new perspective on crime. The task remains for subsequent research to explicate fully its potential.

NOTES

1. Ronald L. Carter, "The Criminal's Image of the City." Ph.D. dissertation, University of Oklahoma (1974); Paul J. Brantingham and Patricia L. Brantingham, "A Theoretical Model of Crime Site Selection." Paper presented at the American Society of Criminology annual meeting, Atlanta, Georgia (1977).

2. For a discussion of the concepts of perception and cognition, see Gary T. Moore and Reginald G. Golledge, "Environmental Knowing: Concepts and Theories," in Moore and Golledge, eds., *Environmental Knowing* (Stroudsburg, Pa.: Dowden, Hutchinson & Ross, 1976), pp. 5–6.

3. Harry A. Scarr, *Patterns of Burglary*, 2d ed. U.S. Department of Justice, Law Enforcement Assistance Administration, National Institute of Law Enforcement and Criminal Justice (1973).

4. Julian Wolpert, "Behavioral Aspects of the Decision to Migrate," Papers and Proceedings of the Regional Science Association (1965); Frank Horton and David Reynolds, "On Investigation of Individual Action Spaces: A Progress Report," *Proceedings of the American Association of Geographers* (1969), 1:70–75; Lawrence Brown and Eric Moore, "The Intra-Urban Migration Process: A Perspective," *Geografiska Annaler* (1970), 526:1–13.

5. Peter Letkemann, *Crime as Work* (Englewood Cliffs, N.J.: Prentice-Hall, 1973), p. 138.

6. Scarr, *Patterns of Burglary*, p. 9.

7. For a more complete explication of this particular characterization of criminal strategy and tactics, see Ronald L. Carter and Kim Quaile Hill, *The Criminal's Image of the City* (in preparation).

8. Pat Burnett, "A Three State Markoff Model of Choice Behavior Within Spatial Structures," *Geographical Analysis* (1974), 10:54.

9. Letkemann, *Crime as Work*, pp. 141–42.

10. Carter and Hill, *The Criminal's Image of the City*.

11. See Sarah L. Boggs, "Urban crime Patterns," *American Sociological Review* (1965), 30:889–908; Carl F. Schmid, "Urban Crime Areas: Parts I and II," *American Sociological Review* (1960), 25:527–42 and 655–78; Kenneth R. Mladenka and Kim Quaile Hill, "A Reexamination of the Etiology of Urban Crime," *Criminology* (1976), 13:491–506; John Baldwin and Anthony E. Bottoms, *The Urban Criminal* (London: Tavistock, 1976).

12. Paul R. David, *The World of the Burglar* (Albuquerque: University of New Mexico Press, 1974), p. 8.

13. Letkemann, *Crime as Work*, p. 138.

14. Joan Petersilia, Peter W. Greenwood, and Marvin Lavin, *Criminal Careers of Habitual Felons* (Santa Monica, Calif.: Rand Corporation, 1077).

15. Thomas A. Reppetto, *Residential Crime* (Cambridge, Mass.: Ballinger, 1974).

16. For published research, see Ronald L. Carter and Kim Quaile Hill, "The Criminal's Image of the City and Urban Crime Patterns," *Social Science Quarterly* (1976), 57:597–607; and Carter and Hill, "Criminals' and Noncriminals' Perceptions of Urban Crime." *Criminology* (1978) 16:353–71.

17. Oscar Newman, *Defensible Space* (New York: Collier Books, 1973).

18. Dennis C. Duffala, "Convenience Stores, Armed Robbery, and Physical Environmental Features," *American Behavioral Scientist* (1976), 20:227–46; C. Ray Jeffery, *Crime Prevention Through Environmental Design*, 2d ed. (Beverly Hills, Calif.: Sage, 1977); George F. Phelan, "Testing 'Academic' Notions of Architectural Design for Burglary Prevention: How Burglars Perceive Cues of Vulnerability in Suburban Apartment Complexes," paper delivered at the American Society of Criminology annual meeting, Atlanta, Georgia (1977).

19. Anthony E. Bottoms, Review of *Defensible Space* by Oscar Newman, *British Journal of Criminology* (1974), 14:203–6; Thomas A. Reppetto, "Crime Prevention Through Environmental Policy: A Critique," *American Behavioral Scientist* (1976), 10:275–88.

卐 14 卐

Cognitive Mapping and the Subjective Geography of Crime

CHRISTOPHER J. SMITH AND GENE E. PATTERSON

IN RECENT YEARS social scientists have studied in detail the characteristic ways people both see and try to understand their visual environment. They have probed the unknown territory inside peoples' heads, trying to discover how people create images of what they see all around them, and how such images influence their subsequent behaviors.

Geographers, architects, and planners were among the first to realize the importance of studying the way people make images of the physical environment. One observer recognized the importance of environmental imagery, and described its function as follows:

> Environmental images function to organize our perceptions, they permit us to code, structure and store visual and spatial information, and directly mediate and regulate our responses to the things we see. By allowing us to recognize, select, register and conserve particular aspects of our unique personal experience in the world, these schematizations constitute the enduring reality which we construct from the phenomena of direct perception. . . .As a mediate pattern in the two way interaction between the observer and the environment, [the image] can also help clarify the nature of style and individual tastes . . . it provides a fundamental reference system for symbolic expression, communication, interpretation and meaning.[1]

After more than a decade of research, the general consensus is to replace the term image with *cognitive map*.[2] A cognitive map is a mental description of an environment, and *cognitive mapping* is the process by which the maps are generated. Downs and Stea have defined a cognitive map as

> a person's organized representation of some part of the spatial environment . . . (it is) . . . a cross-section representing the world at one instant in time.[3]

It is not obvious from this definition that the term cognitive mapping refers both to a *process* and also to *a set of techniques* for assessing the process. The major techniques for eliciting cognitive maps include sketch maps, verbal responses, interpretations of photographs, and simulations.[4] The techniques should in no way be equated with an individual's cognitive map any more than a topographic map should be considered the sole product of a physical geographer. The geographer merely represents some of his data schematically in a map; and in a similar fashion an individual may represent some of his spatial knowledge in a cognitive map. The cognitive map itself is much more than the end product drawn on the page, or the symap drawn from the responses to a semantic differential questionnaire. An individual's cognitive map is a complex network of information, representing events and objects in the environment. Information in the map is used to solve problems, form opinions, and direct actions. In the most general sense a cognitive map both expresses and determines what a person knows about the outside world. Stephen Kaplan has in fact defined cognitive mapping as a process by which an individual acquires and uses the knowledge needed to function adequately in a complex world.[5]

A simple one-dimensional technique cannot adequately represent the process Kaplan has described, and the existing research in the area remains highly speculative.[6] Nevertheless, cognitive mapping studies remain popular, and in this chapter we consider whether they can be useful in studying the incidence and prevention of crime.

Crime and the Geographer

A human geographer studies spatial behavior, but in most cases he observes only its physical manifestations. He describes the behavior, collects data about it, and finally maps it—but the inquisitive mind also wants to know about the origins of behavior. Why did an individual choose route A over route B, for example, and why do people choose one shopping center and not another?

The geographer interested in crime needs to know where crime occurs, but it is more important to find out why it occurs where and when it does, and why certain populations are the most popular targets for crime. A criminal event is one element in the complex interface between humans and their physical environment. This environment is often bewildering in the amount of information it imparts, and because the actors in a criminal event have varying capabilities for dealing with such complexity, there is often very little time to make careful decisions. In any transaction between humans and their environments, the processes that are occurring can be categorized into two major dimensions. First, people are either active toward their environment or they react to it—in other words, it does something to them or they do something to it; and second, the transaction may be physical (and social) or cognitive in essence, implying that the result of the transaction is either tangible or symbolic.[7] Using these categories to classify person/environment events, we see that the spatial aspects of crime are usually studied in the two behavioral modes called *operative* and *responsive* (table 14.1). These two modes cover most of the studies exploring the spatial patterns in crime,[8] and also the impact of the physical environment on patterns of crime.[9] In this paper (and also in Carter's) a case is made for considering crime in the *interpretative* and *evaluative* modes. In other words crime can be studied by considering how individual cognitive maps of the physical environment influence behavior during criminal events (active transactions), and how such maps influence attitudes toward crime, such as fear or tolerance (reactive transactions). By uncovering some features of the cognitive maps of people who are likely to be involved in criminal events, we can hopefully learn more about the behavioral antecedents of crime, and about how crime can be prevented. As we argue for the usefulness of cognitive maps, it will become apparent that such studies should complement rather than replace other crime studies. The work in this field is still rudimentary, but its greatest appeal is that it allows research on crime to be conducted in a positive and

Table 14.1.
Modes of Human-Environmental Transaction and
Related Areas of Research

		Type of Transaction	
		Cognitive	Behavioral
PHASE OF TRANSACTION	Active	INTERPRETIVE Cognitive representation of physical environments Personality and environment	OPERATIVE Experimental studies Spatial behavior studies, including proxemies
	Reactive	EVALUATIVE Environmental attitudes Environmental assessment	RESPONSIVE Impact of physical environment on behavior Ecological psychology

Source: Adapted from Stokols, "Environmental Psychology," p. 259.

predictive fashion, instead of inferring backwards from the data to suggest what might have occurred. A cognitive mapping approach also allows a researcher to consider the actors in criminal events as individuals, and not simply as automatons in a simplistic theoretical model of human behavior of the type used by Newman.[10]

The Subjective Geography of Crime

A cognitive map is a device that helps to make the world an easier place to live in. Extending this argument, Kaplan suggests that cognitive maps have been essential throughout human adaptation because the species has continually had to struggle for survival in a hostile world, without the benefit of speed, ferocity, or fearsome proportions.[11] To solve day-to-day problems, and therefore to survive through time, humans have had to be adept at gathering important knowledge about the world, and also at using their information quickly and effectively. Knowledge in this sense is the key to survival, and Kaplan suggests four domains of knowledge that each individual needs to maintain a minimally functioning cognitive map, namely: recognition, prediction, evaluation, and action.[12] Extending Kaplan's argument to the study of crime, we suggest that each of the actors in an actual or potential crime (including citizens, criminals, and law enforcement officers), must develop appropriate skills at acquiring these four types of knowledge:

Recognition. Involves knowing where you are and being able to identify the common objects in the environment. Individuals need to make sense of their perceived environment, and to make a valid interpretation of new events in familiar terms. Lee has further subdivided recognition into: a) an ability to identify and categorize objects like streets and buildings ("whatness"); and b) an ability to attribute location vis-a-vis other important elements in the environment, such as home, downtown, and safe places ("whereness").[13] A third possible category is the ability to develop temporal knowledge ("whenness"), which helps an individual to know when certain areas are safe or unsafe; when the parking lots close; or how long one is likely to have to wait for a bus.

Prediction. Requires knowing what might happen next and how to make associations between environmental events and objects. In other words, what leads to what? In novel situations this requires guesswork, and unfortunately in many crimes citizens find themselves unable to act quickly enough, which may not necessarily be the case for criminals and police officers. The combination of recognition and prediction abilities helps an individual to develop a probability map to guide his actions. For citizens this map would determine spatial behaviors during shopping trips or when traveling to work; for a patrolman it might determine which parts of the city to consider for his next round of activity.

Evaluation. Using the information gathered during the recognition and prediction stages, an individual must decide what his options are, and most importantly, which of a range of alternatives could have favorable or unfavorable consequences. This activity involves dividing the environment into its elements, the simplest division being those parts of town you would venture to and those you would not. In other circumstances one would need to discriminate between the "good guys" and the "bad guys" one encounters. The need to make such an evaluation rapidly is essential because not only does it determine the success of ones actions (it may, for example, save your life), but also because it often sets an unalterable course for subsequent actions. Usually a decision is made with incomplete information about what the actors think will happen—for example, what are the prospects of being mugged around the next corner? How likely is it that a particular house will be easy to burglarize? Or what are the benefits of patrolling this as opposed to that street? The need to make a clear cut decision, whatever it is, is important as an alternative to ambivalence, and in fact in many criminal events ambivalence could be as costly as making the wrong decision.

Action. Once an evaluation is made, the individual has to select a course of action. The decision requires skill and experience, but in many cases there are limited opportunities to "learn on the job." Decisiveness is essential for the protection of person and property, but when time is short an individual may need to resort to tried and tested routine behavior. Ley, for example, has shown that inner-city Philadelphia residents often choose a substantially longer route to avoid walking through certain parts of the city.[14] To compensate for a lack of information or a lack of time to deliberate in full, some individuals map out a rigid strategy or a plan of action in the event of a crisis.

Kaplan argues that human beings perform these categories of activity as and when they are required. In some cases they are sequential, but at times the first three have to be accelerated or bypassed by a swift action. In such cases a person with the most effective blend of intuition and experience is likely to succeed. Although the skills required to be an effective policeman differ from those required to be a successful criminal, the four processes are to some extent interchangeable and flexible. Arguably, an individual who continually performs well in any sphere has completed these four sets of activities with speed and precision. Someone who continually makes the wrong choices would simply not be around long to tell the story, whether he was a citizen, a criminal, or a policeman. Quite separate from the necessity of acquiring knowledge, however, it seems that humans actually enjoy performing these activities. Most of us relish the task of recognizing things. We love to simplify the world around us; figure out the possible outcomes of our actions; and we delight in solving problems. All people do things to a greater or lesser extent. Some, like mathematicians and chess players, choose to make their world even more complex, and others, including mountaineers, criminals, and policemen, seem to enjoy making their world even more unpredictable than it would be otherwise. Policemen and criminals have chosen an action-packed lifestyle, but often the unwitting citizen has to think and act like a policeman or a criminal to defend his person and property. Unfortunately, short of training citizens to think and act in such ways, preventive solutions to crime are still at the drawing-board stage.

The Uses of Cognitive Maps: Research Activities

The possibilities of conducting cognitive mapping research on the incidence of crime are almost unlimited. One type of study involves asking people to indicate which parts of a city they think are most susceptible to crime. In an exploratory study, students at the University of Oklahoma were asked to identify those parts of Norman they would be afraid to walk around in after midnight. Figure 14.1a is a composite map for all the respondents (n = 51),[15] showing that the most feared part of the city is the downtown area at the junction of Main Street and the Santa Fe railroad tracks. Just to the northeast of the downtown area another fear zone is identified around the state hospital; and lesser zones are identified in the campus area and along the shopping strip of Lindsey Street. Most of the fear responses are oriented to the likelihood of meeting unsavory and possibly dangerous individuals near the university, the hospital, and in the downtown area. The least justifiable in terms of actual crimes committed may be the fear people display of the mental hospital and its surrounding area.

As we know, behavior is strongly influenced by such fears, so it is unlikely that many people would wander along these streets alone after dark in that area. On the other hand, the university area, which is actually much more dangerous in terms of muggings and rapes, is not thought to be as fearsome. Perhaps students feel the campus area is more familiar to them, and that help would be nearby if they needed it. Whether or not this is the case, their responses, and possibly also their behavior, are strongly influenced by stereotyped and often uninformed attitudes about the relative safety of different parts of the city.

Figures 14.1c and 14.1d show the disaggregated responses of the male and female members in the sample. For women, the highest zone of fear in the city is concentrated around the university, with lesser zones in the downtown area, near the hospital, and in the South Base area (an unoccupied naval base in a largely uninhabited part of town). The men indicated a much stronger fear zone around the state hospital than anywhere else in the city. It is possible that men fear the *unknown* parts of the city and the people they may encounter in such areas, whereas women are more fearful of the areas they *know*, and particularly of the areas they *know to be dangerous*. In this sense women's fears may be more realistic, but if both the men and the women were to avoid the areas they feared most, some crimes could be prevented.

It is interesting to note that students who do not live in the city of Norman (commuters), identified only a very limited part of the city as unsafe, notably the area concentrated around the campus area (figure 14.2b). In all probability these students know so little about Norman that the University is the only area they were familiar with. Figures 14.2a and 14.2b provide further insight into the students' cognitive maps of crime by indicating the location of their residences (circles) relative to the closest area of perceived danger (arrows). In general, areas feared by women are much closer to their homes than they are for men, and in fact several of the women indicated that the most dangerous area in the city was actually in their neighborhood (particularly if they live close to the University of Oklahoma).[16] This was much less evident for the men in the sample, most of whom felt that the dangerous parts of the city were spatially separated from them. This response correlates with the response of the seven men in the sample who felt that no parts of the city were dangerous after dark. In general, men feel that they are unlikely to be involved in crimes, and the

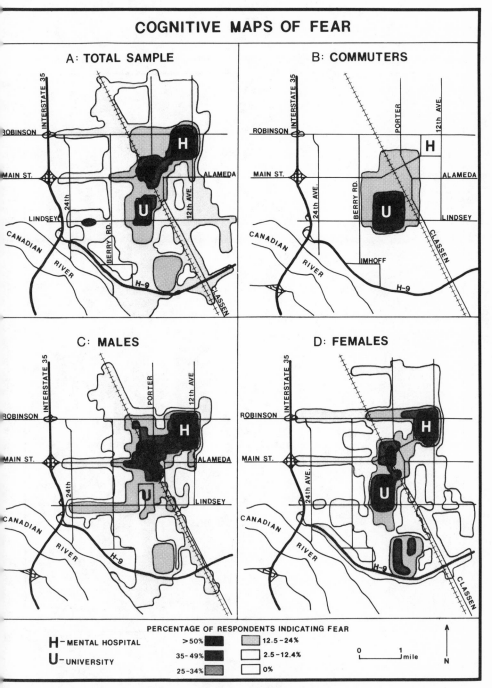

Figure 14.1. Cognitive Maps of Fear

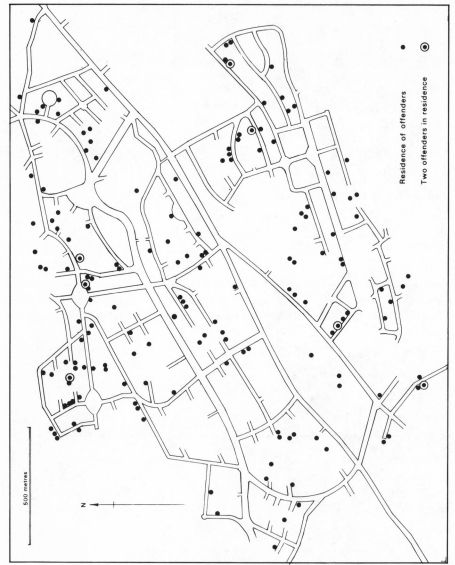

Residence of offenders ●

Two offenders in residence ◉

Figure 14.2. Distance Between Home and Closest Fear

crimes that do occur will probably be located in a part of the city they are not familiar with.

The Uses of Cognitive Maps: Case Studies

Case I: The Blue Knight. Joseph Wambaugh, himself an ex-policemen, has described a "scan" in operation that was observed (recognition), anticipated (prediction and evaluation), and prevented (action) by a car patrolman.[17] The potential thief has chosen a Los Angeles neighborhood he knows well. He knows that people walk around the neighborhood and that at various times throughout the day people are likely to be waiting at the bus stop. Close to the bus stop he selects a tenement house he knows is empty, and sits on the steps of the house as if he lives there. This appears to be a normal afternoon activity in an inner-city neighborhood, and one that is unlikely to attract any attention. When people pass by, particularly women carrying purses, he intends to rob them and flee through a nearby alley to his getaway car. Everything is well-planned and based on information about the neighborhood—the bus schedules, occupancy of the houses, and the availability of suitable targets. The patrolman does not know what is about to happen, so he has to use experience and intuition to predict. This puts him one step ahead of the unsuspecting citizens, and in this instance he was able to prevent a crime. As the patrolman said: "You just don't get suspicious of a guy when he approaches you from the porch of a house in your own neighborhood."[18] According to Oscar Newman's defensible space formulation, the prevention of crimes like this requires that each person know who lives in every house in the neighborhood and therefore everyone has to know who is a stranger. In areas with high resident turnover this is difficult. The only alternative is to be suspicious of everyone, which is an adaptation at perhaps too great a cost.

Case II: The Berkeley Flasher.[19] Several years ago the Berkeley police were puzzled by an epidemic of burglaries in a student neighborhood close to the University of California campus. After days of searching through their files for likely suspects, they concluded that the burglar was either a stranger or someone without a previous record. But, for reasons best known to themselves the police did not accept this possibility, so they produced a familiar "pin map" to show where the crimes occurred. They were clustered, so it looked as if the individual operated on foot. All the apartments burglarized belonged to young women, and all the crimes were committed through the ground-floor doors or windows. The individual appeared to know the neighborhood well and it seemed likely that he even lived there. In all cases only money was stolen, usually from purses; only one room was entered; and there was no evidence of a lengthy search or ransacking—the burglar appeared to know exactly where to locate the womens' purses. The police had to digest and contemplate all this information to figure out what type of person would know exactly where women lived alone; where they kept their money; *and* also to explain why only ground-floor entries were made. One patrolman finally stumbled onto a possible solution by trying to "get inside the head" of such an individual. The pattern of crime appeared to match that of an exhibitionist who wanders around in gardens looking through the windows of ground-floor apartments occupied by women. The police had not considered such a possiblity because they were not used to linking burglary with exhibitionism. As soon as they broke their own cognitive stereotype they had a new lead, and one that was eventually successful. The burglar turned out to be a local "flasher," well-known to the police, but never previously identified as a burglar.

Both of these examples illustrate situations in which the law enforcement officers had to solve problems by either anticipating events or interpreting factual and locational information. By manipulating the information, turning it over in their heads, and juggling it around in a search for new clues and associations, they were able to reach conclusions that led to decisive action. The criminals also showed their expertise and their "eye" for a potentially rewarding situation. Unfortunately, in both cases the amateurs were the citizens, who were unwittingly acting exactly as the criminals wished. Both examples illustrate cognitive mapping interpretation of familiar police activities, and both cases emphasize the importance of seeing (that is, understanding) events from another person's perspective.

Conclusion

We have argued that cognitive maps can be useful for studying spatial patterns of crime, and for considering how crime can be prevented through urban design. An individual's cognitive map helps to determine his behavior, and any knowledge about where and when people think crimes occur will be an essential complement to our overall understanding of the phenomena. If a citizen's cognitive map differs considerably from that of a police officer, an explanation is required. If the perceived pattern of crime does not correspond to the actual pattern, we may learn something important about the perceived and actual environmental instigators and inhibitors to criminal events. A fuller understanding of where it is safe to shop, walk, jog, or drive, is a first step toward both preventive behavior and preventive re-design, and cognitive maps may prove to be useful tools for developing that understanding.

NOTES

1. Charles Burnette, "The Mental Image of Architecture," in Charles Burnette, Jon Lang, and David Vachon, eds., *Architecture for Human Behavior* (Philadelphia: Philadelphia Chapter, American Institute of Architects, 1971), p. 66.

2. Comprehensive reviews of this work have been written by Daniel Stokols, "Environmental Psychology," *Annual Review of Psychology* (1978), 29:253-95; and also by Gary T. Moore and Reginald G. Golledge, eds., *Environmental Knowing: Theories, Research and Methods* (Stroudsberg, Pa.: Dowden, Hutchinson, and Ross, 1976).

3. Roger M. Downs and Davis Stea, *Maps in Minds: Reflections on Cognitive Mapping* (New York: Harper & Row, 1977), p. 6.

4. Reginald G. Golledge, "Methods and Methodological Issues in Environmental Cognition Research," in Moore and Golledge, eds., *Environmental Knowing*, pp. 300-14.

5. Stephen Kaplan, "On Knowing the Environment," in Stephen Kaplan and Rachel Kaplan, ed., *Human Scape: Environment for People* (North Scittuate, Mass.: Duxbury Press, 1978), p. 55.

6. In subsequent papers Kaplan has posited a neural net theory of cognitive maps. See, for example, "Adaptation, Structure, and Knowledge," in Moore and Golledge, eds., *Environmental Knowledge*, pp. 32-45.

7. Stokols, "Environmental Psychology,"

8. For example, Keith Harries, *The Geography of Crime and Justice* (New

York: McGraw-Hill, 1974); Gerald F. Pyle, "Spatial and Temporal Aspects of Crime in Cleveland, Ohio," *American Behavioral Scientist* (November/December 1976), 20:175–98.

9. The best-known study of this type is Oscar Newman's *Defensible Space* (New York: Macmillan, 1972); but for other suggestions, see also H. L. Nieburg, "Crime Prevention by Urban Design," *Society* (November/December 1974), 12:41–47; and also C. Ray Jefferey, "Criminal Behavior and the Physical Environment: A Perspective," *American Behavioral Scientist*, (November/December 1976), 20:149–74.

10. Newman, *Defensible Space*.

11. Stephen Kaplan, "The Challenge of Environmental Psychology," *American Psychologist* (1972), 27:140–43. See also Stephen Kaplan and Rachel Kaplan, eds., *Humanscape: Environments for People* (Belmont, Calif.: Duxberry Press, 1978).

12. Stephen Kaplan, "Cognitive Maps in Perception and Thought," in Downs and Stea, eds., *Image and Environment*, pp. 63–78.

13. Terence Lee, "Urban Neighborhoods as a Socio-Spatial Schema," *Human Relations* (1968), 21:241–67.

14. David Ley, *The Black Inner City as Frontier Outpost* (Washington, D.C.; Association of American Geographers, 1974), pp. 220–26.

15. Seven students, all of them men, said there were no parts of the city they would be afraid of; and three women said they would be afraid of all parts of the city. All ten respondents were excluded from the final analysis.

16. Mean distance between home and closest fear area for women was .3 miles, as compared to 1.1 miles for men.

17. Joseph Wambaugh, *The Blue Knight* (New York: Dell, 1972, pp. 179–80).

18. *Ibid.*, p. 180.

19. This story was related to one of the authors (C. J. S.) by Samuel Chapman, head of the police science program at the University of Oklahoma.

࿕ 15 ࿕

Systematic Sociospatial Variation in Perceptions of Crime Location and Severity

GERALD F. PYLE

RECENTLY, geographers have focused increasing amounts of effort in developing methods of improving our knowledge about variable spatial distributions of crime.[1] As these studies and related social scientific works are examined, it becomes increasingly clear that in the process of developing understandings of socioeconomic "cause and effect" relationships of the criminal justice system, more knowledge must be acquired about multidimensional aspects of attitude and behavior within our cities. Studies of crime in relation to urban environmental design can and have begun to address such issues.[2] In addition to some of the spatial studies of this nature, certain systematic geographic variations in attitudes of criminals in relation to urban locations have been explained.[3] Also, a survey was conducted during 1973–1974 by the Center for Urban studies, the University of Akron, geared toward identifying sociospatial similarities and differences in public perceptions of crime distributions and attitudes toward police actions.[4]

The purpose of this paper is to present an analysis of that part of the above survey pertaining to systematic spatial variations in public perceptions of crime locations and severity. A basic hypothesis of this study is that public reactions to increased awareness of criminal behavior tend to exhibit definite geographic pattern controlled by such indicators as the distribution of crimes, socioeconomic attainment levels of various individuals, differences in suburban and urban lifestyles, and individual interpretations of crime-related information flowing from the news media and other popular sources. The results of this analysis demonstrate, in a fashion similar to studies of the general geographic distribution of reported crimes, that systematic sociospatial variations exist and can be explained within the overall urban ecological context of the settlement patterns comprising American cities. Such information can be an important input to the overall urban planning process as regards urban design and crime, perceived or real.

Traditionally, crime has been regarded as a large-city problem, with converse rural feelings of safety directly attributed to increased "safe" distance from urban boundaries and all of the accompanying problems.[5] Many studies identify the focus of criminal activity as within the core of SMSAs, with FBI crime index reporting generally showing decreasing intensity with distance away from cities. In a growth sense, the American crime pattern does tend to vary with population density and proximity to central cities. However, various crimes often show distinctly different spatial distributions, and this has been explained elsewhere.[6] Nonetheless, attitudes do shape behavior and one of the most significant responses of the American public to the cultural changes during the 1960s was mass migration from urban core areas to more desirable suburban locations. The particular location selected for this analysis reflects many of the current urban-suburban trends found in cities throughout this country.

The Study Area

Situated in the northeast Ohio urban industrial complex, Summit County registered a population of 553, 371 persons during the 1970 census. Slightly more than half of that population resided in Akron, the central city of the SMSA. The Akron area is representative of many similar manufacturing centers wherein much of the economy is dependent upon major industries. Thus, the general urbanized area reflects much of the socioeconomic and demographic characteristics found in medium-sized manufacturing cities. Figures 15.1 and 15.2 show population density and

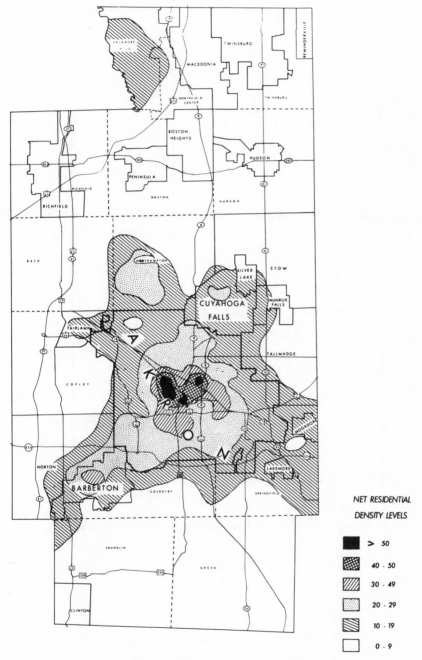

Figure 15.1. Population Density in Summit County

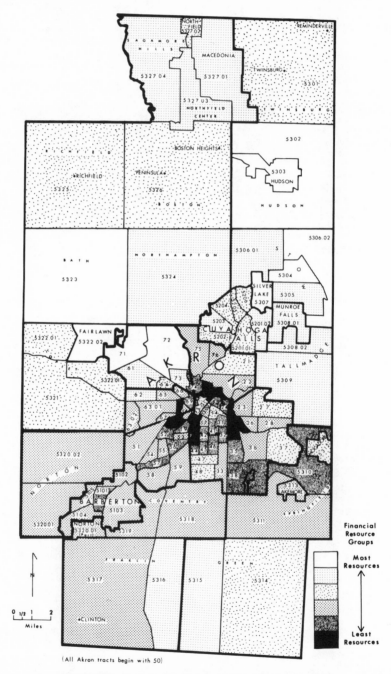

(All Akron tracts begin with 50)

Figure 15.2. Socioeconomic Areas of Summit County, 1970

socioeconomic areas of the county. Essentially the density of population is monocentric, with the most dense areas, in terms of net residential density, to be found within the central city and less dense areas radiating outward in a negative exponential fashion. The sociospatial structure of the area is, again, similar to many such cities. Figure 15.2, for example, shows this overall structure based on a principal components analysis of forty-nine demographic and socioeconomic variables derived from land-use information and 1970 population data.[7] Parts of the Summit County study area with the least resources, primarily those areas with higher percentages of black, poor white, and elderly populations, are to be found within the middle of the city of Akron. As distance increases from the central city, certain directional axes reflect high, middle, or low socioeconomic status. In addition, some of the more youthful populations of the study area reside in suburban locations. These factors were taken into consideration when the public perceptions of crime were derived from surveying the county.

Perceptual Data Acquisition

The general methodological basis for this spatial analysis of attitudes and behavior can be found within the contributions of Cox and Golledge[8] and others. To obtain and subsequently recover the underlying dimensionality of public attitudes about crime location and severity, a questionnaire was administered to a sample population of about 2,500 respondents. Persons interviewed were requested to make numerically scaled judgments about the severity of ten crime categories (nine index and "overall crime") within ten parts, or zones, of the area. The ten zones are indicated within figure 2 and essentially show areas reflecting historical directions of growth and general "familiarity" areas.

The method of acquiring scaled judgments was based on the *semantic differential* technique. Example 15.1 shows the types of polar adjectives used as extremes and major type of question asked. Respondents were requested to rank on the scale of one to seven severity of nine types of Type One offenses and "total crime" for each of the ten general subareas of the study area.

Example 15.1.
Perception Survey Instructions and Sample Statement

The statements on the following pages have a number scale:

1   2   3   4   5   6   7

Please *circle* the number which you feel is the best judgment for each statement.
For example, the statement might be: Auto theft is a serious problem in downtown Akron.

1	2	3	4	5	6	7
Not			Moderately			Very
Serious			Serious			Serious

In other words, if you feel that auto theft is very serious in downtown Akron, *you would circle 7*.

If you feel this is only a moderately serious problem in downtown Akron, you would *circle 3, 4, or 5*, depending upon your judgment. Or if you think this crime does not happen so often, *circle 2*.

In addition to geographical stratification, it was necessary to ask people certain information pertaining to demographic and socioeconomic background in order to obtain a significant sample. A smaller sample of 2,000 respondents, significant at the .001 level, when testing against geographic stratification as well as twenty socioeconomic characteristics, was extracted for the major analytical portions of the study.

Suburban and Central-City Perceptions
of Crime

The first procedure accomplished was to develop some general understanding of the spatial distribution of perceived crime severity. This was accomplished through developing different kinds of response surfaces. These surfaces showed perceived crime severity by the nine Type One offenses and total crime. Maps of perceived crime were then visually compared with distributions showing the intensity of reported crime for the years 1971 and 1972. In addition, Spearman Rank Order correlations were computed, comparing median responses by areas with the reported

225

severity of crime. Each of the ten areas was ranked in terms of perceived crime as well as actual crime, and statistical comparisons were made. Table 15.1 contains the results of the ranked correlations. Due to the small sample size, most of the numbers are larger than would be expected from such methods as Pearson's Product-Moment. Nonetheless, interesting contrasting comparisons can be made.

The correlations contained within table 15.1 indicated at least two major trends. The first trend is that perceived severity of crime and actual crime reporting for crimes against the person generally showed higher correlations than did property crimes. The second and perhaps more meaningful observation is that there

Table 15.1.
Spearman Correlations of Ranked 1971–1972 Average Crime Rating Per 10,000 Persons and Ranked Median Responses from the Ten Study Area Zones

Zones	H	R	UR	AR	AA	RB	NRB	L	AT	Total
					Crimes					
1	.794	.685	.964	.782	.782	.830	.358	.309	.733	.588
2	.939	.721	.891	.855	.855	.746	.479	.406	.830	.855
3	.782	.649	.915	.733	.794	.721	.491	.261	.661	.903
4	.891	.830	.952	.903	.806	.794	.286	.236	.794	.733
5	.915	.697	.842	.770	.661	.552	.285	.321	.649	.600
6	.818	.733	.915	.709	.636	.370	.188	.382	.661	.806
7	.855	.687	.818	.830	.564	.806	.236	.333	.733	.697
8	.842	.842	.927	.855	.733	.758	.382	.333	.818	.673
9	.879	.815	.782	.661	.636	.782	.285	.273	.708	.600
10	.794	.721	.855	.649	.818	.770	.164	.261	.818	.624
Suburban	.768	.732	.817	.720	.573	.468	.503	.091	.830	.721
Central City	.942	.717	.936	.900	.806	.754	.371	.304	.790	.717
Summit County	.891	.721	.903	.770	.806	.745	.333	.321	.794	.612

H = Homicide
R = Rape
UR = Unarmed Robbery
AR = Armed Robbery
AA = Aggravated Assault

RB = Residential Burglary
NRB = Nonresidential Burglary
L = Larceny
AT = Auto Theft
TC = Total Crime

are differences between suburban and central-city perceived/actual correlations, with central-city correlations being higher for more kinds of crimes than either the total county taken as a group or suburbanites compared separately.

Cognitively, a major distinction was made by the entire sample population between central city and suburb. In fact, the distinction generally exaggerated the severity of crime for the entire city of Akron. While overall higher rates of reported Type One offenses are largely confined to the more central parts of Akron, most respondents perceived the entire central city as having crime problems much more serious than the suburbs. While this was true, few persons allowed for the possibility that crimes were committed within particular parts of the area other than the central city. Figures 15.3 and 15.4, containing response surfaces of perceived and actual crime, help explain this. Perceived levels of crime severity on the part of the total sample population are shown within figure 15.3, while figure 15.4 shows the actual crime rate

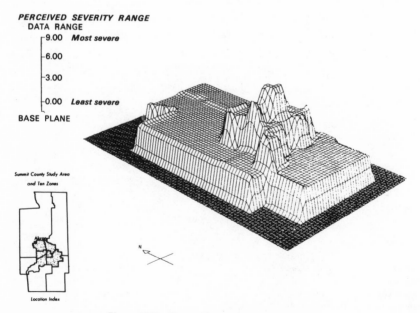

Figure 15.3. County Perception of Total Crime

(as viewed from the southwest)

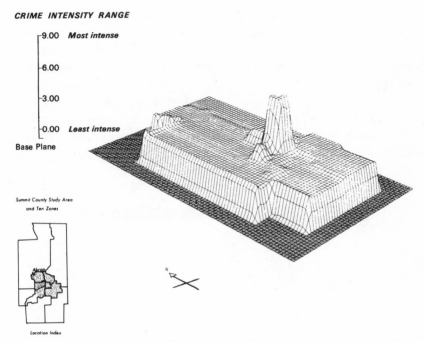

Figure 15.4. Total Crime: Rates per 10,000, 1971-1972
(as viewed from the southwest)

for reporting of Type One offenses for the two-year period prior to the survey.

When individual crime categories were examined in an identical fashion, similar relationships showed up for the most part. Another method utilized was to examine differing perceptions of crime severity by separately extracting the ten zones. Figures 15.5 and 15.6 demonstrate the results of such a comparison. In this instance zone 7, generally characterized by middle- to upper-middle-income suburban families, was extracted and the response surface contained within figure 15.5 was developed. The particular sample from that zone was selected because it is not only upper-income but also 55.2 percent female, of which 52.3 percent surveyed were from 25 to 44 years of age and 70 percent had families with annual incomes of from $10,000 to $25,000. The actual perceived risk of rape, shown within figure 15.6, once again greatly exaggerates the entire central city of Akron.

The key to understanding the differing perceptions of crime within Summit County was explained as generally a manifestation of overriding attitudinal differences between suburbanites and central-city inhabitants. It was thus assumed, on the basis of the severity ratings, that suburban perceptions of central-city crime were exaggerated to the point that distinctions among various central-city neighborhoods were not made, particularly when considering type of crime. On the other hand, while central-city inhabitants demonstrated a better cognition of crime severity within the more populous parts of the study area, their perceptions of suburban crime were not always accurate. A more detailed analysis of responses by socioeconomic and demographic characteristics helped shed some additional light on these disparities.

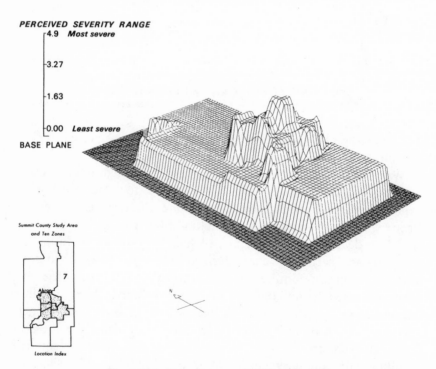

Figure 15.5. Rape: Rates per 10,000, 1971–1972

(*as viewed from the southwest*)

CRIME INTENSITY RANGE

┌─4.90 *Most intense*

├─3.27

├─1.63

├─0.00 *Least intense*

BASE PLANE

Summit County Study Area
and Ten Zones

Akron

Location Index

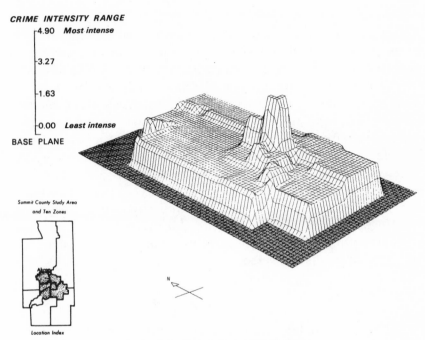

N

Figure 15.6. Zone 7: Perception of Rape
(*as viewed from the southwest*)

Urban Ecological Determinants of Perceived Crime Severity

The suburban–central-city distinctions can be clearly identified. In addition, further evidence of differing spatial perceptions is offered when our sample population is examined by various population characteristics. Median responses were calculated and aggregated into ten areas by ten crime tabulations on the basis of race, age, sex, income, and other indicator characteristics. The overwhelmingly persistent pattern of suburban–central-city differences in perceived crime severity continues to persist.

Race

For example, when comparing black and white responses utilizing a median of 4.00 as a neutral benchmark with the assumption that all collective responses greater than that indicated higher perceived crime rates and those below reflect the converse, a definite pattern of white responses defining the entire central city area (zones 1 through 6) as a generally high crime area stands out.

In general, black perceptions of crime within Summit County were more accurate and realistic than the somewhat exaggerated measures indicated by white respondents. About three-quarters of the central city zones were rated above the 4.00 measure when considering all crime categories. On the other hand, suburban zones were rated slightly higher than they actually are in terms of scaled severity. Since few suburban areas contain any large number of black residents, lack of familiarity may be playing a role in such collective perceptions. Likewise, black and white cognition of many parts of the central city may have explained the exaggerated results recovered.

Sex

Male to female comparisons indicate certain expected systematic regularities. When viewing the entire county, female respondents rated areas by crime type higher than males 98 percent of the time. All suburban female respondents were higher in the aggregate than male responses and 97 percent of the central city collective judgments were higher for females. Still, the suburban–central-city separations were apparent. Most (97 percent) of the male responses from central-city areas were above the 4.00 value and all female responses were above that measure for the same zone. Likewise most suburban judgments of crime severity for both sexes were below the 4.00 level. As a general rule, females rated crime higher throughout the study area (and particularly for central-city areas) than did male respondents.

Age Cohorts

Examination of attitudinal and perceptual differences among various age cohorts show fewer marked contrasts. In general, those persons surveyed who were between the ages of 16 and 19 generally rated most of the study area zone higher than those in both the 20–24 and 25–34 age groups. Still, the overwhelming feature of all of these group responses was the sharp suburban–central-city distinction. Those persons surveyed between the ages of 35 and 44 actually rated some central-city zones lower than suburban zones for the same crimes. This aspect is of particular interest because most of the suburban–central-city dichotomy still showed up when median responses of persons from the latter age cohort appeared to be a little closer to the actual reporting. Conversely, median responses recorded for those persons 45–54 and 55–64 years old were nearly the same as the overall Summit County average ratings. And, median responses of those over 65 tended to be a little less accurate. While the elderly rated some central-city zones higher than suburban locations, nearly one-third of all possible suburban ratings were above 4.00. Conversely, many central-city locations with higher crime rates were rated below the benchmark.

Income

More clearcut distinctions were identified by grouping our sample by income levels. For example, when viewing responses from income groups, $5,000–$10,000, $10,000–$15,000, $15,000–$25,000 and over $25,000 annually, distinctions were more apparent than when age groups were examined. While there were some fluctuations, depending upon knowledge of particular zones, the general trend was for increasingly higher median responses in accordance with increasing income levels. Those persons surveyed who recorded family income levels of less than $5,000 annually rated most crimes lower in central-city zones than did the other income groups. Conversely, median responses from the lowest-income group were higher for all crimes in suburban areas than were responses from those in higher-income brackets. Clearly, this is explained by the fact that most of the lower-income respondents resided within the central city of Akron. As would be expected, higher-income residents rated suburban areas substantially lower. This trend occurred in a very regular and systematic manner, with a major exception being respondents with annual family income in excess of $25,000.

With few exceptions both the central-city and suburban areas were rated higher by this income bracket than any of the other groups. While the central-city–suburban dichotomy in ratings was still clearly apparent, persons from this highest group simply rated all areas higher for all crime categories. These findings parallel perceptions of confidence in the police.[9]

Level of Education

Median responses compared by grouping respondents by level of educational attainment produced trends not so pronounced as with different income groups. In general those with the lowest educational attainment levels rated crime lower for the central city and higher within suburban areas than did those with more education. Once again, the overall suburban–central-city dichotomy was reinforced in two ways. The first and most obvious way was that those with the lowest educational levels tended to dwell more within central-city zones and the second was that regardless of education, suburbs were again rated lower in terms of overall crime. Responses from those who were at least high school graduates were more complex. While some suburban areas were rated generally lower by this group when compared to those with some college, most central-city ratings were not so severe as were those recorded for the other educational groups. These findings reflect better cognition of crime patterns within the county on the part of better-educated individuals.

Length of Residence within an Area

The latter findings suggest more familiarity with the city and, hence, crime problems. This is of particular interest in terms of not only understanding crime patterns but general aspects of urban life. The contention can be made that the longer persons reside in particular neighborhoods, the sharper their perception of crime becomes. These findings are borne out in the Summit County analysis. Respondents grouped in accordance with length of residence within particular locations explained this occurrence. Those who had resided at their present location less than one year during the time of the survey almost uniformly rated all ten zones somewhat lower than those who had lived in particular locations for longer periods of time. Those who had lived at their present residence from one to two years rated most zones lower than those who had resided within their location more than two years. As length of tenure increased, median resonses tended to parallel more closely the scaled crime ratings from within particular neighborhoods.

Other Studies

Aspects of varying cognition of neighborhood and particularly crime seemed to be overshadowed by the general central-city–suburban dichotomy. The Akron area is not unique in this respect, as other cities have shown similar characteristics, though within slightly different methodological frameworks, e.g., Gorse and Beran's study of Lincoln.[10]

By contrast to the suburban study by Grose and Beran, the works of Klinaman and David within the Bedford-Stuyvesant area of Brooklyn show different kinds of results.[11] The Bedford-Stuyvesant study consisted of a sampling of blacks, whites, Puerto Ricans, and in-migrants from the British West Indies. Analyses were formulated on the basis of length of residence, age, sex, and related variables. While within each group a large proportion were long-term residents, the blacks were the most settled in the area, with 48 percent having resided there for more than ten years. Twenty of the respondents from other groups had lived within the community for less than two years. Klinaman and David found "no significant differences in the proportion of men and women in each race-ethnic group who perceived crime in the area as particularly high." However, older blacks and whites perceived crime in the area higher than some of the young residents, but among West Indians and Puerto Ricans age was not a significant factor. Klinaman and David also found a positive correlation between economic status and perception of crime, with respondents at higher educational levels being more crime conscious. This awareness among the more educated and persons of higher economic status was explained in that they had more to lose if they were victimized. Visibility and social contact were also considered as important variables in terms of individual perceptions of crime. This particular study indicated that people with more social contacts had higher levels of perception of crime than those with fewer contacts. And such findings partly related to length of residence, as long-term residents perceived crime to be higher than recent immigrants. Also, residents with relatives within the area perceived crime rates as somewhat higher than those with no kinship ties within Bedford-Stuyvesant.

In corresponding studies of victimization and perception of crime, Biderman found that no relationship existed between victimization and attitudes toward crime.[12] However, Klinaman and David's findings contradicted these earlier findings, indicating that persons who had been more recently victimized perceived crime to be somewhat higher. Klinaman and David attributed these differing conclusions in part to some confusion among researchers over definitions of terms (especially those related to attitude) and the manner in which information is interpreted and categorized. Regardless of method of analysis, however, it becomes increasingly clear within the context of this study that familiarity with various parts of cities plays an important role in understanding perceptions of crime. This contention was explored in more detail through the use of multidimensional scaling techniques.

A Multidimensional Scaling Approach
to Explaining Perception of Crime
within Summit County

Recently many geographers operating within the general area of behavioral science as it related to space have made contributions indicating the importance of perception of geographic phenomena and resultant "behavior." Demko in a study of cognition of location with regard to certain cities in Ontario made note of the importance of perception of geographic phenomena and resultant "behavior."[13] Demko's contribution essentially supports some earlier findings of Cox and Golledge and uses some methods more recently explained by Golledge and Rushton that centered around the basic conception that in many instances and on specific occasions, people's perception of particular places in turn influences their behavior regarding these places. Furthermore, cognition of space is often multidimensional, i.e., there may be some underlying dimensionality not readily identifiable by normal analytical methods.[14]

While it initially appeared that most of the derived scores here were unidimensional, it was possible to identify the true multidimensional nature of many of the aggregated responses from the various ten areas. The method selected to identify these methods was KYST, a program developed by Kruskal, Young, and Seery, working through Bell Laboratories.[15] As with many other multidimensional scaling operations, the basic technique involves the construction of configurations of points in multidimensional space from information obtained about interpoint distances in perceived space of the particular points. KYST initially takes an array of data and performs a partially metric principal components analysis. Then successive iterations are performed, depending upon the size of the data array. Within this study, the basic measure searched for was the minimum amount of stress attained on successive iteration in the multidimensional space. Ten percent stress was taken as an ideal minimum measure. In effect, stress measured the "goodness" or "badness" of fit on successive dimensions. And as explained by Isaac and Poor in *Psychometrika*,[16] it was expected that with increasing numbers of dimensions, the actual stress would decrease. It was therefore the objective of this analysis to minimize stress in as few dimensions as possible, while at the same time attempting to attain some degree of multidimensionality.

Not all solutions were multidimensional. Seventeen percent of the actual cognitive space identified was unidimensional. The bulk of the KYST solutions (77 percent) were two-dimensional and 6 percent were three-dimensional.

Given the actual scaled scores on 100 possible multidimensionality scaling solutions, comparisons were made with urban ecological variables. Making use of PROFIT, a procedure developed by Chang and Carroll,[17] it was possible to test the nonmetric scaled scores against the other known properties. Because of various previous tests, several kinds of information are tested against the KYST scores. The first of these was actual crime information. The second, because of the urban ecological inferences previously made, consisted of testing the scaled scores against the actual socioeconomic characteristics of the zones. The third method, based upon earlier findings by Golledge and Rushton, was to test the perceived distances as measured by geographic distances as measured by geographic distance.[18]

Crime and Perceived Crime

Operating under the assumption that the first dimensions from each of the 100 scaling operations indicated perceived crime, these scores were tested against 1971–1972 crime rates within the ten zones. Table 15.2 shows the results from optimally fitting linear regressions of perceived and actual crime.[19] It was interesting to note that for homicide most of the scaled scores are fairly well correlated with actual crime. The one exception was the perception of homicide by those respondents from zone 6. On the other hand, the most highly correlated perceptions of homicide are those from zone 4 which is, incidentally, not one of the highest homicide areas within the county. It is also of interest that for the crime of larceny, poorly defined and weakly defined earlier, none of the derived measures correlated highly with actual larceny. However, in all but two instances total crime and perceived crime correlated fairly well. A similar result is somewhat true but not so pronounced for nonresidential burglary, wherein one of the zones, 9, did have a fair correlation. But overall total crime correlated more highly. For actual total crime, viewed at the bottom of table 15.2, seven of the ten zones show pairwise correlations above .500 on the first dimension uncovered.

In general, for some zones the first dimension did show a statistically significant correlation. However, there were many weak correlations when comparing perceived crime as indicated by scaled scores on the first dimension with the actual incidence of crime. About 40 percent of ninety possible combinations (exclud-

Table 15.2.
Pairwise Correlations of Crime and Perceived Crime by Zone: First Dimension

nes	1	2	3	4	5	6	7	8	9	10
ᴏmicide	.685	.815	.647	.807	.708	—	.666	.687	.736	.630
ᴛal	—	—	—	.564						
ᴘe	.516	.565	—	.506	.649	.575	.578	—	.577	—
ᴛal	—	—	—	—	.601	.541	—	—	.542	—
ᴀrmed Robbery	.680	.568	—	.597	.666	.680	—	.545	.651	.629
ᴛal	.659	—	—	.541	.619	.631	—	—	.617	.554
med Robbery	.628	.728	.645	.761	.563	.551	.555	.578	.668	.665
ᴛal	.530	.626	.554	.680	—	—	—	—	.617	.571
ᴀggravated Assault		.635	.648	—	.684	—	—	—	—	—
ᴛal		.503	.579	—	.647	—	—	—	—	—
ᴀsidential Burglary	.632	—	—	.605	—	—	.832	.761	.850	.748
ᴛal	—	—	—	—	—	—	.676	—	.633	.586
ᴏnresidential Burglary	—	—	—	—	—	—	—	—	.550	—
ᴛal	—	.554	.527	—	—	—	—	.518	.618	—
ᴀrceny	—	—	—	—	—	—	—	—	—	—
ᴛal	.649	—	.554	.621	.598	.650	.577	—	.538	.522
ᴀto Theft	.516	—	—	.571	.511	.530	—	—	.661	.559
ᴛal	—	—	—	.557	—	—	—	—	.649	.522
ᴛal Crime	—	—	.595	.639	.610	.603	—	.555	.596	.547

ing the total crime category) did not show a strong fit on the first dimension. In addition, another 40 percent of ninety possible correlations of specific perceived crime correlated *not with the crime category but instead with overall crime.*

Several possible explanations are offered. One explanation may be that people's cognition of crime is, in fact, multidimensional. Another possibility is that the crime rate used for comparison was the 1971–1972 average, which possibly was already outdated in 1974. Yet another possibility is that the cognition of respondents of socioeconomic conditions in various parts of the county, for example housing, race, etc., may have influenced their perception of crime. It was therefore decided to test perceived crime within the ten different zones against available socioeconomic variables for those zones.

Perceived Crime and the Social Ecology

When examining the correlation of optimally fitted scaled scores on each crime against twenty-two socioeconomic variables, it was possible to identify some statistical explanation. With homicide, for example, correlations with the multidimensional solutions of perceived homicide showed the strongest correlation among all the zones with percent of males 25–44 years of age. Clearly, neighborhoods containing more younger males were presented as areas of suspicion by most of our sample. Correlations between perceived rape and ecological characteristics also indicated a good statistical match with the variable indicating percent males 25–44. Viewing the multidimensional comparisons, zones 3 and 8 demonstrated strong correlations between perceived rape and the socioeconomic variables on the second dimension. Within zone 3, for example, the variable indicating percent of high school graduates correlated with perceived crime at .622, while the income variable, percent of families with incomes from $10,000 to $15,000, had a correlation of .772. Within zone 8, a suburban area, more variables correlated with the second dimension than with the first.

Other statistical relationships of this nature showed similar results. In terms of armed robbery, for example, most of the best statistical fits were with the first dimension, a minor exception being perception of that crime by those surveyed from zone 6. Correlations for the crime of assault were somewhat similar to those for homicide. Again, and mostly on the first dimensions, some of the highest correlations regardless of zone were with the variable, males 25–44 years of age. It is also of interest that those from zone 6 appear to have scaled scores more highly correlated on the second dimension, thus making (in terms of socioeconomic data) the perceptions of those from zone 6 more multidimensional than some of the others. Also, the scaled scores from zone 10 showed many high correlations on the second dimension. The latter measures include the variable, males 15–24 years of age, as well as several income variables.

In general, the multidimensionality of many of the measures of perception of crime could be demonstrated by testing against socioeconomic measures. In some instances the socioeconomic measures showed better correlations than did the actual crime rates. However, this is to be expected because in many instances respondents no doubt had a better perception of actual socioeconomic conditions in some neighborhoods than they did of reported crime rates. Many persons assumed that some neighborhoods, particularly those with many young males, simply had higher crime rates. In some areas this was true, but other studies[20] have indicated that statistical identification of crime within cities is much more complex and cannot be fully understood through simple correlations of ecological data. It can also be stated that somewhat static correlations of perceived crime with actual socioeconomic data can give us some additional information regarding the perception of crime, but certainly not enough from which to draw major conclusions. It is therefore assumed that additional factors, i.e., those more than actual crime and urban ecological conditions, are contributing to perception of crime within Summit County.

Comparing Derived Cognitive Distance with Actual Geographic Distance

Recently, Golledge and Rivizzigno[21] and others have shown that geographic distance and direction have a definitie relationship with cognition of space over time. Using the PROFIT procedure in a slightly different manner this time, an attempt was made to statistically test those cognitive distances as measured from scaled scores with actual geographic distance from each zone to all others. In this particular procedure, geographic distance was simultaneously compared to the K-dimensional space derived from the scaled scores. One hundred tests indicated that in some instances geographic distance was explaining cognition of crime at least as well as, if not better than, either the actual incidence of crime or the socioeconomic characteristics. For example, table 15.3 shows the correlations derived through the PROFIT procedure for these tests. The most apparent aspect within table 15.3 is that the suburban data from zones 7, 8, 9 and 10 did not correlate well

Table 15.3.
Profit Fits for Geographic Distance and Scaled Scores

Zones	H	R	UR	AR	AA	RB	NRB	L	AT	TC
1	.917	.909	.884	.861	.867	.896	.902	.932	.814	.829
2	.571	.756	.828	.832	.619	.848	—	.787	.748	.636
3	.774	.742	.857	.734	.901	.747	.675	.853	.679	.831
4	.581	.527	.664	.562	.656	.676	.659	.724	—	.535
5	.714	.673	.592	.667	.659	—	.727	.673	.733	.632
6	.554	.722	.753	.738	.877	.541	.755	.862	.869	.734
7	—	.755	—	—	—	—	—	—	.588	—
8	—	—	—	—	—	—	—	—	—	—
9	—	—	—	.674	—	—	—	—	—	.851
10	—	.821	—	—	—	—	.641	—	.699	—

H = Homicide	RB = Residential Burglary
R = Rape	NRB = Nonresidential Burglary
UR = Unarmed Robbery	L = Larceny
AR = Armed Robbery	AT = Auto Theft
AA = Aggravated Assault	TC = Total Crime

when both kinds of distance were compared. However, when the central-city zones were viewed, many strong relationships showed up. For comparative purposes, figures 15.7 and 15.8 explain the relationship between these two kinds of distances.

For example, the two-space solution of the perception of homicide by those from zone 1 showed (correlation −.917) that definite geographic subdivisions of the city could be identified. At the right side of figure 15.7, the CBD is placed in the same cognitive space as parts of the city which are close. Also, the eastern and southern portions of the city clustered. Conversely, western and northwestern Akron were placed in similar cognitive space. However, all suburban areas were perceived in the left or low-crime sections of that space. Further distinctions were made in two ways. The western suburbs are clustered together, as are the eastern suburbs. In fact, this is a realistic cognitive map of homicide within the county. The "mental map" shows west Akron as somewhat high in terms of perceived crime severity, and a clear-cut suburban distinction is made. It should also be noted when viewing suburban perception of homicide that no significant correlations were found between perceived homicide space and geographic distances.

Yet another example can be seen in figure 15.8, the perception of rape by those from zone 7. In this instance, zone 7 is suburban and one of the few of the sixty possible suburban comparisons with a significant correlation. In this example, zones 1 and 3, the commercial core and Akron's lower west side, were placed in similar space within the cognitive map. These were, in fact, two of the areas reporting a higher incidence of rape in 1971 and 1972. The remaining central-city zones were also placed in similar space within this two-dimensional configuration as higher than normal in terms of the incidence of rape. Conversely, at the low end of the

ZONE 1 HOMICIDE

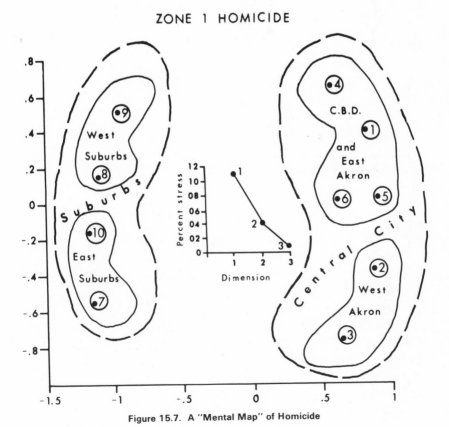

Figure 15.7. A "Mental Map" of Homicide

ZONE 7 RAPE

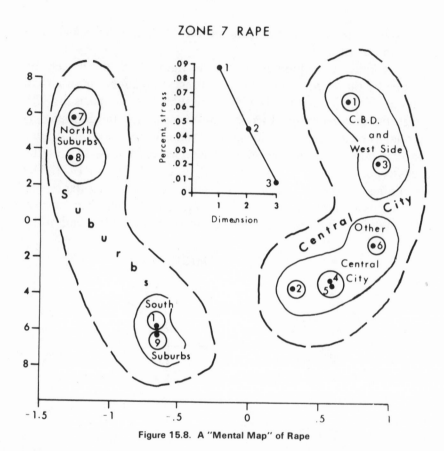

Figure 15.8. A "Mental Map" of Rape

crime scale, northern and southern suburbs were perceived in distinctly different locations. Zones 7 and 8, the northern suburbs, clustered together as having a lower incidence of rape. (In actuality zone 7 had a higher rape reporting rate than zone 8.) At the same time, the southern suburbs, zones 9 and 10, were placed in a similar space. Geographic distance does seem to matter for some kinds of crime, although socioeconomic factors appear to be operating with more strength when suburban cognitions are examined. In general, however, many of the findings earlier within this chapter regarding dichotomous central-city–suburban perceptions of crime are reinforced.

While some of the different perceptions could be identified through the use of univariate measures, it is particularly important to realize that the multidimensional scaling procedures actually *measure* these varying perceptions. Also, the scaled scores derived from the multidimensional scaling procedures were extremely useful for comparison with such measures as those attempted above. It is of particular interest that such notions as geographic familiarity (or lack of it) show up when measuring scaled scores against geographic distance. Multidimensional scaling procedures can be extremely useful in terms of detailed measurement of differing or similar perceptions of crime. If, in fact, Akron and the Summit County area are characteristic of many other locations, then it is assumed that similar multidimensional scaling measures can be derived within other cities.

Conclusions

The most important single finding within this study is that many suburbanites have exaggerated perceptions of crime in the central city of Akron. This has been demonstrated in many ways. One of the strongest methods of identifying this dichotomy is contained in table 15.3, wherein geographic distances were tested against perceived crime in multidimensional space. Again, perceptions of crime vary in terms of sex, with females having more exaggerated notions of the crime problem. Crime perceptions appear to increase as age and income increase, and those who have lived in places longer generally feel that crime rates are higher than those who have lived in areas less time and are not home owners.

It is important that suburbanites are made aware of the fact that many parts of the central city are, in fact, much safer than they realize. The implications of these exaggerated perceptions are many. For example, the lack of use of shopping facilities within many parts of Akron may be due to fear of crime. In addition, fear of crime could be explaining the absence of strong interest in the varied cultural facilities offered within the city of Akron. Another example would be the failure to use many fine recreational facilities. Not all parts of the central city of Akron are high-crime areas. Regardless of crime, different types have higher reporting in different parts of the central city as well as the suburbs; and in many instances, certain suburban locations have a more serious crime problem than the central city.

NOTES

1. See Phillip D. Phillips, "A Prologue to the Geography of Crime," *Proceedings of the Association of American Geographers* (1972), 4:86–91; Keith D. Harries, *The Geography of Crime and Justice* (New York: McGraw-Hill, 1974); Donald L. Capone and Woodrow W. Nichols, Jr., "Crime and Distance: An Analysis of Offenders' Behavior in Space," *Proceedings of the Association of American Geographers* (1975), 7:45–49; Gerald F. Pyle et al., "The Spatial Dynamics of Crime." University of Chicago, Department of Geography, research monograph no. 159 (1974).

2. C. Ray Jeffery, *Crime Prevention Through Environmental Design* (Beverly Hills, Calif.: Sage, 1971).

3. Capone and Nichols, "Crime and Distance."

4. Gerald F. Pyle et al., "An Analysis of Public Perception of Crime and Attitudes Toward the Police." Report prepared for the Summit County Criminal Justice Commission, Akron, Ohio (1975); 310 pp.

5. George Gallup, "City Life Continues to Lose Appeal; Fear for Personal Safety May Be Key Reason," Gallup Poll, December 17, 1972; "The Dimensions of Crime: One Person in Three in Center City Areas Has Been Mugged, Robbed, or Suffered Property Loss," Gallup Poll, January 19, 1973; "Growing Fear of Crime Could Become Number One Issue in November Election," Gallup Poll, April 22, 1972. (Princeton, N.J.: Field Enterprises, Inc.)

6. Pyle et al., "Spatial Dynamics of Crime."

7. Gerald F. Pyle and Bruce Lauer, "Comparing Spatial Configurations: Hospital Service Areas and Disease Rates," *Economic Geography* (1975), 51(1):50–68.

8. Kevin R. Cox and Reginald G. Golledge, eds., *Behavioral Problems in Geography: A Symposium.* Studies in Geography no. 17 (Evanston, Ill. Northwestern University Press, 1969).

9. Gerald F. Pyle, "Systematic Spatial Variations in Attitudes Toward Police Actions " (forthcoming); Frank J. Costa, ed., special issue, *Ohio Journal of Science*, "Public Policy and the Built Environment, 1977."

10. See William J. Gorse and Nancy J. Beran, "The Community Criminal Justice System of Lincoln." Program for the Study of Crime and Delinquency, Ohio State University, Columbus (1973).

11. Paula H. Klinaman and Deborah S. David, "Victimization and Perception of Crime in a Ghetto Community," *Criminology* (November 1973), 11:307–43.

12. A. Biderman, Louise A. Johnson, Jennie McIntyre, and Adrienne Weir, "Field Surveys I: Report on a Pilot Study in the District of Columbia on Victimization and Attitudes Toward Law Enforcement" (Washington, D.C.: U.S. Government Printing Office, 1967).

13. Donald Demko, "Cognition of Southern Ontario Cities in a Potential Migration Context," *Economic Geography* (Janurary 1974), 50:20–34.

14. R. G. Golledge and Gerard Rushton, "Multidimensional Scaling, Review and Geographical Applications," Association of American Geographers, resource paper no. 10, Commission on College Geography, Washington, D.C. (1972).

15. Joseph B. Kruskal, Forrest W. Young, and Judith B. Seery, "How to Use KYST, a Very Flexible Program To Do Multidimensional Scaling and Unfolding." (Murray Hill, N.J.: n.d.). Bell Laboratories, Mimeo.

16. Paul D. Isaac and David D. S. Poor, "On the Determination of Appropriate Dimensionality in Data with Error," *Psychometrika* (March 1974), 39:91–109.

17. J. J. Chang and J. D. Carroll, "How to Use PROFIT, a Computer Program for Property FITing by Optimizing Nonlinear or Linear Correlations," (Murray Hill, N.J.: Bell Laboratories, n.d.). Mimeo.

18. Golledge and Rushton, "Multidimensional Scaling."

19. Chang and Carroll, "How to Use PROFIT."

20. Gerald F. Pyle, "Geographic Perspectives on Crime and the Impact of Anti-Crime Legislation," in John S. Adams, ed., *Urban Policymaking and Metropolitan Dynamics* (Cambridge, Mass.: Ballinger, 1976), pp. 275–91.

21. Reginald G. Golledge and Victoria L. Rivizzingo, "Learning About the City: Analysis by Multidimensional Scaling." Paper presented at the meeting of the Association of American Geographers, Atlanta, Georgia (April 1973).

⚛ 3 ⚛

APPLICATIONS OF
SPATIAL APPROACHES

INTRODUCTION

This section is concerned with the application of geographic techniques to the display and analysis of crime data. Preceding parts of the book have been concerned with pure analysis; here, the gap between "pure" and "applied" is bridged with contributions from criminal justice planner/analysts, from a police department analyst, and from a scholar interested in the law enforcement applications of spatial analytical techniques. The underlying assumption is that the usefulness of academic approaches to analysis is reduced if there is no translation of principles and methods into operational modes.

In the first essay, Joelson and Fishbine provide an informative overview of cartographic techniques which have been utilized in the analysis and display of crime data. They note that the presentation of geographic information of an appropriate level of precision and accuracy is no mean task and that the scale of analysis chosen by a researcher should be constrained by the questions addressed. They acknowledge however, that the method chosen is more often the result of the so-called "law of available data." Joelson and Fishbine posit that the analysis of crime event information from a geographic context calls for the utilization of different cartographic techniques, some of which are suited for microlevel analysis while others are better suited to the macrolevel. These cartographic techniques include choropleth mapping (one means of doing area discrimination), computer graphics technology (which allows for a wide range of unique values to be displayed at one time, i.e., by means of a three-dimensional representation) and, the display of microlevel phenomena, including environments such as bars and adult entertainment facilities. Isopleth mapping techniques may be used to empirically aggregate data into irregularly shaped regions of similar values on variables of interest (e.g., the differing levels of stranger-to-stranger assault seriousness in Minneapolis, as measured by the Sellin-Wolfgang Index).

Makres, in the second essay, provides a succinct but highly interesting view of geographically based techniques applied to the daily data-collection process presently employed by the City of Dallas, Texas, Municipal Police Department. In brief, Makres' article includes a historical perspective of geographic crime analysis in municipal enforcement agencies, problems attending these traditional approaches, data-base structure, an overview of the computerized crime analysis capability in Dallas, and an evaluation of the significance of the Dallas approach to the collection and analysis of geographically-based crime data.

Sanders, in the third contribution, offers us another view of how crime data is analyzed and utilized from a spatial perspective by a police department; more specifically, he examines the application of zone patrol theory as applied in Syracuse, New York, where plans for the implementation of that theoretical approach are underway. He states that an outline of responsibilities provides an operating hierarchy within which functions a new beat/zone configuration whose variable character reflects spatial and temporal differences in the measured demand for police services.

The Display of Geographic Information in Crime Analysis

MITCHELL R. JOELSON AND GLENN M. FISHBINE

IN MANY FACETS of planning and research, the speed at which information can be accessed and processed is critical. But even timely information must be presented in a form which facilitates rapid analysis and interpretation in order to be useful in many criminal justice policy and tactical law enforcement situations. By utilizing computers, planners and researchers can achieve the speed necessary to access and process the enormous amounts of raw information which often must be fed into their decision making; and by utilizing computer-generated graphics as one mode of information presentation, the amount of time which must be devoted to interpretation of analytic results may be drastically reduced. Tremendous amounts of information can be represented in graphic output. Because of this, computer-generated graphics can serve an important role in the communication of analytic results. Maps are perhaps the most lucid form of graphic display in situations where the nature of areawide distributions are of interest. Information which is clearly conveyed will certainly prove to be of more value to policy makers than that which is not. Ac-

The research for this paper was supported by grant #76DF050005, awarded to the Minnesota Crime Prevention Center, Minneapolis, by the Law Enforcement Assistance Administration. Points of view stated in this report are those of the authors and do not necessarily represent the official position of the Minnesota Crime Prevention Center or the Law Enforcement Assistance Administration. This article was originally published by the Minnesota Crime Prevention Center and is used with their permission.

cordingly, the educational value of computer-generated maps, in addition to the analytical value, should not be overlooked.

Our concern here is with the presentation of geographic information, at an appropriate level of analysis, with an appropriate level of precision and accuracy.

One type of crime data often analyzed in a geographic context is crime event information. This kind of information is available from a variety of official sources as both raw and summarized crime incident reports. While the scale of analysis chosen by a researcher should be constrained by the questions asked, the method chosen is more often the result of the so-called "law of available data." As Brantingham, et al. note, most sociological research utilizing crime rate data is conducted at the census tract level because a great quantity of tract level census data is easily available.[1] Many tactical decisions, such as those relating to resource or manpower allocation, are made based on precinct or other grid-level information because that unit of analysis is actually used for tactical deployment, or simply because that is how information is routinely summarized by the agencies involved.[2] While predefined summary area data are often not appropriate for many purposes, their limitations can be overcome by utilizing address-level information and research-specific aggregations.

What follows is a description of display techniques for research, tactical deployment, or policy analysis at levels of aggregation:

1. Predefined summary areas, e.g., tract, precinct, or grid.
2. Address-level, e.g., individual incident sites.
3. Analysis-specific aggregations from address-level information.

Display and Analysis of Area Summary Information

The analysis of crime event data is often accomplished by comparing differences in crime rates across subareas of some jurisdiction. Where the researcher can hypothesize that behavioral differences are a function of some manipulable factor, this kind of analysis can be used directly in the policy-making process. A means of helping the policy maker visually discriminate between subareas can greatly facilitate this process.

Mapping Techniques

One means of doing area discrimination analysis involves using what are called choropleth mapping techniques. Choropleth maps are shaded maps of an area, which discriminate between subareas on the basis of shadings which correspond to the magnitude of the crime rate being mapped.

However, the degree to which a choropleth map distinguishes between subareas depends upon the type of categorization procedure imposed upon the data by the research. Choropleth techniques usually use no more than five or ten distinct categories into which the entire range of observed values must be mapped. This limitation stems from the fact that, as a larger number of shapings are used in a single map, visual fidelity quickly gives way to confusion. Human limitations in the ability to discriminate between shadings are quite pronounced. Accordingly, where the number of unique values being represented on a choropleth map exceeds the number of categories being used, as is usually the case, information is lost in the categorization process.

Two categorization procedures in common use in choropleth mapping are equal membership and equal size interval. The equal membership procedure puts an equal number of subareas into each shading-level category. This results in a ranking of subareas into a fixed number of categories. Unfortunately, very small differences in the values of two subareas may be large enough to place them in separate categories, often resulting in a rather arbitrary discrimination between similar subareas. The equal membership categorization procedure involves a two-step loss of information from the data being mapped: 1) interval information about the distance between rankings is disregarded when assigning cases to categories; and 2) as a categorization procedure, even the ordinal information about the observations within each category is lost. This loss of information can be seen in figure 16.1, an equal membership choropleth representation of commercial robbery frequency in Min-

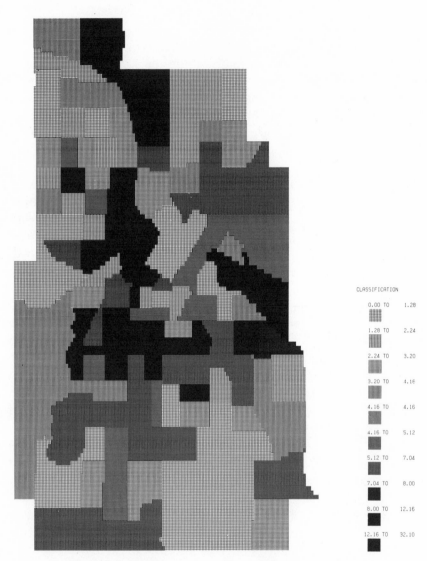

CLASSIFICATION

0.00 TO	1.28
1.28 TO	2.24
2.24 TO	3.20
3.20 TO	4.16
4.16 TO	4.16
4.16 TO	5.12
5.12 TO	7.04
7.04 TO	8.00
8.00 TO	12.16
12.16 TO	32.10

Figure 16.1. Commercial Robbery Frequency (equal membership)
Source: Minneapolis police offense report data,
July 1, 1974 through June 30, 1975.

neapolis.[3] Using five equal membership categories, about 25 tracts must be assigned to each category.

An alternative procedure, equal-size interval categorization, (which, as its name suggests, sets up categories of equal-interval size), solves the problem of somewhat arbitrary classification introduced by the equal-membership procedure, but runs the risk of a different kind of loss of precision. The presence of extreme values in the data set can generate a map with data in only a very few categories. Even though it retains information about the interval size between categories, under certain circumstances, the equal-size interval procedure can introduce a greater loss of information than the equal-membership procedure. This loss of information is demonstrated in the equal-interval representation of commercial robbery frequency in figure 16.2. Due to the presence of a small number of tracts with very high frequencies, virtually all of the tracts are categorized into the lowest or highest categories.

As noted above, choropleth mapping techniques are limited by the inability of persons to discriminate between more than a very few levels of shading, and by the potentially misleading loss of information caused by forcing a wide range of unique values into a much smaller number of categories. These difficulties can be eliminated by using an alternative mapping procedure which neither categorizes nor depends on shading in order to differentiate between levels of the variable being mapped. One such technique involves representing subareas and their associated values as a three-dimensional object (see figure 16.3). The object itself can be mathematically generated and visually displayed through the use of computer graphics technology. The use of three-dimensional representations can provide a net gain of information for use by the researcher or policy maker; true variations in the levels of the variable being mapped are exactly represented. When all of the subareas being mapped are viewed as a single three-dimensional object, subtle variations between subareas, and patterns among subareas become clearly apparent. Differences in analytic perspective can be easily compared through the use of three-dimensional mapping techniques. Three-dimensional representations of commercial robbery in Minneapolis (figure 16.4) give quite different views of the problem when

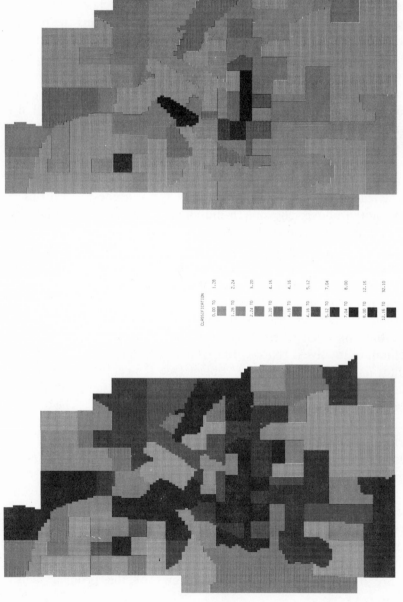

COMMERCIAL ROBBERY FREQUENCY
(EQUAL INTERVAL)

COMMERCIAL ROBBERY FREQUENCY
(EQUAL MEMBERSHIP)

Figure 16.2. Contrasting Choropleth Classification Procedures

Source: same as figure 16.1.

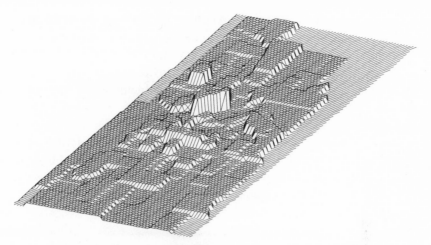

Figure 16.3. Three-Dimensional Representation of Commercial Robbery Frequency by Tract

Source: same as figure 16.1.

mapped from the perspective of frequency (over one year) and risk (proportion of commercial units robbed over one year). Note that the downtown business district is the highest "hill" in the frequency representation and the lowest "valley" in the risk representation. Although figure 16.4 does not clearly demarcate particular city features, it is an easy task to display features such as tracts, or rivers found on other maps. Additionally, the research viewing such a representation is of necessity familiar with the location of city features long before this representation of data is generated.

Data and Analysis of Address Level Information

The most basic element of crime-related geographic information is the individual address, usually that of an offense site. When crime-related information is aggregated to any geographic area, it is this address-level information which is summarized. In the process of summarization, information about individual addresses is lost (see figure 16.5). And yet, address-level information is necessary for many purposes. Analysis of microlevel phenomena, such as crime around specified nodes like bars, adult entertainment facilities, or even police precinct stations, can only be done with address-level information. The identification of "hot spots" or commercial strips with special crime problems also necessitates the use of address-level information.

Resource allocation strategies, such as physical redesign or intensive manpower allocation, become more practical and potentially more cost-effective when small but severe trouble spots can be identified. The process of identifying these trouble spots can best be accomplished with address-level information.

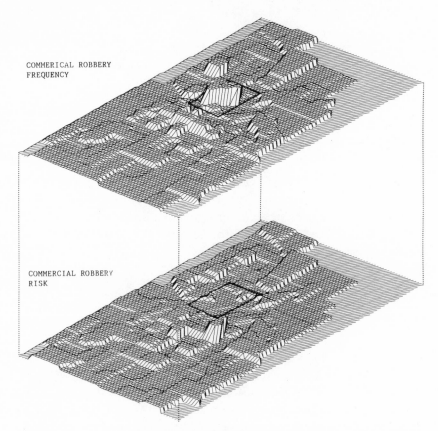

COMMERICAL ROBBERY
FREQUENCY

COMMERCIAL ROBBERY
RISK

Figure 16.4. Three-Dimensional Comparisons of Commercial Robbery Frequency and Commercial Robbery Risk

Source: same as figure 16.1.

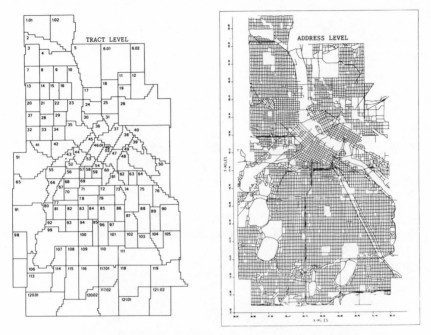

Figure 16.5. Contrasting Levels of Analysis in Minneapolis

Our analysis of stranger-to-stranger assault in Minneapolis on the tract level identified the entire downtown area as a trouble spot, while, as can be seen in figure 16.6, the more detailed address-level analysis pinpointed Hennepin Avenue, or more specifically, a row of adult entertainment establishments, as the site of nearly all of the offenses in the area.

The Display of Analysis-Specific Aggregations

Address-level information need not be applied exclusively at the microanalytic level. Analysis-specific aggregations are directly recoverable as needed from address-level data. For instance, when asked by the Minneapolis City Council to determine if crime rates near a specific bar in Minneapolis were higher than those in other areas of the city, our research design called for computing the

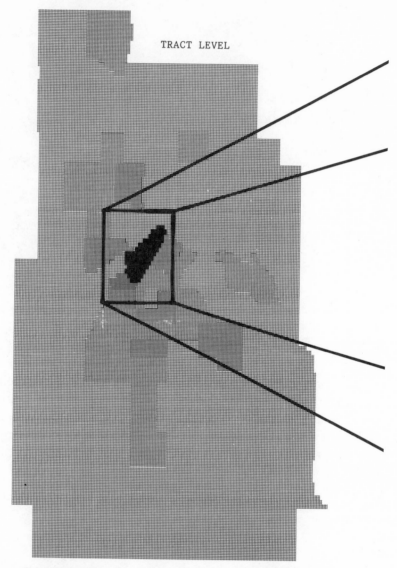

Figure 16.6. Contrasting Levels of Analysis for Assault in Minneapolis
Source: same as figure 16.1.

ADDRESS LEVEL

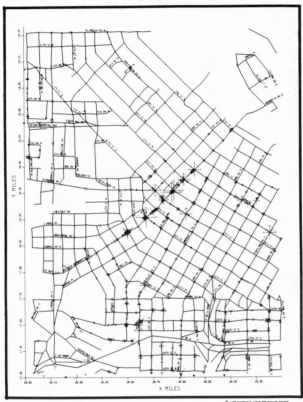

CRIME SYMBOL KEY
ASSAULTS-DOWNTOWN MPLS

SIZE INCREASES WITH NUMBER OF CRIMES

× ASSAULT-SEXUAL
✛ ASSAULT-STRANGER
Y ASSAULT-NONSTRANGER
Y ASSAULT-OTHER

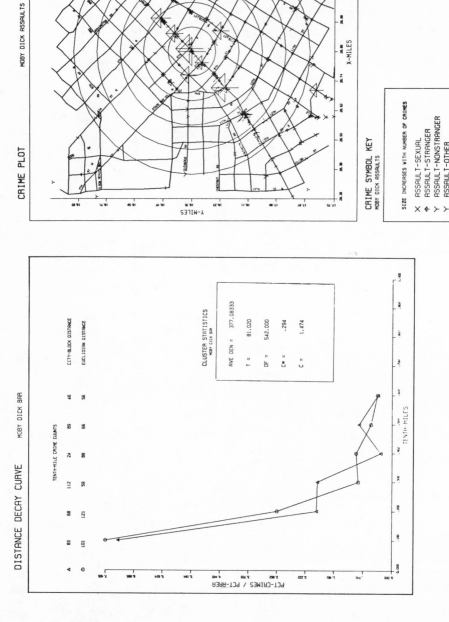

Figure 16.7. A Node Analysis of Crime Around Moby Dick's Bar in Minneapolis

Source: same as figure 16.1

NODEMAP DENSITY PLOT   MOBY DICK BAR

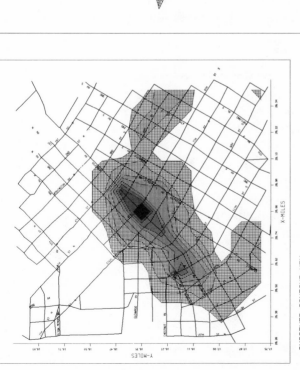

DENSITY OF CRIMES

SMOOTHED CONTOUR MAP   ASSAULTS AROUND MOBY DICKS

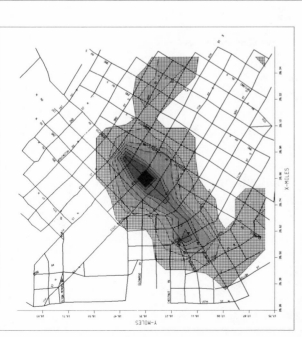

SMOOTHED CONTOUR KEY
ASSAULTS AROUND MOBY DICKS

GRID SIZE .0085 SQ MILES
EQUAL INTERVAL

	0.0 TO 3.1
	3.2 TO 6.2
	6.3 TO 9.4
	9.5 TO 12.6
	12.7 TO 15.7
	15.8 TO 18.9
	19.0 TO 22.1
	22.2 TO 25.2
	25.3 TO 28.4
	28.5 TO 31.6
	31.7 TO 34.7

**Figure 16.8. Isopleth Maps of Assault Around Moby Dick's Bar
in Minneapolis**

Source: same as figure 16.1.

crime rate (in crimes per square mile) for circular bands of increasing radii from that site, in order to construct a distance-decay curve. A distance-decay curve displays the change in crime density as one approaches the immediate vicinity of some site of interest, in this case, Moby Dick's Bar (see figure 16.7).

Using address-level data, spatial analyses of any level of sophistication can be applied to an entire city, resulting in a view of the city which reflects global behaviors which may be lost through aggregate analyses. Detailed identification of barriers to crime, streets or facilities conducive to crime, or even changes in levels of seriousness of crime can be generated for an entire city from address-level data. Isopleth mapping techniques can be used to empirically aggregate data into irregularly shaped contour regions of similar values on a variable of interest. These regions can be represented in a variety of ways, such as contour lines, shaded contour bands, or as a three-dimensional object. For example, note in figure 16.8 the pattern of differing levels of assault in the vicinity of Moby Dick's Bar in Minneapolis uncovered by use of this technique.

Conclusion

The use of computer-generated graphics as one form of presentation for geographically-related crime information provides speed and versatility of analysis to the researcher and policy-maker. A wide range of techniques exist for the analysis and display of both aggregated and address-level information. Computer-generated mapping techniques are useful not only in analysis, but in the presentation of analytical results as well. For many purposes, they can convey enormous quantities of information with a clarity which is unsurpassed by other forms of information display.

NOTES

1. Paul J. Brantingham, Delmar A, Dyreson, Patricia L. Brantingham, "Crime Seen Through a Cone of Resolution," *American Behavioral Scientist* (1976), 20:261–73.

2. Of course, statements made from empirical analysis of such aggregated data about the behavior of individuals may suffer assertions about individual behavior made from purely aggregated data.

3. All computer-generated graphics in this report were produced by THENA, a comprehensive package for planning, resource allocation, and analysis, now undergoing preliminary implementation by the authors at the Minnesota Crime Control Planning Board.

࿊ 17 ࿊

A Geographically Based Crime Problem
Identification System—
Its Application to the Analysis
and Prevention of Crime

CARL MAKRES

TRADITIONALLY, police patrol forces have been deployed to geographical areas (i.e., police beats) primarily to reduce response times to citizens' calls for service. Crime prevention in the patrol mode has therefore been characterized by random success because of the primary responsibility of patrol units to respond to dispatched calls. Consequently, special or tactical units have generally been given the responsiblity of developing successful deployment strategies to prevent crime. These strategies, however, have usually been based on historical information rather than on current real-time information. This has been caused by the inability of police planners to collect and analyze detailed area-specific crime data on a timely basis. Local area crime patterns tend to change rapidly, thus making it mandatory to obtain analysis information quickly if success is to be achieved.

In the early 1900s August Vollmer first introduced to this country the concept of pin- or spot-mapping to visually identify areas where crime and service calls were concentrated.[1] In subsequent years, this technique has been adopted by virtually all police departments as the basis of their crime analysis activities. Even in police departments where no formal geographic crime analysis function exists, it is not uncommon to find pin- or spot-mapping occurring independently on the divisional or precinct level (e.g., the New York City Police Department).

By determining areas of high crime concentration through pin- or spot-mapping techniques, police departments are able to more efficiently utilize their resources through area-specific deployment strategies. Routine patrol activities in high-crime areas can be supplemented with tactical deployments designed to alleviate specific crime problems. Once a high-crime area is identified via spot-mapping, other crime analysis activities generally follow to support the ultimate resource deployment. Information on suspect/vehicle descriptions, modus operandi, etc. can be obtained from the offense/incident reports relating to the area while intelligence, previous arrest and informant data can be obtained about the area and the present crime problem from other departmental sources. Such activities ordinarily comprise a modern geographically-based crime analysis operation.

The Manual Crime Analysis Approach

The activities of a typical crime analysis operation (e.g., the Dallas Police Department circa 1969–1975) may be described as follows:

Each morning, crime analysis personnel receive copies of all offense/incident reports, arrest reports, and supplemental reports turned in to the department during the preceding twenty-four-hour period. Robbery, burglary, and auto theft offense reports are manually separated, along with supplement and arrest reports for the same crime categories.

Any arrest reports containing nicknames or vehicle information are saved. Upon request, offense reports for other crime categories (bicycle theft, rape, etc.) are also retained for a specific crime problem.

Once the offense/incident reports are sorted into the proper categories, each offense is posted on a wall map. The posting consists of placing a 1/4 inch round adhesive coding dot on acetate overlays covering large 6 by 7 foot wall maps of the city. A separate map exists for auto theft, business burglary, residence burglary, and robbery (half-dots are used to distinguish robbery of individuals from business robberies). The coding dots are color-coded by month, and the date of the occurrence of the offense is written on each coding dot. Although the acetate overlays are changed periodically, at least a two-month accumulation of offenses is always present on each wall map. When an overlay is removed, it may be rolled and stored for future reference.

By studying the crime reports daily, and noting the location and time of occurrence, modes of operation, and automobiles and suspects involved, crime analysis personnel are able to identify geographic offense concentrations, establish connections between offenses, and detect crime trends.

After the crime reports are sorted, studied, and their locations posted on the wall maps, they are filed by type of offense, beat, and date. Files are maintained for each of the posted offense categories. Supplements concerning any offense on file are placed with that offense. If a supplement indicates that an offense or group of offenses has been cleared, the offenses are so marked and the supplement filed with the offense report.

Periodic meetings are held with patrol district station representatives and representatives from the Criminal Investigation Division, the Tactical Section, the Community Services Division, the Intelligence Division, the Helicopter Division, etc. The wall maps are reviewed and problem areas discussed at those times.

When requested, bulletins are prepared on the problem areas. A bulletin is a summary of the crime occurrence in a police beat over the time period of interest. The bulletin may list the date, time, and location of each offense. Depending on the type of offense being treated, it may also describe the method of entry, type of property stolen, weapon used, suspect description, and suspect vehicle description.

Problems Involved with the Traditional Approach

In a high-crime volume environment (i.e., larger cities), the basically manual nature of the traditional approach results in a significant time delay between crime problem identification and the implementation of possible solution strategies (e.g., tactical deployment). Typically, the time delay develops as follows:

1. When a crime is committed, it is generally not available for analysis until the following day. It takes approximately eight hours for offense reports to arrive at a particular destination from officers in the field. The reports are usually turned in at the end of a tour of duty (work shift) or collected at various intervals during the duty tour and turned in. Each report must then be reviewed, UCR-coded,[2] selected data captured for computer records (if automation is available), reproduced and distributed to the various departmental user groups (e.g., investigators, crime analysts, etc.). Since crime analysis personnel are normally available on only one work shift per day in most police departments, the majority of the offense reports are received one day late.
2. In the crime analysis area, the offense reports are sorted, read, posted to a wall map, and filed. If a geographic concentration or offense/offender pattern is discovered, an analysis of the situation is made. Since the first part of each day is normally devoted to sorting, posting, and filing offense reports from the day before, crime problem analysis is generally not started until the afternoon and not concluded until the end of the day.
3. After analysis, a handwritten report may be prepared and typed onto a standard format for deployment personnel. Depending on the work load of the secretarial staff, typing may be completed either in the morning or afternoon of the third day.

Thus, a significant time lag may frequently accompany the utilization of the traditional approach to geographic crime analysis in many police departments. When this occurs, tactical deployment personnel are too often placed in the position of chasing or following crime problems rather than interpreting them.

Computerized Crime Analysis in Dallas

The RTD Project

One possible solution to the time delay between crime problem identification and preventive action is the utilization of the computer to speed up the processing of crime information.[3] If the data gathering, tabulating, and report formatting are automated, a significant portion of the delay time can be eliminated. The computer can be utilized to provide the identification of geographic crime concentrations and process all the associated information about each specific concentration identified. The Dallas Police Department adopted this solution to the time-delay problem in its Real-Time Tactical Deployment (RTD) Project.

The RTD Project was financed through Law Enforcement Assistance Administration (LEAA) funding under the Impact Cities Program[4] (Grant No. IA-74-B05-2530). The System Development Corporation (SDC)[5] of Santa Monica, California, was selected to provide technical support for the project. Documentation of the user requirements and system specifications was initiated in March 1974, with the developmental phase of the project beginning in July 1974. The RTD Project was completed on September 30, 1976.

The purpose of the project was to achieve faster deployment on acute crime problems by achieving the following objectives:

> Minimize the time required to detect a crime problem.
> Minimize the time required to process the data related to a detected, crime problem.
> Minimize the time required to provide the department's Tactical Section with information needed to respond to the crime problem.
> Improve both the quality and quantity of information made available to tactical units about a given crime problem.

The RTD system is operated daily by the Dallas Police Department's Crime Analysis Section to identify and analyze "hot" crime areas in the city. To date, crime analysis personnel have concentrated the use of the system on residential burglaries during the week and business burglaries on the weekends. Other crime types are addressed as needed.

Each of the 157 patrol beats[6] in Dallas is evaluated each morning for burglary problems. The problems are identified through examination of summary reports provided by the RTD system (figure 17.1). The information provided in these reports reviews the crime occurrence history of the past fourteen days. Hot areas

Hot Adjacency Summary Report
11/18/76–12/2/76

	Hot Beats	Total Crimes Last 14 Days	1st 7-Day Ont	*1st Week* 14-Day History							*2d Week*							2d 7-Day Ont	Report Day THU	DIFF. 1st–2d 7 Days	14-Day Average
				THU	FRI	SAT	SUN	MON	TUE	WED	THU	FRI	SAT	SUN	MON	TUE	WED				
1.	416	16	7	2	1		1		2	2	1	3		2	2	2	1		9		+2	1.1
2.	452	16	7	1	1	1	1	1	2	1		3		1	1	1	4		9	2	+2	1.1
3.	422	15	9	1	4	1		1	2	1		1	2	2		1	1		6	2	−3	1.0
4.	345	12	8	2	1	1	1	1	1		1	1		1			1		4	3	−4	.4
5.	415	12	6		1	1		1	1	2	1	1		1	1				6			.8
6.	513	12	7		1	2	2	1		1	2	1		1	1				5	1	−2	.8
7.	426	11	6	1		2	1	1		3	3	1	1	1	1				5	1	−1	.7
8.	143	10	2					3	2		1	2	1			2	1		8		+6	.7
9.	222	10	7		1	1	3		2	1	2	1		1		1	1		3		−4	.7
10.	330	10	7	1		2		1	2	1	1								3		−4	.7
11.	117	9	7	2	2		1	1	2		1	1	1	1		1			2		−5	.6
12.	311	9	3		1		1	1		1	1	1	2	2			2		6	1	+3	.6
13.	317	9	6	1	2		1			1	1	2				1			3		−3	.6
14.	334	9	4	1	1			1			1	3		1					5		+1	.6
15.	361	9	4		2			1	1	1	1	1	1	1	1				5	1	+1	.6
16.	423	9	5			1	1	1	2		1	1	1	1		1			4	3	−1	.6
17.	433	9	4				1	1		1	1	1	1	1	1	1			5		+1	.6
18.	364	8	5		1			2	1	2	1			1		1	1		3		−2	.5
19.	366	8	5			2	1	1	2	1	1		1	1		1	1		3		−2	.5
20.	116	7	4		2					2	2	1							3	1	−1	.5
21.	124	7	4	2	1	1	1	4		1	1		1	1					3		−1	.5
22.	212	7	7								1										−7	.5

Figure 17.1

are identified by evaluating the daily occurrence frequency for beats experiencing an abnormally high number of crimes during the fourteen-day period.

The report is output separately in two sort orders to provide the crime analysis with two independent perspectives of viewing current crime patterns. The first sort order is by number of crimes occurring within a beat during the past fourteen days (i.e., figure 17.1). This report immediately identifies the high-crime areas to the analysts.

The second order is by beat and allows the crime analyst to determine if beats adjacent to the problem beats are also experiencing an upward trend.

If an increasing trend is indicated (e.g., more burglaries during the past seven days), then that area is designated "hot" and analyzed further.

For such further analysis, detailed reports are provided daily in a format that can be disseminated to the department's Tactical Section and Helicopter Division. These reports include a fourteen-day burglary review of each hot beat (see figure 17.2), all suspect descriptions, and all suspect vehicle descriptions for the preceding fourteen days. Other information provided on an as-needed basis includes people arrested in hot areas, partial license plate checks against traffic citations and wanted-vehicle files, known offenders living in hot areas and reviews of other repressible crime types. Utilizing this process, the RTD system provides the department's tactical forces with the information necessary for deployment within three to twenty-four hours of crime problem occurrence.

In addition, an on-line terminal is provided for supplemental information retrieval and report production by the department's various user groups.

RTD System Description

The two major software components of the RTD system are:

—Adjacency Program, which performs the analysis of crime occurrences and produces the summary and detail crime occurrence reports discussed above;

—DS/3 Data Management System, which produces reports containing supplemental information to support crime problems analysis and deployment operations.

The system also provides generation of special ad hoc reports on a same-day basis, using either the on-line terminal or the computer center batch procedure.

The RTD system operates on several existing data files, including offense, arrest, known offender, traffic citation, wanted person, and vehicle files. The information contained in these files is entered daily via on-line data entry terminals. The offense information is entered within one to three hours of crime reporting.[7]

Adjacency Program Description. The adjacency Program reviews the occurrence of crime in each beat of the city on a daily basis. It calculates the following statistics for each beat:

Number of crimes occurring on report day[8]
Total number of crimes occurring in the previous fourteen days
Fourteen-day crime occurrence history
Fourteen-day crime occurrence average
First seven-day total
Second seven-day total
Difference between first and second seven-day totals.

Operation of the adjacency program calculations is controlled through user-specified options in the program's run deck. These options include:

The ability to specify the size of the basic geographical unit used. This unit is called an adjacency cluster and can consist of one or more beats or reporting areas
The crime types to be included in the calculations
The reports to be output
The dates and time spans to be used for calculations.

The results of the calculations are displayed in a series of reports (e.g., figure 17.1).

The Adjaceny Program also initiates the operation of the DS/3

Residential Burglaries
for TAC
for Beat 332

Date Span From	To	Day	TOF 1	TOF 2	Street	Object of Attack	Property	Burg. M.O.	Burg. Entry	Status	Service Number	Non Susp	Num Veh	Evid Cole
5/28		WED	1500	1800	SPANISHFCR	APT		OTHER	DOOR F	SUSPENDE	0175658G	1	0	0
5/29		THU	530	1615	SPANISHFCR	APT	TV/RADI	PRY	WIND F	SUSPENDE	0176784G	0	0	0
5/29		THU	900	1900	SOUTHERNCA	APT	TV	PRY	DOOR F	SUSPENDE	0771910	0	0	0
5/30		FRI	930	1300	SOUTHERNCA	APT	GUN/MISC	UNLOCK	DOOR F	SUSPENDE	0179124G	0	0	0
5/31		SAT	1030	1500	SPANISHFCR	APT	FOOD	UNLOCK	DOOR F	SUSPENDE	01835850	0	0	0
6/01/-	6/02/75	SUN	2020	200	SOUTHERNCA	APT	TV/RADI	PRY	WIND F	SUSPENDE	0181353G	0	0	0
6/02		MON	930		MIESTBLVD	APT	RADI/MISC	PRY	WIND S	SUSPENDE	0161798G	2	1	0
6/03		TUE	900	2100	SOUTHERACA	APT	TV/CLOT	OTHER	UNK	OPEN	0183553G	0	0	0
6/03/-	6/04/75	TUE	2200	800	LIESTELVD	APT	MONY	PRY	DOOR F	OPEN	0184038G	0	0	0
6/04		WED	2130	2300	BONNIEVIEW	APT	RADI/MISC	PRY	WIND S	OPEN	0185080G	2	1	0
6/06		FRI	700	1800	SOUTHERNCA	APT	TV/MISC	PRY	DOOR F	SUSPENDE	0187506G	0	0	0
6/06		FRI	1600	1630	PROSPERITY	SINGLE/FAM	RADI	KEY	DOOR F	SUSPENDE	0187606G	0	0	0
6/06/-	6/08/75	FRI	2000	1800	PROSPERITY	SINGLE/FAM	TV	PRY	WIND R	SUSPENDE	0189756G	0	0	0
6/07		SAT	330	400	KIESTBLVD	APT	MIXC/MONY	UNLOCK	UNK	OPEN	0187947G	0	0	0
6/07/-	6/08/75	SAT	2200	300	OVERTICNRD	APT	RADI	KEY	DOOR F	SUSPENDE	0189094G	1	1	0
6/09		MON	30	430	SCSUTHERN	APT	MISC/MONY	OTHER	DOOR R	SUSPENDE	0150148G	0	0	0
6/09		MON	1300	1530	SOUTHERNCA	APT	TV/GUN	OTHER	UNK	SUSPENDE	0190673G	0	0	0
6/09		MON	1530	2330	SOUTHERNCA	APT	TV/RADI	UNLOCK	DOOR R	SUSPENDE	0191312G	0	0	0
6/10		TUE	600	1700	SPANISECH	APT	TV/	PRY	DOOR R	SUSPENDE	0192018G	0	0	0
CNT														
19														

Figure 17.2

system to produce user-specified reports providing supplemental suspect, vehicle, and crime description information (e.g., figure 17.2).

DS/3 Data Management System Description. The DS/3 Management System[9] provides the crime analyst with the capability to selectively search and obtain additional information from the data base to support their deployment strategies and crime investigations. DS/3 is available for use from an on-line terminal, in batch processing mode or via linkage with the Adjacency Program.

Crime analysis and police data processing personnel in Dallas use the DS/3 system through an on-line terminal to obtain additional information for tactical and helicopter deployment. In addition to the files used for crime analysis, several other files are avaliable to DS/3, including wanted vehicles/persons, arrested persons, property identification, traffic citations, accidents, and all files associated with the computer-aided dispatch system and known offender information.

DS/3 also provides the user with the capability to develop and produce tailored reports on a same-day basis. The desired report may be formatted and run with the output being received at the terminal or at the high-speed printer in the city's computer room. The combination of on-line information retrieval and report generation capability allows crime analysis personnel to develop, produce, and receive the output of a report during the same day without the assistance of programming personnel.

Significance of the Dallas Approach

The Dallas experience has shown that automation provides a viable solution to the time-lag problem encountered when deploying police resources to active high-crime areas. The information provided by the RTD system is of a significantly higher quality and is more comprehensive than that available with the previously employed manual method. This is due to the following reasons:

—Information is more current. Information associated with the identified problems is given to the Tactical Section and Helicopter

Division within three to twenty-four hours of problem occurrence. With the manual system previously employed, problem information averaged three days old.

—Information is more accurate and complete. The RTD system reports always reflect the latest status (open, closed, etc.) of every crime report. The manual system did not provide this capability. In addition, crime reports were sometimes lost in duplication and transmittal to the Crime Analysis Section.

—Information is more comprehensive. Each of the city's 157 beats is evaluated every twenty-four hours and all of the related information is available for analysis. This information includes all basic crime information, all vehicle descriptions, and all suspect descriptions.

—Information is prioritized. Beats are listed and ranked by the number of crimes occurring during a specified data period. The manual system's spot maps tended to become too cluttered for careful analysis. It was also difficult to read and analyze every related crime report and manually correlate the data.

—Supplemental information is available to support deployed field units. Information on persons perviously arrested in a problem area for the offense type in question or people who live in the problem area and who have been arrested elsewhere for the same type of offense can be obtained for each problem.

—The supplemental information can be obtained on-line for immediate results. It is not necessary to wait for follow-up or additional information. Results of any query into the data base can be obtained within minutes.

—The information is output in a report format approved by the users, thereby alleviating the need for retyping before dissemination.

Thus, the development of the RTD Project has resulted in a field-proven resource deployment system for police agencies that is responsive in a real-time mode. Not only are crime problem areas detected more quickly with the system, but also deployment analysis reports are much more comprehensive and accurate through the use of the correlation capabilities available with automated data processing. The ultimate result is that better informed field forces can now respond much faster to rising crime problems than previously possible.

NOTES

1. *Crime Analysis Systems Manual* (preliminary draft) (Washington, D.C.: U.S. Department of Justice, Law Enforcement Administration), pp. 1–2, describes a mapping technique first introduced by August Vollmer in the early 1900s.

2. Uniform Crime Reporting is a standardized method of crime classification initiated by the F.B.I. and used by most police agencies.

3. Other possible solutions, if feasible, are to increase staff size and/or to decentralize the analysis staff (to decrease the volume of offenses to be processed at any given time).

4. The Impact Cities Program was a special LEAA (Law Enforcement Assistance Administration Program) in which eight major city/county governments were given federal funding to develop innovative and effective law enforcement programs or techniques.

5. SDC has been involved in a number of law-enforcement related projects, including PATRIC for the Los Angeles Police Department.

6. A beat is the patrol area of one police element (car or foot patrolman) during a given work shift.

7. Offense information is entered via the department's direct entry procedure, whereby crime reports are called in by patrol officers and recorded onto computer records by data entry personnel.

8. Depending on what time of day the adjacency program is processed, the currency of the latest crime information is usually within the past two or three hours.

9. DS/3 is a trade name for a proprietory software system developed and sold through the System Development Corporation.

࿖ 18 ࿖

Theory and Practice
in Urban Police Response

A Case Study of Syracuse, New York

RALPH A. SANDERS

THE 1970s have been years of urban police reform in the United States. Police response to rising social, economic, political, and internal pressures for improved services has been surprisingly uniform in its direction, at least according to the results of a recent survey.[1] A recent study for the Syracuse, New York, Police Department (SPD) reflects this generality, both in terms of reorganization objectives and in the complex of pressures for change.[2] This chapter draws heavily upon that Syracuse study. In what follows, we examine both the principal causes and goals of recent policy reform initiatives, and consider in some detail the recently completed reorganization plans for the Syracuse Police Department.

A General Urban Context

The history of urban policing reflects a long-term evolution toward specialization and professionalization, toward more complete public accountability, toward the centralization of authority, and toward increasing force sizes and operating costs.[3] More recently, the growth of information processing activities, particularly those which address the volatile issues of police productivity,[4] increasing levels of technological sophistication, especially that which enhances police mobility,[5] and strengthening police unionization,[6] have come to the fore. In several of these respects, in both the long and the recent short run, there are few important differences between the evolution of urban police forces and that for other governmental organizations in the public eye.

For urban police departments within metropolitan areas in the 1970s, this rapid evolution is likely to continue for some time in response to the changing pattern of urbanization, particularly within the central cities of metropolitan areas. Central-city outmigration, sufficiently large and rapid to cause outright population loss in virtually every American metropolis, has changed the nature of, and the demand for, urban police services.[7] An emerging crime ecology, itself a reflection of the social ecology of the city, can be seen to spring from ethnic and racial concentrations, and the centralization of the unemployed, the poor. Increased levels of privation and a heightened awareness of deprivation, real or perceived, absolute or relative, create central-city crime increases through growing personal frustration, alienation, social disadvantage, and economic hardship.

Central-city population losses are both a cause and a consequence of declining commercial and industrial bases, both major contributors to the local government revenue base. Losses in the urban economic base ultimately translate into shortages of urban revenue, and these into strains on police budgets. In order to justify continuing high levels of public expenditure for police operations, demands for evidence of improving police productivity are often the rule. As with most labor-intensive organizations, susceptibility of police budgets to rising operating costs acts to constrain police output in a tight fiscal environment.

Internally, departments are generating their own demands for improved performance; from the police union point of view, gains are most likely when work equity and the full range of benefits, from higher wages to greater pension benefits and occupational security, better match the high skill level increasingly sought in an ever-professionalizing police force.[8] As if these pressures for reform were not enough, they combine at a time when police visibility is in public focus. Television glorification of police work and police success is sharply contrasted in the public mind with rising local crime rates, power abuses, and police inefficacy.

In this environment, political demands upon the police for results beyond the immediate control of either the police or the city's elected officials tend to produce an aura of reformist expectation; reform merely for the sake of progressive appearance may be no small explanation of recent trends in urban police departments.

Police Reform Strategy

Contemporary urban police reorganization strategies may be lumped into three qualitatively different but overlapping categories: (1) increasing police information-handling capacity; (2) police image alteration; and (3) increasing police productivity. Each of these categories is examined separately.

Information handling is a rising tide within the total police effort. An improved ability to collect, process, and disseminate a large range of information, information on police performance, information facilitating police operations and aiding mobility, represents the beginnings of a virtual revolution in urban police work. Estimates of costly upgrading of information-related machinery, from mobile reception and transmission to in-house data analysis and display, are offset by the promises it offers in the areas of crime analysis, intradepartmental communications, and reductions of storage space for voluminous police records. Crime prediction is now a budding art.[9] The rapid retrieval of criminal records is seen as one means for improving the arrest-prosecution ratio.[10]

One important corollary of this electronic revolution is found in police labor-management relations. Newly generated demands for measures of work productivity by police planners and police overseers lead inevitably toward closely monitored data-based evaluation of individual work performance. While close monitoring may lead to a reduction of genuinely wasted time, it may lead as well to unhealthy competition among officers, and the development of police programs oriented toward those aspects of policing for which measurement is taking place. Measurements of police success may become self-fulfilling, and initiatives toward problem solving and orientations toward the civil well-being diminished.

Strategies focusing on *image alteration* reflect concerns both inside and outside police departments. Internally, the long-standing military appearance and organization has both its supporters and detractors. Opposition, while not extending its disaffection to uniformed apparel and the system of ranks, tends to reflect that overly rigid rank-command systems of intramural communication may be antithetical to modern business practices. More importantly, the problems and options requiring police decisions and actions are more complex than the rank system of decision authority is able to accommodate. The need is to enhance departmental decision-making flexibility, and that need suggests designifying the military *modus operandi*.

A recent image-related focus is on police-community relations. Defining mutual police-community goals and establishing regular lines of communication are integral to this process. In Cincinnati, Ohio, for example, the police are manning beats designed on the basis of a community perception survey.[11] The image of police as adversaries in some neighborhoods is of long-standing concern; police involvement with youth groups, parades, and "Officer Friendly" programs are a growing portion of the community relations operation. Although it would be easy to exaggerate the importance of this image manipulation in fostering police-community accord, admiration, and cooperation, not the least advantage of improved community relations would be a *measurable* change in community attitudes toward police, a lessening of police performance as a political liability.

Easily the most complex of the three categories of police reform strategy outlined here is that dealing with increasing *police productivity*. In this area, there is only limited agreement on what is to be measured. Productivity has been forcefully argued to be the combined elements of police *effectiveness* and police *efficiency*. Effectiveness is demonstrated ability of the police to accomplish some goal. Efficiency combines the results of police activity with the resources expended to accomplish the result. Great productivity, then, is the accomplishment of specified goals at little cost.[12]

In these definitions, urban police departments are more and more charged with increasing efficiency to raise productivity, since raising effectiveness without improved efficiency must necessarily involve greater resource outlays, exactly that which urban police departments are asked to forego. Issues of police efficiency lie both within departmental organization and externally, at the interface between the police and the public.

The flow of information throughout a large organization is the subject of management science. That police today should wish to take advantage of such knowledge is a reflection of modern beliefs that police, despite a conventional military appearance, must conduct their operation in a business-like manner. This involves reevaluation of the specific roles of departmental bureaus and the various ranks of sworn personnel within them. The degree of reform is the degree to which the functioning of ranks and bureaus has been brought into question. The functions of bureaus are called line functions, the tasks each is charged to perform. By bringing together the role definitions of personnel and their ranks with the line functions of bureaus, judgments can be made as to the efficiency of extent organizations. Misallocations of ranked personnel, overly diffused communications structures in specific line functions, and the need for new role definitions are typical results of such inquiry.

Police service to the public is delivered in a variety of ways. The main arm is through the patrolman, whose task it is to fill the role definition supplied by the department. There are, consequently, many types of patrolman activity and these differ considerably from department to department, and occasionally even within departments. As patrolman roles are important definitions by which the police relate to the public, they are the subject of much attention in police planning. In general terms, patrolman roles vary in breadth, (the number of line functions to carry out), depth (the extent to which decision authority resides with the patrolman for each line function), and location (the area, or areas of the city in which his responsibility lies). In line with a reevaluation of patrolman roles lies the question of deployment, the fielding pattern of patrol officers in space and time. As the ecology of crime changes with an unstable residential pattern, the responsiveness with which a police department can alter its deployment schedules has much to say about police effectiveness.

The Case of Syracuse, New York

The issue of police reform is highly complex; in this section we hope to illuminate a variety of police planning principles by reviewing the recent reorganization study of the Syracuse, New York Police Department.

The City of Syracuse is a central city of a Standard Metropolitan Statistical Area whose population in 1970 was approximately one-third of the metropolitan total of 637,000. Like many of its older northeastern counterparts, the central city has experienced net population losses since the 1950s, and holds a residuum of economic problems for its remaining, heavily blue-collar and one-tenth black population. Sharply rising fuel costs, a declining commercial and industrial base, and lingering high levels of unemployment counter some significant attempts at downtown renewal during the 1960s and 1970s.

In recent years, Syracuse has experienced a marked upswing in crime consistent with trends reported elsewhere. Increases in serious criminal offenses have been particularly significant in crimes against property, a pattern expected perhaps in view of consistently high rates of unemployment in the years of record. Although the incidence of crime has been growing in recent years, the Syracuse Police Department has managed to hold a line in maintaining a consistent crime clearance rate; in fact more crimes have been cleared than ever before. Nonetheless, most categories of crime have risen so sharply in the past twenty years that merely maintaining consistent clearance rates results in an ever greater number of crimes which remain unsolved. In the past ten years, for example, the number of serious offenses in Syracuse which were not cleared grew from approximately 4000 to over 11,000.

Responding to the perceived need for innovative action against a rapidly rising demand for police services, the SPD established a Crime Control Team (CCT) on an experimental basis in 1967. A corps of highly trained officers with expanded work definitions assumed policing responsibility for seven of the twenty-three beats for the city. Based in part on CCT success, the SPD engaged a team of four Syracuse University faculty members to determine the feasibility of reorganization along the lines of zone patrol theory, and to provide a set of reorganization options for the SPD to consider.[13] The following discussion outlines this work which, as of December 1977, has received police favor in most of its aspects. Where options were presented for the SPD to evaluate for eventual implementation, this discussion presents only those alternatives which the SPD eventually chose.

Internal Organization

Within the Syracuse Police Department internal organization, four broad areas were identified as subjects of recommendations for improvement.

1. The location of decision-making. The tendency for bureaucratic structures to lead to centralization of decision-making is well-known. This is particularly true where well-defined operating roles and bureaucratic responsibilities have not been clearly outlined. Highly centralized structures require long chains of information flow, and tend to be sluggish in responding to demands for action. For the police operation, a tendency for ineffective patrolman performance lies in the traditional roles the officer is asked to carry out. Recent trends have focused upon decentralized decision making and an expanded work definition, providing more scope for immediate effective patrolman action. Although few are prepared to argue that decentralization will lower the overall crime rate, many do believe that deployment of personnel with a larger stake in significant decisions can lower incident response times, eliminate investigative red tape, improve both the effectiveness of patrol operations and police public relations, and increase overall police morale. Such innovations are thought to maximize criminal deterrence within the constraints imposed by limitations in personnel, equipment, and police budgets.

For the SPD, then, a primary target involved decentralizing police authority. In concert with the aforementioned CCT experience, patrolmen are asked to conduct their own investigations in certain classes of criminal offense and to engage in community relations activity beyond the scope of traditional patrolman requirements. Beyond the advantages already reviewed, such a definition promises to reduce the heavy workload of the Criminal Investigations Bureau and to reduce the time spent in wasteful, largely unproductive mobile patrol activity.

2. The consolidation of line functions. In a long-term evolutionary sense, the changing emphasis of the overall police operation results in the blurring of line function responsibilities in the various police departmental bureaus. To the extent that the same or similar functions lodge within different bureaus of a department, the need for lateral information flows between performing in an uncoordinated manner increases, giving rise to more effort at intradepartmental communication, poor line function productivity, and the duplication of services. Virtually every bureau within the SPD, for example, currently has an independent responsibility within the area of community relations; prospects for coordination and effective action, especially with the growing emphasis on improving police images, lay in centralizing community relations activities and raising the overall effectiveness of community relations output.

3. The technology of intradepartmental communication. Upgrading police efficiency is increasingly dependent upon the rapid retrieval and dissemination of information. A growing reliance upon computer technology and scientific police deployment to raise productivity carries several concomitants: the need to automate and regularize the reporting of incidents and other events related to police workload on a small-area basis for the city, the need to design simple, effective, and reliable police data outputs to facilitate police decision making for persons not skilled in the evaluation of numeric information, and the need to collect meaningful information for use in crime analysis and crime prediction. Regular exchanges of such information within the department should enable departments to effectively respond to changing demands for its services.

4. The location and duration of command responsibility. Police command responsibilities can be defined with respect to time or place or both. Ongoing SPD operations, for example, invest in

middle-echelon command personnel a temporal (eight hour per day) responsibility for given subareas of the city, the exact number of which is closely related to the higher-ranking personnel within the department over a period of years. Such temporally-based hierarchical command structures are vulnerable during daily transition periods between work shifts, and necessitate a regular assembling of all command officers to devise community-related (that is, areally based) policing policies. For any area of the city, at least four persons have significant command responsibility and accountability.

The newly designed alternative invests authority in the middle ranks on a twenty-four-hour, zonal, basis. For the City of Syracuse, three permanent zones have been outlined, incorporating approximately equal demand and police manpower requirements. Within zones, ten- and eleven-man teams are headed by team leaders, each of whom assumes twenty-four-hour responsibility for a small area, or subzone, of which there are fifteen in all. In general, the hierarchy of police command mirrors the hierarchy of areal delineations of police authority; time is removed as a basis for authority. The issue of areally defined policing, or zone patrol, is most fundamental to modern police planning, and seems to govern many recent strategies of police deployment.[14]

Police Deployment

A large number of recent police initiatives fall under the blanket notion of zone patrol. Although there are many variations on this theme, an axiom of the theory in all cases signifies the importance of local area knowledge, responsibility, and accountability for the patrolling officer. Patrolling officers themselves are thought to be either generalists, who assume a wide range of responsibilities with decision-making authority, or specialists, whose narrow range of duties is complemented by a system of intramural referrals and reporting. In line with department-wide initiatives toward decentralization, and increasing amount of authority is accumulating in the patrol officer function; decentralization for the police is in large part a redefinition of patrolling officers as generalists in police work. The physical decentralization of police facilities is not a necessary concomitant.

For the Syracuse Police Department, the generalist's role has been defined to include several aspects: (1) responding to incidents, or calls for assistance; (2) follow-up, or investigation of certain classes of criminal offenses; (3) regular surveillance of junior and senior high schools and school grounds during the academic day, for the academic year; (4) carrying out administrative duties, such as serving warrants, and filing reports; (5) community relations activities; and (6) routine patrolling.

To enable patrol officers to carry out assigned responsibilities productively, a system of police beats must be created, keeping the design simple to administer and easy to police. Beats are argued to be most successful when they are free of internal barriers to movement, facilitating a rapid response to calls by police, internally homogeneous on a range of variables depicting the social areas of the city; they should equalize workloads for the system of beats, and should be areally compact, to reduce street mileages and response distances within each beat.

Effective design matches the manpower with the maximum number of beats that manpower can police, within the constraints of personnel unavailability. The relationship is straightforward:

$$B = \frac{(A)(N)(W)}{(F)(H)},$$

where

B = number of beats per shift;
A = number of working hours per man per week;
F = assignment availability factor, which allows for all lost time due to illness, leave, vacations, and the the like;
H = number of hours per day per man, usually 8.0;
N = total number of patrol officers employed, and
W = percentage of average weekly workload within the shift.[15]

Using a generalist definition of police workload previously discussed, adding in a factor for workload queuing,[16] and setting the number of patrolmen available to the SPD for 1977 (161) solutions were found for the twenty-one shifts of the average work week, for a period from September, 1976 to March, 1977. Based upon the data, the City of Syracuse could best match manpower with workload by employing a maximum of thirty-six beats (Friday, evening watch) to a low of ten (weekdays, 11:00 P.M. to 7:00 A.M.). But because a number of solutions were numerically identical, and because a highly variable beat structure poses severe administrative and deployment scheduling problems, the optimal solution was taken to be a simple variable beat structure in which fifteen beats for the city could be patrolled during the ten least busy watches, and thirty during the remaining more demanding eleven watches. This design partitioned the original measurement

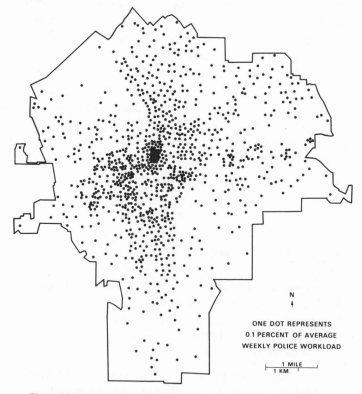

N

ONE DOT REPRESENTS
0.1 PERCENT OF AVERAGE
WEEKLY POLICE WORKLOAD

1 MILE
1 KM.

Figure 18.1. Demand for Police Services, Syracuse, N.Y., 1975–1977
The demand for police services is the sum of all elements of patrolman workload for the average week for each of 257 small areas of the city. For further details on the elements of workload, see text. The author expresses his gratitude for map design assistance to Mark Monmonier of the Syracuse University Geography Department and for map drafting to Michael Kirchoff of the U.S. Cartographic Laboratory.

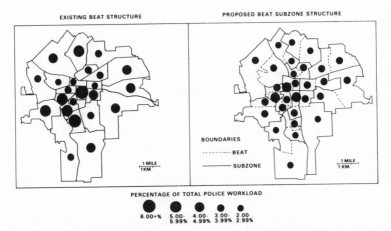

Figure 18.2. Distribution of Police Workload, Syracuse, N.Y.
The existing twenty-three beat structure (left) operates throughout the entire week. The proposed thirty beat structure (right) is to be used for the eleven busier watches, and the fifteen subzones into which these are combined for the other ten watches. Beyond equalizing workload for patrolling areas of the city, the variable (30-15) beat structure facilitates an optimal match between the demand for police service and the deployment of officers.

of workload into a simple variable beat structure which equalized the distribution of workload in a greatly improved manner over that previously employed in Syracuse. See figures 18.1 and 18.2.

The full complement of patrolmen was then divided into ten and eleven-man teams, each team being assigned to cover one subzone (one of the larger beats of the fifteen previously described) and the two beats (of the thirty) which comprise the subzone. The team structure is argued to facilitate cooperative policing ventures, to simplify administration, and to provide an identifiable unit responsible for the police activities in a small area of the city. Felicitous scheduling of area- and time-specific assignments guarantee an optimal match of individuals within the team to the areas they are expected to know.

Overview

Modern urban police planners widely share the assumption that the combined effects of technological sophistication, public education, the scientific redeployment of patrol officers, and the reorganization of departments can be used to elevate levels of criminal deterrence and apprehension. Police reform seeks closure of the triangular polarities of police-criminal-public, to a simpler dyad of criminal-public, by raising levels of trust, cooperation, and identification of the police with a widely shared community interest. This thinking suggests, however, that expectations for great success should be tempered by knowledge of the constraints common to urban police departments everywhere in the United States. In the police view, police reform should be couched in the context of a more general critique of the criminal justice system. This is because of the unparalleled increases in crime incidence, and knowledge of the general public unwillingness to engage in, and to pay for, higher levels of deterrence activities.

NOTES

1. An informal survey of twenty urban police departments in many parts of the United States conducted in 1976 provides the basis for generalizations about urban policing in America. See note 2.

2. R. A. Rowntree, R. A. Sanders, M. S. Monmonier, and L. G. Nigro, *Decentralizing Police Services through Zone Patrol: A Feasibility Study for the Syracuse Police Department*. Syracuse Police Department Xerox (July 31, 1977), 386 pp. The significant contributions of Sgt. E. G. Van Der Water of the SPD in this study are gratefully acknowledged.

3. J. F. Richardson, "The Police in the City: A History," in R. A. Mohl and J. F. Richardson, eds., *The Urban Experience* (Belmont, Calif.: Wadsworth Press, 1973), pp. 164–181.

4. G. H. Kuper, "Productivity: A National Concern," in J. Wolfle and J. Heaphy, eds., *Readings on Productivity in Policing* (Washington, D.C.: Police Foundation, 1975), pp. 1–10.

5. See, for example, O. W. Wilson and R. C. McLaren, *Police Administration*, 4th ed. (New York: McGraw-Hill, 1976); and R. C. Larson, *Urban Police Patrol Analysis*, (Cambridge, Mass.: MIT Press, 1972), for wide-ranging discussions of the uses and effectives of modern technology as it affects police mobility.

6. J. A. Grimes, "The Police, the Union, and the Productivity Imperative," in Wolfe and Heaphy, eds., *Readings on Productivity in Policing*, pp. 47–85.

7. For a discussion of recent populations trends in metropolitan areas, see P. Morrison and J. Wheeler, "Population Bulletin: Rural Renaissance in America?" *Population Reference Bureau* (October 1976), 31:3.

8. Grimes, "The Police, the Union."

9. I have been unable to locate a source which deals specifically with crime prediction techniques, and information on such techniques stems from the survey by Rowntree, et al., *Decentralizing Police Services*. These prediction equations are based on the assumption that crime, the victim, and the perpetrator are usually found in close proximity. Ecological correlations between social and physical data and crime incidence form the logical basis for proceeding, and the regression analyses provide the formal predictions.

10. For a full discussion of the meaning and danger of this ratio as a measure of police productivity, see H. P. Hatry, "Wrestling with Police Crime Control Productivity Measurement," in Wolfe and Heaphy, eds., *Readings on Productivity in Policing*, pp. 86–128.

11. S. N. Clarren and A. I. Schwartz, *An Evaluation of Cincinnati's Team Policing Program*. Paper presented at the American Psychological Association's Convention in New Orleans, Louisiana, August 30, 1974 (Washington, D.C.: Urban Institute, 1974).

12. Kuper, "Productivity," especially pp. 2–3.

13. I should like to distinguish here between the report submitted to the SPD on July 31, 1977 and the materials I wish to address here. Interpretation of the data and selectivity in discussion for this paper are my own, and should not be thought necessarily to reflect those of the other authors of the police report, nor those of personnel within the SPD. I would also like to acknowledge the considerable assistance of Mark Monmonier of the Geography Department at Syracuse University in several phases of both the police report and the drafting of this article.

14. Zone patrol theory is a broad idea set which reflects no specific method of patrolling, except in emphasizing the importance of the areal base in police deployment and administrative and command responsibilities.

15. The definition of workload as used here excludes the function of routine patrolling. For this study, patrolling by one officer was viewed as a use of residual time, the difference between eight hours and the number of hours used for all other functions. Alternative definitions could be employed if *directed* patrol (the stationing of officers at prescribed locations for deterrence effects) is viewed as desirable; for this study, all locations were assumed uniform with respect to the needs for police visibility, the direct effects of other aspects of police work having been taken into account.

16. Queuing is defined as the piling up of work at particular times in the 257 areas for which police data was available. Queuing is viewed as a curvilinear function of measured workload, adding hours to the total measured workload to compensate for the harrying effects of work backlogs.

CONCLUSION

The eighteen original essays presented here contain a rich variety of topic, perspective, and method, with place-to-place variations in crime constituting the central theme. What are the theoretical implications of this research, and what are its implications for future research in the spatial ecology of crime?

The key concept that, at least partially answers all three questions, is *eclecticism*. This concept is particularly helpful in explaining why there is a relative lack of emphasis on theoretical constructs in the essays. Strongly theoretical approaches to the interpretation of criminal behaviors tend to focus on a particular sociological or cultural phenomenon (e.g., labeling theory), and to the extent that such approaches *are* focused they inhibit comprehensive interpretation. This is not, of course, a criticism of theoretical constructs or interpretations, but rather a recognition that criminal behavior is so complex that only a combination of theoretical arguments can approximate an explanation. When several theories themselves inherently complex are combined, it is questionable whether the ensuing explanation can be within the realm of human comprehension.

Studies of criminal areas and of the spatial patterns and relationships affecting criminal behavior present extraordinary difficulties from the point of view of theory building. The entire physical/social milieu must form the framework within which theory development occurs, and it is clear that many of the most fundamental questions do not yet have widely accepted answers. Data availability problems continue to be crucial; although some progress has been made in measurement methodology, basic measurement models remain largely unchanged and, in conjunction with the lack of comprehensiveness of criminal justice information systems, continue to confound many primary research efforts that could form the basis of consensus theory building in crime geography.

A brief example of the kinds of difficulties involved in building spatial theory may be drawn from the concept of the "journey-to-crime" discussed here by Nichols and Phillips. The simplest theoretical formulation would suggest that the principle of effort minimization should govern journey-to-crime behavior, just as it should explain shopping behavior, at least at its simplest level.

Insofar as both types of travel behavior are well approximated by log normal distance-decay curves, the least-effort principle is vindicated. However, the studies cited draw attention to distance variations associated with age, sex, race, and type of offense. When one pauses to consider that within a given offense category, many behavioral subcategories are encompassed, and that opportunity patterns are highly variegated, then it is appreciated that the development of adequate *descriptive* models is difficult, quite apart from the problems encountered in simulation or prediction efforts. Such problems tend to encourage comprehensive eclectic empiricism, rather than focused theorization. However, the eclecticism is for most researchers a matter of necessity, given the data inadequacies and the inconsistencies of many prior research efforts.

A coherent and comprehensive research agenda is needed, one that will assist in convergence of the behavioral (individual-based) and ecological (aggregate-based) schools of criminology. Books such as *Crime: A Spatial Perspective* serve the purpose of presenting recent research findings in a coordinated format in order to focus attention on research themes that have been attracting significant attention. The present work would suggest several topics for a research agenda: improvements in area-based statistics and methodological refinements in general; the spatial interface between laws, crimes, and justice; refinements in approaches to regional and interurban analysis; the journey-to-crime and other distance-related phenomena; threat perception (both the threat of being victimized and the threat of being arrested); and the applications of findings to the development of crime inhibiting strategies.

AUTHOR INDEX

SUBJECT INDEX